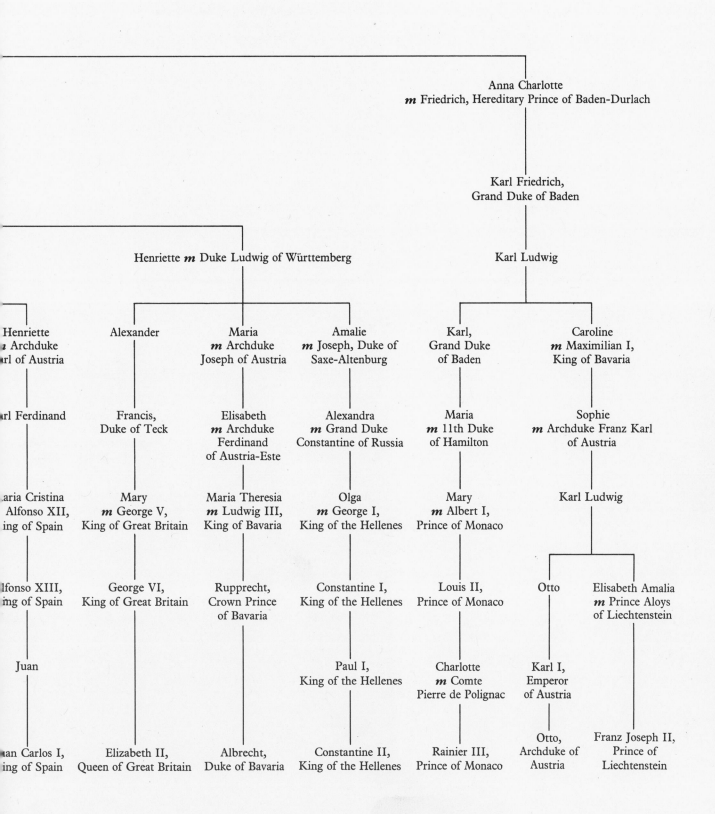

Anna Charlotte
m Friedrich, Hereditary Prince of Baden-Durlach

Karl Friedrich,
Grand Duke of Baden

Henriette *m* Duke Ludwig of Württemberg

Karl Ludwig

Henriette
m Archduke
Karl of Austria

Alexander

Maria
m Archduke
Joseph of Austria

Amalie
m Joseph, Duke of
Saxe-Altenburg

Karl,
Grand Duke
of Baden

Caroline
m Maximilian I,
King of Bavaria

Karl Ferdinand

Francis,
Duke of Teck

Elisabeth
m Archduke
Ferdinand
of Austria-Este

Alexandra
m Grand Duke
Constantine of Russia

Maria
m 11th Duke
of Hamilton

Sophie
m Archduke Franz Karl
of Austria

Maria Cristina
m Alfonso XII,
King of Spain

Mary
m George V,
King of Great Britain

Maria Theresia
m Ludwig III,
King of Bavaria

Olga
m George I,
King of the Hellenes

Mary
m Albert I,
Prince of Monaco

Karl Ludwig

Alfonso XIII,
King of Spain

George VI,
King of Great Britain

Rupprecht,
Crown Prince
of Bavaria

Constantine I,
King of the Hellenes

Louis II,
Prince of Monaco

Otto

Elisabeth Amalia
m Prince Aloys
of Liechtenstein

Juan

Paul I,
King of the Hellenes

Charlotte
m Comte
Pierre de Polignac

Karl I,
Emperor
of Austria

Juan Carlos I,
King of Spain

Elizabeth II,
Queen of Great Britain

Albrecht,
Duke of Bavaria

Constantine II,
King of the Hellenes

Rainier III,
Prince of Monaco

Otto,
Archduke of
Austria

Franz Joseph II,
Prince of
Liechtenstein

EUROPE'S ROYAL FAMILIES

The *Country Life Book of*

EUROPE'S
ROYAL FAMILIES

Maria Kroll · Jason Lindsey

With photographs by
Lichfield

COUNTRY LIFE BOOKS

Published by Country Life Books and distributed for
them by The Hamlyn Publishing Group Limited
London · New York · Sydney · Toronto
Astronaut House, Feltham, Middlesex, England

First published 1979
ISBN 0 600 376311

Typeset by City Engraving Limited, Hull
Edited, designed and produced by Burke's Peerage
Limited, 56 Walton Street, London SW3.
Printed in Great Britain by Hazell, Watson & Viney Ltd.,
Aylesbury, Bucks.

Contents

Foreword

As might be expected, the contributors to *Europe's Royal Families* have a common regard for the soundly practical, and the romantic virtues of monarchy as a form of government for free people. However, this book is more than just a panegyric on royalty; it has a wider purpose than merely to chart the familiar arguments in favour of monarchy, or to vindicate Europe's various royalist causes: in this, it was felt, one either preaches to the converted, or embarks on a lost cause.

Instead, there was a more catholic approach: to portray, for a twentieth century increasingly short of colour and pageantry, the superb style, and the great diversity of human character to be found within the family of European royalty. Indeed, every conceivable type is here, from the hero to the coward, from soldiers to saints, from politicians to poets; there are scholars, libertines, financial geniuses, connoisseurs, scientists, sportsmen, artists, doyens of fashion, eccentrics and bores. If *Europe's Royal Families* has a dedication, it is to the most colourful of these characters, and also to those who suffer with dignity that intractable social ill—being royal without a throne.

It would be impossible to list all the people and organisations who have given invaluable help to the authors and editor in their work: the private secretaries of most of the families featured have, for example, been truly generous in their support. However, we do have special debts of gratitude to King Simeon of the Bulgarians; to King Umberto of Italy; to the royal families of Norway, Liechtenstein and Roumania; to Mark Bence-Jones; to Maurice Quick for making available his excellent collection of historic photographs; to Sally Harris for her research and to Fiona Grafton, who knows better than anyone what the work has entailed.

Europe, 1360

What is usually understood as medieval, Christian Europe had completely developed by the mid- to late-fourteenth century. Geographically, its largest component was the Holy Roman Empire. This was the grand, but loose political concept created by arrangement between the Popes and the strongest secular rulers to emerge in western Europe after the decline of the Roman Empire in the west and the increasingly separate course followed by the Eastern, or Byzantine Roman Empire had made it relatively useless for the purpose of defending Christendom against the Barbarians. Thus, the Frankish king, Charlemagne, was recognized by the Pope as Holy Roman Emperor from 800, and after the decline of his power, the German Otto I and his successors held the title from 962. The loss of their Italian territories, and quarrels with the Popes, reduced the Holy Roman Emperors to no more than the titular heads of a princely federation of German states by the time that Rudolph, the first Habsburg Emperor, succeeded in 1273. The seven greatest princes of the confederation elected the Emperor.

Other boundaries on this map indicate independent states, but in France, as in the Empire, the key semi-independent feudal principalities are marked. At this time, the English kings had lost their French domains, but retained Aquitaine as a fief from the French crown. Dauphiny, in theory part of the Empire, is marked as French because it was the personal domain of the heir to the French throne.

In eastern Europe, the Turks had forced the Byzantine Empire out of Asia Minor, and the growth of the Slav kingdoms confined it to a modest area in the vicinity of Constantinople.

8

WAY

Oslo •

Stockholm •

SWEDEN

NMARK

Copenhagen •

mburg

POMERANIA

BRANDENBURG

HOLY

ROMAN

SILESIA

Prague •

BOHEMIA

EMPIRE *Danube* MORAVIA

BAVARIA

Vienna •

AUSTRIA

an

Venice •

REPUBLIC OF VENICE

Florence •

PAPAL STATES

Rome •

KINGDOM

OF NAPLES

Naples •

Palermo •

KINGDOM

OF SICILY

MALTA *Mediterranean Sea*

TEUTONIC KNIGHTS

Königsberg •

Warsaw •

POLAND

LITHUANIA

UKRAINE

Pest •

• Buda

HUNGARY

MOLDAVIA

WALLACHIA

Danube

BOSNIA

SERBIAN

PRINCES

BULGARIA

PRIN.

OF

ALBANIA

DUCHY OF

Athens •

ACHAEA ATHENS

CRETE

RUSSIAN STATES *Volga*

PRINCIPALITY

Moscow •

OF MOSCOW

KHANATE OF THE GOLDEN HORDE

CRIMEA

GEORGIA

Black Sea

EMPIRE

OF

TREBIZOND

BYZANTINE EMPIRE

• Constantinople

OTTOMAN TURKS

ARMENIA

CHIOS SELJUK TURKS

KNIGHTS

OF RHODES

KINGDOM

OF CYPRUS

ARABIA

9

Europe, 1721

At the beginning of the eighteenth century there existed the group of European states—often described as the "Powers"—which were to dominate the continent's history for the next two centuries. They were: Britain, powerful at sea, with increasing colonial ambitions; France, very powerful and potentially dominant on the mainland; Austria, with its possessions along the Danube; Prussia, still in its infancy, having recently acquired the status of kingdom and likewise Savoy-Sardinia.

The struggle between these states at the beginning of the eighteenth century has been described as the first of the world wars, and this map shows the boundaries of Europe in 1721 after the treaties which ended the conflict.

The circumstances which took Europe to war was the rise of France at the same time as the decline of Spain. When in 1700 the last of the Habsburg kings of Spain died without an immediate heir, Louis XIV of France and the Austrian Habsburgs voiced their rival claims to the throne. England and Holland formed an alliance with the Habsburgs against France, for if the Bourbons were to control Spain and her enormous possessions in the New World together with the Spanish Netherlands, the commercial well-being of those two emergent trading nations would be seriously threatened.

The outcome of the ensuing War of the Spanish Succession was that while Louis XIV had his grandson confirmed as Philip V of Spain, the Spanish Empire was divided, Spain retaining Spanish America, and Austria taking the Spanish Netherlands. Overall, Great Britain (so called since the union of England with Scotland in 1707) emerged with the best terms.

10

FINLAND

INGRIA

KINGDOM OF SWEDEN

ESTONIA

• Stockholm

LIVONIA

• Moscow

COURLAND

GOTLAND

RUSSIAN EMPIRE

LITHUANIA

• Copenhagen

Königsberg
• PRUSSIA

ıburg

BRANDENBURG

POLAND

Volga

ER

Warsaw

SAXONY

SILESIA

Prague

MORAVIA

ROMAN EMPIRE

BOHEMIA

BAVARIA Danube

Vienna

CRIMEA

AUSTRIA

Budapest

KINGDOM OF

TRANSYLVANIA

Black Sea

CROATIA

HUNGARY

SLAVONIA

WALLACHIA

REPUBLIC OF VENICE

Venice

BOSNIA

Florence

BULGARIA

SCANY

PAPAL STATES

SERBIA

MONTENEGRO

OTTOMAN EMPIRE

Rome

KINGDOM

OF NAPLES

• Constantinople

Naples

CORFU

SICILY

MOREA

Athens

CYPRUS

Mediterranean Sea

MALTA

CRETE

Napoleon's Era

At the end of the eighteenth century, Europe was again at war, on this occasion because revolutionary France threatened to expand at the expense of the European monarchies.

Before Napoleon seized control in 1799, the French Republic had extended its boundaries to the Rhine and caused similar republics to be declared in Holland, Switzerland and Italy. Inspired by his vision of a European Empire, Napoleon went on to defeat coalitions of his opponents at the battles of Marengo (1800), Austerlitz (1805), Jena (1806) and Friedland (1807), assuming, in 1804, the title of Emperor of the French. The map on page twelve shows the high tide of his achievement, with central Europe, Italy and Spain under his direct control, and the Scandinavian and eastern European powers forced into alliances with him. Great Britain remained outside this system,

confirming her control of the sea at the Battle of Trafalgar in 1805.

The process of the dissolution of Napoleon's Empire began almost immediately. There was resistance to his reforms, defeats at the hands of Wellington in the Peninsular War and the disastrous invasion of Russia in 1812. The British invaded France across the Pyrenees; Prussia and Austria joined in alliance with Britain and Russia; widespread revolts broke out against French rule and Napoleon was forced to abdicate in 1814.

The map on page thirteen shows how after Napoleon's fall the *status quo* of Europe was restored at the Congress of Vienna. The Bourbons returned to the thrones of France, Spain and Naples. In return for various compromises, the British had their colonial gains during the war period confirmed.

There was no restoration of the Holy Roman Empire, but in its stead a confederation of German states was created. Within this, Bavaria and Württemberg kept their new status, conferred by Napoleon, as kingdoms. To contain the strength of France, Belgium and Holland were joined, the House of Orange becoming a monarchy; the King of Sardinia took Genoa; Austria gained Lombardy and Venetia and Prussia the Rhineland. Poland was partitioned to prevent its complete absorption by Russia, which took Finland. In return for this loss, Sweden was permitted to annexe Norway.

The underlying principle of the treaty was to preserve peace by compensation and by creating a balance of power. On the whole, it was a long-lasting settlement – there was no war involving all of Europe for more than a century afterwards.

The First World War

The First World War changed Europe—and indeed modern civilization—more fundamentally than any previous conflict. To understand how the continent went to war in 1914, it is first necessary to appreciate the various powers' fears and ambitions.

The map on page fourteen shows Europe before the outbreak of war. Prussia had for some decades been the rising German power and Bismarck was determined to maintain this trend, for this reason allying his state against France with Austria-Hungary.

The latter, which had been united in the 1860s, wished to expand southeast into the Balkans. The Balkan peoples, especially the southern Slavs of Serbia, Bosnia, Herzegovina, Montenegro and Dalmatia, had long been fired by nationalism, and felt that they should belong to a single, Yugoslav nation— a development which Austria-Hungary saw

as ultimately divisive of its own empire.

Russia also had Balkan ambitions, which it had been furthering by assisting some Balkan nationalities in their rebellions against the Turks, and which it saw threatened by Austria-Hungary's annexation of Bosnia-Herzegovina in 1908. Thus France and Russia were united in opposition to Prussia and Austria-Hungary, an alliance which was joined by Great Britain in 1907. Italy had joined the German alliance in 1882, but did not support it when war broke out.

The famed assassination of Archduke Franz Ferdinand at Sarajevo made Austria decide finally to put an end to southern Slav agitation. When the southern Slavs rejected the ensuing Austrian ultimatum, they were supported by Russia. Germany was bound to support Austria, as was France to support Russia, and Great Britain to aid France. Italy, in the event of war, opposed the German alliance and Bulgaria cast in its lot with the German Empire. The Turks, fearing Russia, also sided with Germany. These were the alliances which entered the war in 1914.

The political boundaries which resulted from the eventual settlement of all the disputes by 1922 are shown on the map on page fifteen. Alsace-Lorraine passed from Germany to France; Poland was reconstituted as a state; the Austro-Hungarian Empire was dismantled so that out of its former territories of Bohemia, Moravia and Slovakia were created Czechoslovakia; the southern Slav states formed the new Yugoslavia; Austria and Hungary were divided into separate countries. Finland, Lithuania, Latvia and Estonia became independent of Russia, whose Tsarist Empire had collapsed in 1917.

Reigning Families

BELGIUM	**Wettin**
DENMARK	**Oldenburg**
GREAT BRITAIN AND NORTHERN IRELAND	**Windsor**
LIECHTENSTEIN	**Liechtenstein**
LUXEMBOURG	**Nassau**
MONACO	**Grimaldi**
NETHERLANDS	**Orange-Nassau**
NORWAY	**Oldenburg**
SPAIN	**Borbón**
SWEDEN	**Bernadotte**

BELGIUM

Ruling Flemings and Walloons

When King Baudouin ascended the Belgian throne in 1951 he keenly felt the insults which had been heaped on his father and step-mother as a result of the controversy over their conduct when Germany invaded Belgium in 1940. He was at first a reluctant king who made no secret of his outraged feelings. But if his subjects regarded him with apprehension at first, all that has changed.

He is now a well-loved, hardworking, much-travelled monarch who has visited most continents and received visits from most of the world's leaders, while Brussels, his capital and that of the E.E.C., is of course the market-place where all Europe meets.

The King and his Spanish Queen, Fabiola, attend endless functions—both are as conscientious as they are popular. Their presence at concerts, lectures and charitable events is unfailingly sought after: they are the focal point, the unifying symbol for the Flemings and Walloons who make up the Belgian nation.

There are no children, and the heir to the throne is the King's brother Albert. The Prince and his wife Paola undertake many of the royal duties, and their son, Prince Philippe, spends much time with his uncle, the King, to obtain a foretaste of his future responsibilities.

The family has been linked with Belgium ever since it took its first step to nationhood in 1830 when the Flemings and Walloons rose against the Dutch fifteen years after having been united, against their desires, with

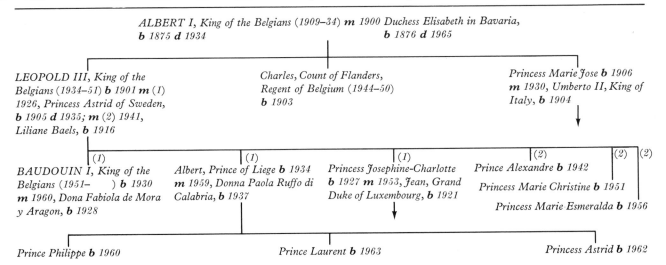

ALBERT I, *King of the Belgians (1909–34)* **m** *1900 Duchess Elisabeth in Bavaria,*
b *1875* **d** *1934*   **b** *1876* **d** *1965*

LEOPOLD III, *King of the Belgians (1934–51)* **b** *1901* **m** (*1*) *1926, Princess Astrid of Sweden,* **b** *1905* **d** *1935;* **m** (*2*) *1941, Liliane Baels,* **b** *1916*

Charles, Count of Flanders, Regent of Belgium (1944–50) **b** *1903*

Princess Marie José **b** *1906* **m** *1930, Umberto II, King of Italy,* **b** *1904*

(*1*) BAUDOUIN I, *King of the Belgians (1951–)* **b** *1930* **m** *1960, Dona Fabiola de Mora y Aragon,* **b** *1928*

(*1*) *Albert, Prince of Liege* **b** *1934* **m** *1959, Donna Paola Ruffo di Calabria,* **b** *1937*

(*1*) *Princess Josephine-Charlotte* **b** *1927* **m** *1953, Jean, Grand Duke of Luxembourg,* **b** *1921*

(*2*) *Prince Alexandre* **b** *1942*

Princess Marie Christine **b** *1951*

(*2*) (*2*) *Princess Marie-Esmeralda* **b** *1956*

Prince Philippe **b** *1960*

Prince Laurent **b** *1963*

Princess Astrid **b** *1962*

The Netherlands by the Congress of Vienna. Before that, these southern provinces of the Netherlands (called *Gallia Belgica* in Roman times) had been known as the Spanish, and then the Austrian, Netherlands. Apart from a short spell of independence from 1598 to 1628 under a Spanish infanta and her Austrian husband, they had never been a separate entity. Now a new state was proclaimed, with a constitution embodying the latest liberal principles. It was to become the envy of frustrated reformers in more autocratically ruled kingdoms: among the constitution's articles was one that required any act by the king to be "countersigned by a minister who, in doing so, renders himself responsible therefore". Belgian monarchs have found this limiting but it holds good to this day.

The new state's provisional government wisely thought that to proclaim a republic would mean quarrelling with all the world, so they duly elected Leopold of Saxe-Coburg and Gotha as king.

This prince, a member of the House of Wettin, was the handsome,

King Baudouin is the only reigning male of the House of Coburg, a dynasty which gave sovereigns to England, Bulgaria and Portugal as well as Belgium, and a sprinkling of consorts throughout the world. As an arbitrator, Baudouin has a considerable reputation and, at 49, he is already regarded as a wise old man among sovereigns. The almost oriental immoveability of his features seem to indicate that he would be a hard man to surprise. His wife, Queen Fabiola, wears the sadness of being childless with dignity.

Albert and Paola, Prince and Princess of Liège, were once described as European royalty's ideal couple: they lend great panache to royal occasions in Belgium and elsewhere. Albert is the heir to the throne, his brother Baudouin having no children. Paola, a stately blonde, is the daughter of an Italian duke. They spent their honeymoon as guests of Britain's Queen Mother in Scotland. In recent years, each has maintained an independence within the marriage, but both undertake royal duties. Albert sometimes takes advantage of his right to address the Senate, particularly on economic matters.

Prince Philippe, right, his uncle, centre and father. Philippe, as eventual heir to the Belgian crown, spends as much time as possible with his uncle to gain a taste of his future responsibilities. Life at the Belgian court, well-known for its strictness, cannot permit him or his brother and sister Laurent and Astrid the sort of freedom other royal teenagers enjoy.

ambitious, younger son of the late Duke Franz, and brother of the reigning Duke Ernst I. He had been brought up in Coburg, and through the Russian marriage of one of his sisters had held positions in the Tsar's army since the age of six. In 1814, aged twenty-three (now as a lieutenant-general) he went to England in the suite of the Tsar, met King George IV's daughter, Princess Charlotte (at the time engaged to the Prince of Orange known as Young Frog, but in love with Prince Frederick of Prussia) and married her in 1816. Her death soon after in childbirth was a double blow for Leopold, because with her died his hope of being the power behind the throne of England. He mended matters as best he could by arranging the marriage of his sister to the King's brother, the Duke of Kent. Later he kept an avuncular eye on his niece, Victoria—she called him "my second papa" —as well as on his Coburg nephews Albert and Ernst with another possible match in view.

Leopold's powerful English connections made him an acceptable candidate for more than one of the crowns than on offer. After some

The king who abdicated: Leopold III, in his late seventies, lives quietly at Argenteuil, near Brussels and in the south of France. With this greatly maligned man one is immediately aware of being in the presence of a king. He is insistently majestic by nature. Physically large and rugged, King Leopold is interested in non-competitive sports and when fishing or hiking, might be taken for a retired ski instructor or mountain guide. He has few intimate friends, preferring the company of his own family, although Prince Bertil and Princess Liliane of Sweden, whom he sees in France, are an exception.

Princesses Marie Christine, left, and
Marie Esmeralda are the daughters of
King Leopold and his second wife.
They have a brother, Alexandre, who
is considerably older.

vacillation, he declined Greece, but when it came to Belgium, he thought it wise to accept, provided there were enough safeguards to enable him to rule, and provided that the powers made up their minds about the frontiers. Even when these had been successfully negotiated, people abroad found it hard to understand over whom Leopold was to rule. Certain towns within the new state, such as Brabant and Ghent, were familiar. Limburg was known for cheese, and the Duchy of Luxembourg for dukes. Of course everyone had heard of Flanders, if not for the crusading counts who had furnished more than one medieval King Baudouin for the throne of Jerusalem, then because it had been the cockpit of endless battles, including Waterloo. Finally Hainault was familiar because of Philippa, mother of England's Black Prince—but who were the Belgians of whom Leopold was to be king?

Talleyrand, winkled out of retirement to represent France at the conference deliberating Belgium's creation, said there was no such people, and he was right. There were Flemings and Walloons, that was all.

Above, Charles, Count of Flanders, photographed in 1945. He is the Howard Hughes of European princes: a true recluse, protected from contact with the outside world by loyal staff of his house near Liège. The Count was educated in England at Eton, served in the British navy, and was a successful Regent in 1944-50 during the crisis which ended with the abdication of his brother, King Leopold. Then he retired altogether from public and social life and since has made one recorded public appearance. This was at a Belgian court in 1972, for a case against a former financial adviser accused of misappropriation of funds. Charles uttered not a word, lost the case, paid the costs and went back into retirement.

Liliane, Princess of Belgium, is the second wife of King Leopold III. Born Liliane Baels, she married the King six years after the death of his first wife, Queen Astrid, in a motor accident.

21

Leopold I

Nonetheless these dissimilar peoples were to be united, and when King Leopold I entered his new country, its motto was *L'Union fait la Force*. It will be noted that this is expressed in French. There was a new national anthem, *La Brabanconne*, which in previous years had been the battle hymn of the revolutionaries. All seemed set for a stable reign.

The powers had agreed a long list of articles to safeguard the country's independence, including its neutrality in perpetuity. The borders were fixed by common agreement, which did not prevent King William II of the Netherlands from at once invading. Leopold, constitutionally the chief of the Belgian armed forces, rode into battle but to no avail: as a result of this conflict, which lasted ten days, Belgium's borders were reduced after all. It was some proof of Leopold's diplomatic finesse that this setback was accepted by his subjects, though they were always keenly to mourn the loss of Luxembourg, which King William gained back in his capacity as Grand Duke.

In 1832, King Leopold married, for political reasons, Louise, a daughter of Louis Philippe, King of the French. She was self-effacing, generally regarded as an angel. It was Leopold's third marriage, counting a morganatic one to an actress in England. There was, in fact, nothing strait-laced about most Coburg princes. Leopold's nephew, Duke Ernst II, who was to succeed in 1844, was a notoriously unfaithful husband, in whose time the Coburg court became decidedly raffish. The shining exception was Ernst's brother, Prince Albert, whom, to Leopold's intense joy, Queen Victoria married in 1840.

This was not the end of the Coburg matches arranged by Leopold: one of his nephews married the Queen of Portugal and a niece married Louis Philippe's son, the Duc de Nemours, whose sister Princess Clementine went to another nephew of Leopold's.

Leopold's own children naturally made fitting marriages: his heir, Leopold, known as the Duke of Brabant, tall, unprepossessing, with a beak of a nose, married an archduchess of Austria; Leopold's second son, the

Belgium

Brussels' cavernous royal palace dates from when Napoleon's brother, Louis, was King of Belgium and, at least in theory resided for six months of the year in Brussels and six in Amsterdam. The superb gates which open on to the Palace Square have a pinched look because they do not lie in line with the walls and railings. The building is sited on a slope so that it looks like a piece of cake about to slip off a carelessly balanced plate. The furnishings are French of the First Empire—suitably gorgeous. The Venetian Staircase is justly famous and one of the state bedrooms is unique, containing a pair of canopied beds in a style (which never really got off the ground) known as Queen Louise. The chandeliers are blindingly beautiful and the carpets much too fine to walk on. One modest entrance hall, for the special use of the sovereign, is exquisitely designed and furnished. The palace is now used for state occasions or for lodging visiting heads of state.

Count of Flanders, married a Prussian princess; his youngest daughter, Charlotte, married the Archduke Maximilian of Austria, and was to become the poor, demented Empress Carlotta of Mexico. Leopold was highly satisfied when Queen Victoria's daughter married the Crown Prince of Prussia. While that stiff and pompous court looked askance at this lively *Engländerin*, she remained a Coburg to Leopold, as she did to Germany's Chancellor Bismarck who called the House of Coburg the stud-farm of Europe. When Leopold wanted to marry yet another nephew to the Queen of Spain, Queen Victoria called a halt. She said that the Coburg influence had spread wide enough, and Leopold, who prided himself all his life on being his niece's mentor, did not pursue the matter further.

In his seventy-sixth year, Leopold was made up to the teeth, still sporting a black wig with a central curl over the forehead and showing every outward sign of youth and health. The wig, someone suggested, was meant to indicate vigour in senility, but the King said he needed it to keep his head warm. As pleased with himself as ever, he claimed that he had advanced the affairs of Belgium by a century in a quarter of that time, and when he died in 1865 he was sincerely mourned by his people. He had grown in stature from a man with a strong penchant for a crown to the "Nestor of Sovereigns", respected, though not necessarily liked.

The unprepossessing Leopold II was thirty years old on his succession. Highly sarcastic, he could never resist saying disagreeable things to people and his chief interest was in the amassing of wealth. His marriage, which was not a great success, yielded a son, who died at the age of nine to the extreme grief of the father, and three daughters to whom he was less than kind. If Leopold I had found the constitution limiting—he had said "it is obvious there was no monarch present to defend his interest when they drew it up"—Leopold II found it a heavy chain which prevented him from acting as he wished. What he wished, in fact, was to obtain colonies for Belgium. The government, maddeningly, refused to be interested, so he went it alone.

Empress Carlotta

23

*The Château de Laeken, in Brussels'
northern outskirts, is King Baudouin's
and Queen Fabiola's private residence
and few have had the privilege of
glimpsing the interior. Though gloomy,
it has architectural merit. Wiring,
drains, bathrooms and kitchens have been
completely modernised. The principal
drawing rooms are attractive, but
elsewhere the furniture is ordinary.*

In a way that was not strictly above-board, he called, in 1876, a conference of explorers and geographers and begged them to interest their governments in the possibility of opening up Africa and of abolishing the slave trade. To this purpose, he founded the *Alliance Internationale Africaine*. This soon became the *Alliance Internationale du Congo*, a company of which he was the sole shareholder, and which started the general scramble for Africa. Employing the services of Henry Morton Stanley, of Livingstone fame, Leopold II had the entire Congo in his personal control, and privately exploited its vast natural resources. The world thought of the A.I.C. as mainly a philanthropic organisation, but when astonishing rumours of hair-raising brutalities inflicted on the population scotched this illusion, Leopold II became the most reviled monarch in Europe. The King's apologists said that he was motivated not by greed, but by an understandable desire to buttress his successors so that they might act more freely under the restrictive constitution. As for atrocities—if the Congoese dropped dead in large numbers, not the King but an epidemic of sleeping sickness was to blame. One contemporary observer, seeing him peel a grape with long nails and a cruel glint in his eye, thought that "he looked as though he was skinning alive the president and all the members of the Aborigines' Protection Society". Finally, the state took over the Congo, but not before the king had transferred the assets of the A.I.C. to Coburg.

Leopold II died at the age of seventy-four. Almost to the last, he had pursued young women of uncertain reputation up and down the Riviera on his motor-tricycle, huge white beard streaming in the wind. He played a final practical joke on his relations by rising from what was practically his deathbed, and, in his long, white dressing-gown morganatically marrying his *maitresse en titre*, who was dressed in black. After the ceremony, he turned: "Gentlemen", he said, "meet my widow". The king's daughters, however, made short work of her after Leopold II's death four days later. They also upset his will, in which they did not feature.

Leopold II

King Albert I, who succeeded his uncle in 1909, was the first King of the Belgians to take his oath in both French and Flemish, the reason for this being that the question of Belgium's official language, French, had become a great political issue. His life was devoted to developing the spirit of unity in his country. Both he and his wife Elisabeth of the ducal Wittelsbach line (and with all the talents and the spirit, some of the eccentricity and none of the neuroses of that family), became genuinely popular. It was the First World War that made heroes of them both.

The King, as head of the armed forces, defended to the last ditch the twenty square miles that remained of free Belgium, while the rest was occupied by the Kaiser's army in defiance of Belgium's neutrality. The Queen worked tirelessly for the wounded, exposing herself to real danger in the field hospitals. "Plucky little Belgium" became a catch phrase and at the war's end all the world saluted the king's noble and heroic stand. He was described as the best constitutional monarch who ever reigned in Europe. In 1934 he was killed in a rock-climbing accident in his beloved Ardennes and succeeded by his son Leopold III.

Albert I

In the first year of the new King's reign, his beautiful and much-loved wife, Queen Astrid, who had borne him three children—Baudouin, Albert and Josephine-Charlotte (the Grand Duke of Luxembourg's wife)— died in a car crash. It was a tragic beginning to a difficult reign. What concerned Leopold most was to strengthen his country: Belgium needed to be strong to deter other nations from making her, yet again, a battlefield. As the Second World War loomed, her defences were indeed built up. Broadcasts by the King appealing for peace (one was made in conjunction with Queen Wilhelmina of Holland) fell on deaf ears. When in 1940 Hitler's armies invaded Belgium King Leopold took command of his army which fought until, inevitably, it was forced to capitulate. He decided to remain with his people instead of continuing Belgian resistance from abroad, as Queen Wilhelmina had done, and as his ministers were about to do. This decision still arouses controversy, and at the time caused great bitterness between monarch and government. In 1941, the government-in-exile issued a decree declaring him unfit to rule. Leopold and his second wife Mary Liliane Baels, Princess de Rethy, guarded by the Germans, stayed at his palace of Laeken until being taken to Germany in 1944. He was liberated by the Americans in 1945, but remained in exile for another five years while the politicians argued about the future of the monarchy. Then he abdicated in favour of his son.

Queen Astrid

DENMARK

Ancient Line

Queen Margrethe of Denmark positively enjoys her job: "It is no strain", she has said, "one enjoys doing it. It is a happy duty." When at the age of thirteen she discovered she was to become heiress to throne, she was delighted because "it meant I would always live in Denmark."

Her succession was established in 1953 by a referendum. The country was so used to male sovereigns, and Margrethe's father, Frederik IX, had no sons and three daughters. The heir was his brother, Knud, but the King's intelligent daughter Margrethe was clearly a more suitable long-term choice. The question was put to a national vote, which favoured Margrethe. She became the first Queen regnant of Denmark in six hundred years, breaking a line of alternating Frederiks and Christians which had continued since 1513. Since then, the Danish public have shown no signs of regretting their choice. A recent poll showed 88 per cent of the electorate in favour of retaining the monarchy.

Even by royal standards of the second half of the twentieth century, Queen Margrethe has had a remarkable all-round education. First there was boarding school in England (North Foreland Lodge, near Basingstoke), where she made several good friends. Then she embarked on her university career: philosophy and administration and constitutional law at Copenhagen University; international law and archaeology at Cambridge; civics at Aarhus (Denmark's second great university); French and jurisprudence at the Sorbonne and finally sociology at the London School of Economics. She is fluent in Danish, Swedish, English and French and also knows some German and Faroese. She did a domestic science course; travelled ex-

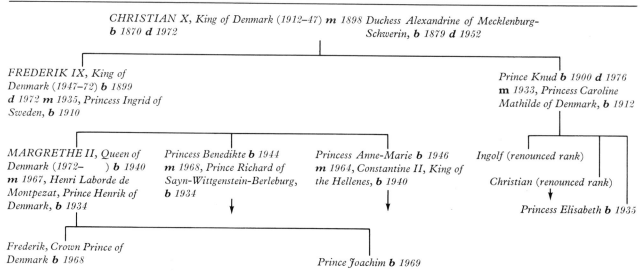

CHRISTIAN X, *King of Denmark (1912–47)* **m** *1898 Duchess Alexandrine of Mecklenburg-*
b *1870* **d** *1972*   *Schwerin,* **b** *1879* **d** *1952*

FREDERIK IX, *King of*
Denmark (1947–72) **b** *1899*
d *1972* **m** *1935, Princess Ingrid of*
Sweden, **b** *1910*

Prince Knud **b** *1900* **d** *1976*
m *1933, Princess Caroline*
Mathilde of Denmark, **b** *1912*

MARGRETHE II, *Queen of*
Denmark (1972–   ) **b** *1940*
m *1967, Henri Laborde de*
Montpezat, Prince Henrik of
Denmark, **b** *1934*

Princess Benedikte **b** *1944*
m *1968, Prince Richard of*
Sayn-Wittgenstein-Berleburg,
b *1934*

Princess Anne-Marie **b** *1946*
m *1964, Constantine II, King of*
the Hellenes, **b** *1940*

Ingolf (renounced rank)

Christian (renounced rank)

Princess Elisabeth **b** *1935*

Frederik, Crown Prince of
Denmark **b** *1968*

Prince Joachim **b** *1969*

tensively; won a bronze badge at judo and practised shooting with a rifle. But of all these interests and accomplishments, one, archaeology, became, and remains a passion.

Family life is important to Queen Margrethe, and she appears to combine it successfully with the heavy demands of royal duties. When her sons Frederik and Joachim were younger, she devoted two hours each evening between six and eight either to reading to them, or to playing or watching television with them. They have had as normal an upbringing as possible for their circumstances, and partly to this end there is a family cottage south of Copenhagen to which they and their parents escape for relaxed, informal living.

Denmark's monarchy is surrounded, in fact, by a minimum of ceremony:

Queen Margrethe, her husband Prince Henrik, her eldest son Prince Frederik and second son Prince Joachim. Queen Margrethe, called "Daisy" by her close friends and family, is good-natured, easy to talk to, unwilling to pull rank, and intellectually accomplished. She is a graduate of five universities, fluent in several languages, with a passion for archaeology. She is also passionate about clothes, and hats especially, designing much of her wardrobe herself. After her gowns have been worn a few times, she redesigns them, changing bits from one to another. The two princes, who are happiest when out of doors, are keen on skiing and have a gratifyingly Danish love of sailing and the sea.

Ingrid, Queen Mother of Denmark, lives, as privately as possible, in the newly restored and redecorated Chancellery in the park of Fredensborg Castle, near Copenhagen. From the day she ceased to be Queen Consort, she has refused, as a matter of principle, to grant audiences outside her immediate circle of family and friends. She has endeared herself to very nearly the whole of contemporary European royalty, especially to newcomers. Her ability to wear many jewels has not been carried off with such splendid effect since the heyday of Queen Mary. She is the only surviving daughter of Gustaf VI Adolf, the late King of Sweden.

Henrik, Prince of Denmark, is a Frenchman by birth- he was Third Secretary at the French Embassy in London when he met his future wife in 1963. His hard work for Danish export campaigns has reaped some fine rewards.

Right, Prince and Princess Georg of Denmark: he is the great-grandson of King Christian IX, and his mother, Princess Margretha, was a sister of Queen Astrid of Belgium and Crown Princess Märtha of Norway. Princess Georg, the former Viscountess Anson, and a niece of Great Britain's Queen Mother, is the mother of the photographer the Earl of Lichfield, whose photographs appear in this book. Prince Georg has been an attaché at the Danish Embassies in London and Paris. Prince and Princess Georg were married at Glamis Castle in 1950.

the sovereign's success depends rather on gaining the people's affection than acting as a figurehead. There is no coronation, simply a proclamation from the royal balcony of the parliament building. Margrethe is a constitutional monarch, power being exercised in her name by the ministers. Her chief duty is presiding over the Council of State's fortnightly meetings and the most exacting decision required of her is the choice of a prime minister in the event of a stalemate general election. A singular feature of the Danish royal routine is the audience held fortnightly at the Christiansborg Palace where, by immemorial custom, any Dane may meet his sovereign for an informal talk.

The Danish monarchy has close links with several other European royal families. Its "parent" dynasty, the House of Oldenburg, besides giving Kings to Denmark, Grand Dukes to Oldenburg, Dukes to Schleswig-Holstein and Emperors to Russia, has also provided Kings of Norway, Sweden and Greece. Members of the latter royal family are styled princes, or princesses of Greece and Denmark; one such is Philip, Duke of Edinburgh, so that, technically, Oldenburg will, in the next generation, give Great Britain her next sovereign in the person of Prince Charles.

Denmark is one of the oldest kingdoms in Europe. Its recorded history emerges from the myths and legends of the norse sagas with King Gorm the Old (living in about 900 AD), from whom descend all subsequent monarchs of Denmark. His grandson conquered England in 1013, and Sweyn's son Knud (Canute) conquered Norway in 1030.

His descendant, the remarkable Queen Margrethe I (after whom the present Queen is named), who died in 1412, temporarily united the three Scandinavian kingdoms of Denmark, Norway and Sweden. In 1448 the succession passed to her kinsman, the Count of Oldenburg, who was elected king. Thereafter, although the crown passed in practice from father to son, it was in theory elective, the heir being elected in his father's lifetime. The monarchy was only made officially hereditary in 1660.

Much of the visible, architectural splendour of Copenhagen, with which one associates the Danish monarchy, may be traced to an eighteenth-century King of Denmark, Frederik V, who acceded in 1746. His court was noted for its gaiety and he encouraged the arts. A new theatre was opened in 1747, and an Academy of Art was founded in 1754. Having completed his father's palace of Christiansborg, he planned to extend Copenhagen by building a new quarter called Frederiksstaden. Much of the scheme had to be abandoned because of lack of funds, but among the new buildings which were completed were the four matching Rococo palaces of Amalien-

Queen Margarethe's younger sister, Princess Benedikte, is married to Prince Richard of Sayn-Wittgenstein-Berleburg, and lives at Bad Berleburg, West Germany. When Queen Margrethe is away from Copenhagen, Princess Benedikte sometimes performs royal duties in Denmark on her sister's behalf.

borg. They were originally intended for noblemen, but were acquired by the crown at the end of the century.

Frederik was an easy-going and approachable King, but he devoted himself entirely to his pleasures, leaving the business of ruling to his ministers. He was succeeded by his seventeen year-old son, Christian VII, who was intelligent, but even more dissipated than his father. Soon after coming to the throne, he showed signs of insanity, alternating between lethargy and fierce outbursts of drunken rage. He married Caroline Matilda, the fifteen year-old sister of George III of Great Britain and treated her with cruelty and contempt. The King was surrounded by favourites, who began to take the place of the ministers bequeathed him by his father. Then came the sudden rise of Struensee, the court physician. By 1770, he had gained complete ascendancy over the King as well as the Queen, who became his mistress. He made himself the virtual dictator of Denmark and for sixteen months subjected the country to radical reforms, sweeping away many old Danish institutions. In 1772, he was arrested following a coup and beheaded. The Queen was taken away in a British warship and the country ruled by a triumvirate dominated by the King's step-mother, Juliana Maria. Twelve years later, when the King's son Frederik reached the age of sixteen, he ran a successful coup against her and obtained the powers of Regent for himself.

Though only of moderate intelligence and mainly interested in military exercises and uniforms, he took his duties seriously and enlisted the help of some talented advisers. A long period of reform followed, which ended when Denmark became involved in the Napoleonic wars. Provoked by Britain's high-handed action in attacking Copenhagen and seizing the Danish fleet in 1807, Frederik entered the war on the side of France. This proved a disaster for Denmark, putting an end to her valuable trade with Britain and severely damaging the economy. It also led to the seccession of Norway, which had long been a dominion of the Danish crown.

Frederik was succeeded in 1839 by his fifty-three year-old first cousin, Christian VIII. He was cultured, and his reign was a period of literary and artistic activity under the influence of the movement known as National Romanticism, which produced Johan Lundbye's paintings, Friedrich Kuhlau's music and the fairy tales of Hans Christian Andersen. The return of prosperity made the people more politically conscious and agitation increased during the months following the succession of Christian's son, Frederik VII.

As a result, Frederik granted a new constitution in 1848. It was thoroughly democratic, and for it he was widely acclaimed by his subjects. The

29

When King Christian IX of Denmark was "the father-in-law of Europe" (his daughters-in-law were Queen Olga of Greece; the Crown Princess of Denmark; Princess Marie of Orléans. His sons-in-law were the King of England; the Tsar of Russia, the Crown Prince of Hanover), it was almost impossible to pick up an illustrated periodical that did not contain photographs of Fredensborg with all the Royal relatives arranged stiffly on the entrance steps. Begun in 1720, Fredensborg, near Copenhagen, was set on the crest of a slope so that from any part of the park the view of the building was rewarding. The main block is dramatised by an octagonal forecourt, once entirely enclosed, but now open to the approach street. The whole is very plain and predominantly Italian in style with French overtones.

royal family, however, disapproved. Frederik had already scandalized them by his matrimonial entanglements: having been twice divorced, he was now living with a former dancer and milliner, Louise Rasmussen, whom he afterwards married morganatically, creating her Countess Danner.

The fact that Frederik VII was childless raised a problem of succession. There were no male heirs in the immediate royal family, so it was finally agreed that the crown should go to Prince Christian of Schleswig-Holstein-Sonderburg-Glücksburg whose father was head of a junior branch of the Danish Royal House. As the younger son of an impoverished cadet branch, he had been destined for nothing more than the army. But while he had grown up far from the throne, he had long been an adopted member of the royal family, for King Frederik VI had been his guardian and like a father to him. He was good-looking, with a pleasant, unassuming manner and he was intelligent, with an exemplary character. By his marriage in 1842 to Princess Louise of Hesse-Cassel, he had come much closer to the Danish succession, for her mother was a sister of Christian VIII.

The succession problem was tied up with the Schleswig-Holstein question, which bedevilled the political life of Denmark and her foreign relations for a quarter of a century. The Duchies of Schleswig and Holstein, which had long been merged with the Danish crown, could not be inherited by a female. The chief reason for choosing Christian as heir was that he was eligible to succeed to the Duchies as well as to Denmark itself, thus retaining the Danish dominions intact.

Unfortunately, the Duke of Augustenburg, a more senior Schleswig-Holstein, had a better claim to the Duchies than Christian. He also had the backing of a majority of Holsteiners as well as of German-speaking elements of Schleswig, who wished to be independent of Denmark under his rule. Also, the German-speaking inhabitants of the Duchies looked towards the united Germany that would shortly come into being, while the Danish-speaking elements in Schleswig wished to be more closely tied to Denmark. In 1848, the German-speaking Schleswig-Holsteiners rose in rebellion, and there a followed a civil war lasting two years. The Danish

Christian IX

31

army prevailed and in 1852, at the Treaty of London, the Great Powers recognized Christian's right to succeed to the Duchies as well as to Denmark. But the question of the Duchies' position within the Danish state was still unresolved when Christian succeeded as Christian IX in 1863.

Less than week after his accession, Christian gave away to Danish public opinion and agreed to a constitution which was regarded by the Schleswig-Holsteiners, and by the Powers, as being contrary to the undertakings given by Denmark at the end of the civil war. The Duke of Augustenburg proclaimed himself Duke of Schleswig-Holstein, and Bismarck, who had already decided to go to war with Denmark to deprive her once and for all of the Duchies, immediately came to his support. The Danes fought bravely, but were no match for the Prussians and their Austrian allies. Denmark was defeated and the Duchies were lost to her.

This catastrophe, which reduced Denmark's European territory by almost half, was blamed on Christian. Also, some of his subjects now mistrusted him on the grounds that he was German, although he had shown himself to be entirely Danish in outlook since early youth. But as the unhappy events of the war receded, King Christian's sense of duty, and his integrity, gradually won his people over. King Christian had, in addition, a particularly honoured place among European monarchs on account of the importance of his three children. His second son William had been elected King of Greece in 1863 and now reigned as George I. His eldest daughter, Alexandra, was married to the Prince of Wales and his second daughter, Dagmar, was now the Empress Marie of Russia. Being the "father-in-law of Europe" put a severe strain on the King's finances, for as kings went, he was a poor man. He could not afford to go to St. Petersburg for his daughter's wedding because of the largesse which the Russians would have expected him to distribute.

But if it was beyond his means to pay visits to his illustrious children,

Alexandra, Princess of Wales

they often visited their parents. The annual family reunions at the Castle of Fredensborg, when all the King and Queen's children came together with sons- and daughters-in-law, grandchildren and great-grandchildren, became an institution much talked about in royal circles. The Prince of Wales, who was used to more sophisticated entertainments, found them a little trying, especially after King Christian had become rather deaf. Just before he died, the King had the final satisfaction of seeing his grandson Prince Carl, second son of Crown Prince Frederik, elected King of Norway.

Crown Prince Frederik outlived his father by only six years, so that his reign seems rather like a continuation of King Christian's. The long reign of his son, King Christian X, spanned the two world wars. In the First World War, Denmark managed to remain neutral, while remaining on particularly good terms with Britain owing in part to the warm friendship between King Christian and his first cousin, King George V. At the end of the war, the Danish-speaking part of Schleswig was restored to Denmark.

During the Second World War, when Denmark was under Nazi occupation, King Christian lived quietly in his palace. His attitude to the Nazis was correct, dignified and aloof: when Hitler sent him greetings on his birthday, he annoyed the Führer by simply replying, "thank-you".

Tall and erect, King Christian looked a splendid figure. He had a great love of the sea and was a good yachtsman. His son, Frederik IX, who succeeded him in 1947, was also very much a sailor, a delightfully relaxed and down-to-earth man, who boasted some splendid tatoos. A talented musician, he would conduct the Danish State Orchestra in private, occasionally making records, which were sold for charity. Like his grandfather, he looked to Sweden for his bride, marrying Princess Ingrid, daughter of Gustaf VI Adolph. King Frederik's youngest daughter, Princess Anne-Marie, married King Constantine II of the Hellenes in 1964, thus uniting the two main branches of the Danish Royal House.

Frederik IX

33

GREAT BRITAIN
Family Business

According to Queen Victoria, nothing was so salutary for a monarch as not having been born to the purple. She was heiress presumptive from the age of eleven, when her uncle, William IV, was crowned, but her mother kept this fact from her, discouraging enquiries about the succession. Queen Elizabeth II of Great Britain had the same salutary early experience.

When she was born Princess Elizabeth of York on 21st April 1926, in the reign of her grandfather King George V, there was no reason to suppose that sovereignty was her destiny. Her father's elder brother, at the age of thirty-two, was an immensely popular Prince of Wales—though even then a "certain lack of seriousness, excusable . . . to healthy youth, disquieting in the mature man" was being noticed. Ten years on, came his abdication; Princess Elizabeth's father became King George VI and she herself heiress presumptive.

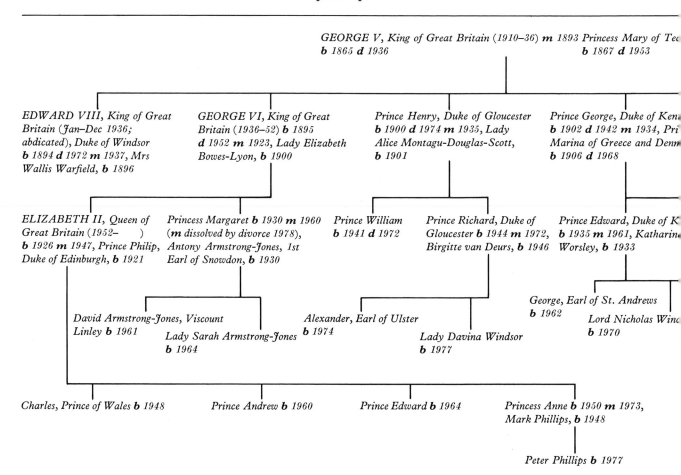

GEORGE V, *King of Great Britain (1910–36)* **m** *1893 Princess Mary of Te* **b** *1865* **d** *1936* **b** *1867* **d** *1953*

EDWARD VIII, *King of Great Britain (Jan–Dec 1936; abdicated), Duke of Windsor* **b** *1894* **d** *1972* **m** *1937, Mrs Wallis Warfield,* **b** *1896*

GEORGE VI, *King of Great Britain (1936–52)* **b** *1895* **d** *1952* **m** *1923, Lady Elizabeth Bowes-Lyon,* **b** *1900*

Prince Henry, Duke of Gloucester **b** *1900* **d** *1974* **m** *1935, Lady Alice Montagu-Douglas-Scott,* **b** *1901*

Prince George, Duke of Ken **b** *1902* **d** *1942* **m** *1934, Pri Marina of Greece and Denn* **b** *1906* **d** *1968*

ELIZABETH II, *Queen of Great Britain (1952–)* **b** *1926* **m** *1947, Prince Philip, Duke of Edinburgh,* **b** *1921*

Princess Margaret **b** *1930* **m** *1960 (m dissolved by divorce 1978), Antony Armstrong-Jones, 1st Earl of Snowdon,* **b** *1930*

Prince William **b** *1941* **d** *1972*

Prince Richard, Duke of Gloucester **b** *1944* **m** *1972, Birgitte van Deurs,* **b** *1946*

Prince Edward, Duke of K **b** *1935* **m** *1961, Katharine Worsley,* **b** *1933*

David Armstrong-Jones, Viscount Linley **b** *1961*

Lady Sarah Armstrong-Jones **b** *1964*

Alexander, Earl of Ulster **b** *1974*

Lady Davina Windsor **b** *1977*

George, Earl of St. Andrews **b** *1962*

Lord Nicholas Wind **b** *1970*

Charles, Prince of Wales **b** *1948*

Prince Andrew **b** *1960*

Prince Edward **b** *1964*

Princess Anne **b** *1950* **m** *1973, Mark Phillips,* **b** *1948*

Peter Phillips **b** *1977*

Her childhood was not so very different from that of other privileged children of the day — except that she was tutored in constitutional history and law. The Second World War broke out in 1939. Next year, aged fourteen, Princess Elizabeth, together with her sister Margaret, four years her junior, made a first public broadcast. Her first public engagement came in 1942, with an inspection of the Grenadier Guards.

After the war, the Princess, who had of course often accompanied the King and Queen on their wartime journeys across Britain, joined them on their South African tour. She celebrated her twenty-first birthday in Cape Town, and from there broadcast her now famous "solemn act of dedication" to the Commonwealth.

Shortly after this voyage, in 1947, the King announced her engagement to Lieutenant Philip Mountbatten. Prince Philip, nephew of Lord Mountbatten of Burma, was a Prince of Greece, and belongs, like all members of that royal house, to the family of Schleswig-Holstein-Sonderburg-Glücksburg. He had renounced his foreign titles on becoming a British subject in the spring of 1947 and adopted the name of Mountbatten — anglicized from Battenberg, his mother's maiden name. His marriage to Princess Elizabeth was celebrated in November that year, the first grand royal occasion since the war.

Princess Elizabeth became Queen in 1952, learning of her accession — in the words of a contemporary diarist — "up a tree watching the rhinoceroses drink". She was in Kenya at the time, accompanied by her husband, and planning to visit Australia and New Zealand on behalf of the ailing King George VI. The sad news of his death came suddenly, and the young Queen at once returned home to make her accession declaration to

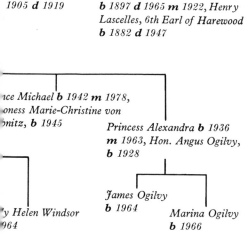

Prince John *b 1905 d 1919*

Princess Mary, Princess Royal *b 1897 d 1965 m 1922, Henry Lascelles, 6th Earl of Harewood b 1882 d 1947*

nce Michael *b 1942 m 1978,* oness Marie-Christine von nitz, *b 1945*

Princess Alexandra *b 1936 m 1963, Hon. Angus Ogilvy, b 1928*

'y Helen Windsor 964

James Ogilvy *b 1964*

Marina Ogilvy *b 1966*

Prince Philip has a reputation for outspokenness, for "opening my big mouth and putting my foot in it", as he once said. In spite of this, or perhaps because of it, he has found a place in the British public's consciousness which another prince consort, Prince Albert, was never able to achieve. Prince Philip once characteristically summed up his approach by saying, "Stick your neck out, but don't actually pass them the axe." His sixtieth birthday is in 1981.

The British ask a great deal of their Queen. She must be regal, and at the same time natural, as if she were an "ordinary" person living a "normal" life, albeit under extraordinary circumstances. She must be continuously adapting to the occasion, always taking a personal interest in everyone she meets, never making a false step. Caught up in the excitement and glamour of a public event, few stop to consider how lonely and demanding the Queen's job can be, for she performs it with apparent ease and grace. Only on rare occasions have her private feelings been revealed in public, but always to her advantage. One such instance was when the Prince of Wales was being installed as Great Master of the Order of the Bath in Westminster Abbey in 1975. For a change, the Prince had precedence, since he was leading the procession, and the Queen's face showed her obvious pride in the way her son was fulfilling his role.

Above: Princess Anne, her husband Captain Mark Phillips and son Peter. Anne's perfectionism has made her a champion on horseback, but it has not helped in her relations with the press. Outwardly tense in public, she explains: "If one stops having nerves, one isn't doing the job as well as one should." She is the only royal lady to have driven both a London double-decker bus and a Chieftain tank, the latter at considerable speed, though it was her riding skill that won her a place at the 1976 Montreal Olympics.

Charles, Prince of Wales and heir to the throne of Great Britain and Northern Ireland, is one of the world's most eligible bachelors, seldom short of female admirers. Seldom either is he at a loss for words, no matter how dismal the situation, and this easy manner has brought him to the heights of popularity. This was well illustrated at a ceremony in Wales, when he overheard two old women talking in Welsh. "He's gorgeous", said one. "Yes", responded the other, "I could eat him with a spoon." Charles turned to them with a wink and a smile and in perfect Welsh said: "Thank you very much, girls."

Above: Prince Andrew, in spite of being the younger brother of a personable Prince of Wales, has emerged as an individual in his own right. It is well known that during his period of enrolment at Gordonstoun, the Scottish public school attended by his father and elder brother before him, he spent three terms at a school near Toronto and made many firm friends there. Not such common knowledge is the fact that he is a capable water colourist, some of his most telling pictures having captured the rugged beauty of the Canadian landscape.

Above: Prince Edward, youngest of Queen Elizabeth's children. His happy smile and his penchant for hats, sometimes of an unusual variety, have already warmed hearts across the world. Lately eased into the royal routine of unveiling this and that and turning the first spadeful of earth, Edward has a mischievous quality about him which invites attention and disguises a serious approach to even the most everyday problems.

the Privy Council: "I shall always work, as my father did, throughout his reign, to uphold constitutional government and to advance the happiness and prosperity of my people, spread as they are the world over."

The British constitution is not a written set of rules, though parts of it are in statutory form. It is, simply, the system of government now in force: a system subject to changes in the future (as it had been subject to changes in the past), to a pattern set by law and convention. The sovereign is its corner stone and is also the head of the armed forces and the Church of England. The monarch has a vast number of formal functions which are, in practice, performed in the monarch's name by ministers, and all legislation passed is described as being "enacted" by the sovereign.

The British sovereign, however, is far from being a mere figure-head: in any given reign, governments come and go; the monarch remains, providing a lifetime's experience and an element of continuity. In the words of Bagehot, it is the function, and the right of the monarch "to be consulted, to encourage and to warn." It is generally realized that the advantage of the British monarchical system lies not in the wide powers exercised from the throne, but in the fact that this power, represented in the person of the King or Queen, cannot be assumed by others. In order that the Queen may be kept minutely informed in every field, red boxes of state papers and ambassadorial reports follow her wherever she goes at home or abroad — "doing the boxes" is a relentless task.

Modern communications have enabled Queen Elizabeth, who is not only the sovereign of Great Britain but also of the self-governing monarchies of the Commonwealth, to visit her domains more often than any of her predecessors. She also pays a prodigious number of state visits. She has been seen, dressed in light, bright colours for maximum visibility, hat well off the face, by an amazing number of people the world over.

On her journeys, Queen Elizabeth is invariably accompanied by Prince Philip, created Duke of Edinburgh on his wedding day. Besides quietly supporting her, the Duke undertakes a great many engagements of his own — the list of his chairmanships and presidencies is awesomely long.

The maintenance of the monarchy in Great Britain compares well with the cost of heads of state in other forms of government, yet the Civil List — her annuity from the state — and the state's financial contribution to the members of her family, all of whom share the duties inherent in the family business, remains a sensitive subject, often aired in the British Parliament and press. It is, however, a bonus for the country and for the Queen that there is such a large and capable team willing to make a contribution.

People everywhere display an insatiable curiosity about the British royals: a curiosity which is the expression of the fact that royalty still has its potent mystique. Whether, for all their blue blood, the members of the charmed circle are "just ordinary people", their every utterance and gesture is seen as special. Their physical presence causes awe and excitement: to shake a royal hand is a privilege so eagerly sought that royal hands have been known to swell up quite painfully by the end of the day. And it is a statistical fact, causing less hardship to Queen Elizabeth, that she, of all well-known personalities, appears most frequently in the dreams of her sleeping subjects.

After the Queen, with the possible exception of Princess Margaret, no member of the English royal family is the subject of so much attention from the media as the Prince of Wales, heir to the throne.

He has a strong sense of duty, of humour, of history and of politeness,

Queen Elizabeth The Queen Mother has great strength of character combined with such a delightfully feminine charm that a fleeting glimpse of her has cheered sad hearts. Although born at the turn of the century, her gift for putting strangers naturally and effortlessly at their ease remains quite undiminished.

A look of real happiness transforms Princess Margaret's face when she is with her children David and Sarah. The press photographers have persistently, and often unfairly, caught her at her worst moments, rarely conveying the sense of humour which seldom deserts her. Even when she was a child, her governess noted in Margaret the "born comic". Her talents include gifted piano playing and a wide interest in the arts.

Right: Prince Richard of Gloucester, photographed in 1972 with his future wife, Birgitte. Harry Truman, who said he felt as if the sun, the moon and the stars had fallen on him when he succeeded to the American presidency on the death of Roosevelt, would have understood the retiring Prince Richard's feelings on suddenly becoming heir to a royal dukedom after his elder brother's death in 1972. Once absorbed in his profession as an architect, Prince Richard now fulfils his share of royal duties with dedication. He is a talented photographer.

Above: Princess Alice, Duchess of Gloucester, widow of the late Duke, was born a Montagu-Douglas-Scott. Her parents-in-law, King George V and Queen Mary, considered this daughter of the 7th Duke of Buccleuch a fine choice as wife for their son Henry. The Duchess has risen with great dignity above her sorrows, most tragic of which must have been the death of her eldest son William in a plane crash in 1972. Her consideration for others, even at the most difficult times, was typified by the way in which she arranged for one of her former cooks to sit with the family at her husband's memorial service.

and of what is due to him as Prince of Wales. He has intelligence and culture, a quick wit and a quick understanding.

With a long neck, bright blue eyes, the high complexion of the Guelphs, good teeth and his father's stance, he photographs well: but although in life the Prince is perhaps a shade less handsome, his charm makes him far more attractive. The question "Sir, to what do you ascribe your amazing success with the opposite sex?" might well have been asked even if he were not who he is.

Prince Charles looks young for his age, and has been called a late developer. "All my life I've been learning", he says, which is hardly surprising in view of the part for which he is cast. Any heir to any throne must have a feeling of waiting in the wings. There simply is no distinctive role for any Prince of Wales to play — which is why the dangers of an Edward VII or Edward VIII situation are much discussed.

Naturally, the question of his marriage looms large and will continue to do so until it is settled. He is on record as saying that he had better marry a royal princess because only such a girl would know what would be required of her, and he must rue the day when he said that thirty seemed a good age for marrying. Since he reached this magic age, still a bachelor, and no announcement followed, speculation has continued.

According to the constitution, he is perfectly free to marry a commoner, or indeed a royal princess, provided that she is a Protestant. Should he

Prince Michael of Kent, younger brother of the Duke of Kent, and familiar as a hero of the bobsleigh run, was born on American Independence Day, 4th July 1942, a circumstance happily commemorated by the fact that President Franklin Delano Roosevelt became his godfather, and that the Prince was christened Michael George Charles Franklin. His Roman Catholic wife, the former Baroness von Reibnitz, whom he married in Vienna in 1978, has the elegant beauty typical of some Edwardian duchesses and is a welcome addition to the English royal family. There was disappointment that the couple's wedding could not take place with the full blessing of either the Roman Catholic or the Anglican Church.

Princess Alexandra, the Duke of Kent's sister, with her children Marina and James, and her husband the Hon. Angus Ogilvy, board member and businessman. Alexandra is a clever manager, elegant and unruffled, one of the most popular and hardworking members of the British royal family. Her resemblance to her mother, the late Princess Marina, is remarkable.

marry a Catholic, the law of the land would have to be changed, even if the Catholic Church were to allow the children of such a marriage to be brought up as Protestants. In view of the suggestion that he might marry Marie Astrid, the daughter of Grand Duke Jean of Luxembourg (and in the face of denials from the Palace, naturally anxious to preserve the royal privacy), the religious question is much discussed. All shades of opinion are represented in the country: some people would like to see the unification of the Churches, even though the Prince, on his succession will be the head of the Church of England and become, like all kings of England from Henry VIII onwards, the Defender of the Faith. Others feel that even if the Christian Church remained disunited, legislation could easily solve such a problem. And then there are those who view the matter radically, as Queen Victoria did when one of her younger sons, Prince Alfred, married a Russian grand duchess: "What I feel painfully in the religion is that it is the first departure since two hundred years nearly from the practice in our family since the Revolution of 1688. We must be very firm — or else we may pack up — and call back the descendants of the Stuarts."

The link between Queen Victoria's House and that of Stuart, which preceded it, was formed by James I's granddaughter, Sophie, Electress of Hanover. A daughter of Elizabeth Stuart, Electress Palatine and Winter Queen of Bohemia, Princess Sophie was born into the reformed religion,

Princess Alice, Countess of Athlone, the last surviving grandchild of Queen Victoria, is much loved by her family, for whom she is a living link with the past. Born in 1883, the daughter of Queen Victoria's fourth and youngest son Leopold, Duke of Albany, she is the longest-lived British princess in history, having attained an even greater age than Augusta, Grand Duchess of Mecklenburg-Strelitz, the grand-daughter of George III who died when she was ninety-four. Princess Alice now lives in Kensington Palace, with other members of the family as neighbours.

Left: the Duke and Duchess of Kent with their children Lady Helen Windsor (left), Lord Nicholas Windsor (standing, centre) and the Earl of St. Andrews. The Duke of Kent, like the Duke of Gloucester, is a first cousin of the Queen, and after her children, Princess Margaret and her children and the Duke of Gloucester and his children, is in line of succession to the British throne. The Duke, his brother and sister have a double connection with the Queen, for their mother, the late Princess Marina, was a cousin of Prince Philip. One of the happiest moments in the Duke's life came in 1961 when he married Miss Katherine Worsley, who has proved to be a worthy successor to her enormously admired mother-in-law.

and remained a Protestant, while her Stuart cousins, Charles II and James II, especially the latter, veered towards Catholicism. After William of Orange, another cousin, had been called to throne and had failed to furnish heirs, as had his successor, Queen Anne, "Sophia and the Heirs of her Body" were the logical choice for the throne of Great Britain — and as an extra bonus, Sophie had produced Protestant sons. (That there was also a Catholic among them was a fact kept dark by the genealogists, for all his mother's indignant references to "poor Max, quite ignored".).

The ancestry of Princess Sophie, and consequently that of Queen Victoria, and therefore that of Queen Elizabeth II, is deeply rooted and traceable to the medieval British kings and beyond to the elected warrior priests who were invested with every kind of magic property by their followers. In due course, these sanctified tribal rulers made way for the medieval kings of England—the Saxons, Normans, Plantagenets, Yorkists and Lancastrians followed by the Tudors and Stuarts.

Queen Anne died at forty-nine, a few weeks after the aged Sophie of Hanover. Indeed, Queen Anne's extremely curt letter, yet again declining the honour of a visit from the Electoral Prince of Hanover—the future George II — is said to have hastened the death of Sophie, a spry old lady of eighty-four.

So it was Sophie's eldest son, George I, who succeeded to the three kingdoms in his mother's stead. Although he had not set foot in England — and, unlike his son, had little desire to do so — he was far from being an unknown quantity: Hanover had turned into "a little England" long since, with large groups of Whigs and many Tories paying their respects to the heiress's family, for all that many of them also flirted with the Stuarts.

As George I had been separated from his wife (and cousin) Sophie Dorothea of Celle for some time, England had to do without a Queen. Instead, the new King brought his son, George August, now Prince of Wales, and Princess Caroline. They in turn left their son, Frederick, in

George III

40

Germany: relations between the Hanoverians and their heirs were seldom, if ever, happy. George I had, from the age of fifteen, been difficult with his own parents, especially with his mother, who grieved to see her eldest boy grow from an ardent, communicative child into a dour, taciturn and parsimonious man, less enthusiastic about England than she might have wished. However, her misgivings were nothing compared to the insane loathings felt by George I for George II and by George II and Queen Caroline for the luckless Frederick, father of George III, known as poor Fred: he died before he could succeed. There was little love lost between George III and George IV; and a modified coolness, by now proverbial, between the sovereigns of England and their successors stretched right to the time of Queen Victoria and her son Edward.

The first three Georges were mocked by the novelist Thackeray for stupidity, for their un-English ways and their thick German accents, which had not quite faded even with George III. George I's German entourage was heartily disliked, especially the two ladies, called the Elephant and the Maypole, who were generally taken to be his mistresses.

In the reign of the Georges, British constitutional monarchy became firmly established: the pattern of government as England knows it now had largely, if not entirely, emerged. Moreover, the quite domesticated life of George III and his Queen, Charlotte of Mecklenburg-Strelitz, brought into being the notion of the royal family as the "guardians of the nation's morals" — though this idea received a setback in the reign of George IV.

Prince George ascended in 1820 after acting for a decade as Regent for his father, who was stricken with a disease that periodically produced symptoms of insanity. As Prince of Wales, George IV had agreed to marry Princess Caroline of Brunswick, renouncing the twice-widowed Maria Fitzherbert whom he had married in a Catholic ceremony — meaningless in English law. A gifted, high-living profligate with a taste for the arts and a lifelong passion for building and interior decoration, Prince George was

George IV

41

Princess Margaret's apartments in Kensington Palace express her own taste and that of Lord Snowdon, but the parts of the Palace open to the public reflect earlier ages. The portions added by Wren for William and Mary are particularly fine, though Kensington Palace is perhaps most often visited because it is where Queen Victoria was born, and where, as a girl of eighteen, she received the news of her accession. Prince Philip spent the night there before his wedding in 1947.

Balmoral, in Aberdeenshire, is affectionately called The Scotch House by those whose names regularly appear on the Queen's guest list there, for it flaunts more tartan yardage than the London shop of that name. Prince Albert bought the Balmoral estate in 1852 and had the house rebuilt in Scottish baronial style to provide the retreat which, for Queen Victoria, was "this dear paradise".

deeply in debt and only a suitable marriage, approved by Parliament, would bring him the increased annuity he needed.

Queen Charlotte had a good deal of private information regarding her future daughter-in-law, who was also her husband's niece, and tried to speak out against the marriage. The bride was considered by her German relations to be unfit for society and not allowed to stir, even from one room to another, unaccompanied by her governess because "her passions are so strong". At dances, she had been known to make an exhibition of herself by indecent conversations with men. Her flamboyance might not have been such a drawback in the eyes of the Prince, but her limited physical attractions, her grubbiness and her lack of style caused him to ask for a glass of brandy as soon as he had clapped eyes on her.

The marriage was a disaster. The royal couple ceased to share a bed after a very short time, and Princess Charlotte, born nine months after the wedding almost to the day, remained an only child. After his accession, King George IV brought a divorce suit against the Queen, whose subsequent behaviour suggests that she must have been a little mad. This caused an enormous scandal, even though her threat to call the King's mistresses as witnesses for her defence remained unrealized. The King had also been much criticized for his unkindness to his only daughter, Princess Charlotte. Her life was miserable until she married Leopold of Saxe-Coburg, future King of the Belgians. Soon afterwards, she died in childbirth, her son still-born.

Since the King had not been able to rid himself of his wife, there was no way in which he, personally, could secure the succession. A number of his brothers therefore gave up their mistresses or morganatic wives of long standing, and plunged into such matrimonial connections as did not contravene the Royal Marriage Act.

The King, his popularity restored soon after the abortive divorce, "as if he were the most virtuous, the most fatherly, the greatest of Kings", amused himself with mistresses of a mature and motherly type, and gave wonderful house parties at his new pleasance in Brighton—the pavilion that looked to one of the wits "as though St Paul's had gone to Brighton and pupped", and was described as the Kremlin by another. As he grew older, the King's passion for architecture increased. He rebuilt Buckingham Palace and made Windsor Castle his Versailles — albeit in the Gothick style — and was the first English king to create a splendid setting for the monarchy, a setting expressing its grandeur in visible terms. It was on phaeton drives in Windsor's Great Park that the King's young niece,

42

Victoria of Kent, sometimes accompanied him: she was the daughter of the King's brother and of Victoria of Saxe-Coburg, the sister of Prince Leopold who had been married to the late Princess Charlotte.

Before she became England's greatest queen regnant after Elizabeth I, the King's brother, William IV, ascended the throne, ruling from 1830 to 1837. Sailor Bill, simple, down to earth, and unaffected, had a real desire to make the people happy. To this end he walked among his subjects, and with Queen Adelaide, became far more accessible than any British monarch before him. Gentle Queen Adelaide was "much admired for her comportment and mien", as well she might have been in comparison with the flamboyant and dishonoured Caroline, dead long since.

On 28th June 1837, a contemporary wrote "the poor King expired last night. He is a great loss to *All*, even to the young Queen, who would have derived benefit from a few years' more experience."

Queen Victoria, now aged eighteen, won all hearts by admirably speaking her accession declaration in the Council. All agreed on the "harmony and sweetness of her voice", and on the excellent sense she showed in all important matters right from the start. After a visit to Windsor a guest reported "the Queen is as great a wonder in her way, as Fair Star or any other enchanted princess. What luck it is for this country to have such a jewel to raise the character of royalty."

Three years later, the character of royalty was raised even further with the Queen's marriage to the dutiful and good Prince Albert of Saxe-Coburg. The Queen's Uncle Leopold had helped to arrange this marriage for Albert, who was one of his nephews.

Because in later life when Queen Victoria made such a cult of widowhood and mourning in general, she almost invariably looked grim, it is easy to forget she was particularly noticed for her humour and ability to enjoy life. As a girl, and into her old age, the private Queen was often very amused indeed. If the public Queen was painted looking solemn, one may trace this to contemporary conventions in portrait painting. As for photographs of the Queen, the necessity for long exposures meant that subjects had to keep a straight face if the picture was to be sharp: there *is* one smiling snap of Queen Victoria (showing too much gum) but it is blurred, not sharp.

Queen Victoria had nine children, by whose marriages she became the beloved grandmother of all Europe: as a mother she was awe-inspiring, fond of her offspring while they were between three and six, which she considered the only attractive age, less so before and after. Even her eldest son, Edward, called Bertie, managed to please her in those years, not least for "his fairy figure", which then resembled his "adored Papa's". He soon, she thought, grew into "a caricature of myself" in looks, and his voice made her so nervous that she could hardly bear it. At the age of seventeen, he struck his mother "by systematic idleness, laziness — disregard of everything" — it was she said, enough to break one's heart, and filled her with indignation, vigorously expressed both by the Queen and Albert. When the Prince Consort died in 1861, leaving his widow disconsolate for many years to come, she could not look at Bertie — "Oh that boy!" — without a shudder. She thought that one of his youthful indiscretions — called "Bertie's fall" — had hastened Prince Albert's death, lowering his resistance to typhoid fever caused by defective drains at Windsor.

No time was to be lost in marrying off the fallen Prince of Wales. He had, apparently, been unimpressed by Princess Alexandra of Denmark, "that sweet lovely young flower which would make most men's hearts

Prince Philip calls the London residence of the British sovereign a "tied cottage" and is fond of pointing out that he and the Queen "live above the shop". A somewhat prosaic description is appropriate, for Buckingham Palace is not one of Europe's most attractive royal dwellings. The familiar east-facing facade is a 1913 addition, made of Portland stone rather than the Bath stone of the rest. With the exception of the private apartments and some of the guest suites, the interior has little charm. Prince Philip has endeavoured to introduce some twentieth-century conveniences, for instance by converting part of a dressing room between his suite and the Queen's into a small pantry and kitchen for private use.

Queen Victoria

The Royal Pavilion at Brighton began as a relatively humble hideaway for the future George IV, but by 1812, the first year of his regency, the Prince was tired of the simple villa and engaged Nash to redesign the place in what is usually described as the Indian style. The result, with its clumps of onion-shaped domes and slender pillars, is a delightful anachronism.

George V

beat fire and flames", at a meeting kindly arranged as though by accident by his sister of Prussia. But in November 1862, Queen Victoria declared his marriage, which in view of the loss of her own happiness "is dreadful for me". However, the presence of dear Alix, good, kind, bright, cheerful, quiet, gentle, deep, serious, reasonable and sensible, quite soothed the Queen and made her wonder if Bertie "quite deserved such a sweet wife"

The Prince and Princess of Wales were married at Windsor in March 1863. The Queen watched the ceremony from a gallery — and described the occasion as a fearful ordeal. She felt helpless and alone, and when she received good accounts from Osborne where the young couple had gone for a week's honeymoon — "love has shed its sunshine on these dear young hearts" — she felt an understandable pang.

For many years, she remained in sad retirement and became known as the Widow of Windsor, which earned her much adverse comment. Winkled out of her retirement by Disraeli who made her Empress of India, much to her delight, she became a positively venerated figure, always dressed in black, even for festive occasions when, however, pearls or stunning diamonds would adorn her white cap. Queen Victoria died in 1901, in the arms of her visiting grandson, the Kaiser, and the Prince of Wales became Edward VII, adopting his father's surname, that of Saxe-Coburg and Gotha. (In 1917, this Germanic name was changed to Windsor by King George V, and it is not unlikely that it will change to Mountbatten-Windsor in the reign following the present Queen's.).

England's Edwardian age had begun when Edward, as a gregarious Prince of Wales, had transformed the social scene. He was still fond of women (though his affairs never quite undermined his marriage) but a wise and tactful mistress, Mrs. Derek Keppel, took the place of the more turbulent ladies of the past.

In the year of his accession, on his sixtieth birthday, King Edward created his son George Prince of Wales. This Prince had been heir to the throne since his elder brother, the Duke of Clarence, had died in 1892. In the following year he had married his late brother's fiancée, Princess Mary of Teck.

As Edward VII, when Prince of Wales, had often complained, with justice, that his mother "would not tell him things", so did Prince George and so, it was confidently believed, would the little Prince Edward, the eldest of Edward and Alexandra's grandchildren, who was called David at home. The future George V did not, however, complain for long: his father arranged for him to see documents of major importance, discussed problems with him as they arose, and, unlike his own mother, was genuinely delighted when the Prince and Princess of Wales were acclaimed on their journeys abroad. When King Edward died in 1910, King George V wrote in his diary that he had lost his best friend and the best of fathers.

The last vestiges of Edwardian society — the gay whirl of the lavish house parties, the elegance of the season, the improprieties that were winked at as long as no public scandals were caused — were swept away with the First World War. King George had never been a part of these: his inclinations lay in domesticity.

His Silver Jubilee in 1935 showed him in no uncertain terms how much he was loved. Every night during Jubilee week, enthusiastic crowds cheered in delirium as he appeared on the balcony of Buckingham Palace with the Queen by his side, and so many people waved flags and showed him their devotion as he toured the streets that he said "I had no idea they felt like

Possibly the most beguiling room in the Royal Pavilion (opposite page), is the Prince Regent's Bedroom, later called the King's Bedroom. The furniture is splendid, each piece designed for the spot it occupies. The most oriental room is the entrance hall, with its delicate-looking twin staircases equipped with railings apparently made of bamboo, although in fact of cast iron.

that about me. I am beginning to think they must really like me for myself!"

George V had no time for modernism, whether this was expressed as innovations in matters of procedure or in clothes — particularly in the case of his children, whom he was trying to imbue with his own views and ideas, and intimidated in the process.

There were difficulties, especially, between King George V and his eldest son. Though a dutiful and indeed loving son, David, created Prince of Wales at Caernarvon in 1911 — "the dear boy did it all remarkably well" — was a somewhat aggressively modern member of the nightclub generation. There were family rows about the Prince's cut of trousers (he went in for turn-ups, anathema to the King), about his hair-cuts, and, apparently about things that might be regarded as less trivial, though even the trivialities were, of course, the outward expression of more fundamental differences in character and approach: thus the King, congratulating his second son, George, on the occasion of his marriage to Lady Elizabeth Bowes-Lyon wrote, significantly, "you have always been ready to listen to any advice and to agree with my opinions . . . very different to dear David". Relations between parents and their eldest son were frigid: both King and Queen were shy of discussing with him the disquieting news of his attachment to the twice-divorced American, Mrs. Simpson. King George V died before the matter had been broached, and after a brief reign — less than a year — as Edward VIII, the new King found himself obliged to abdicate in order to be able to marry Mrs. Simpson. He became the Duke of Windsor, and his brother succeeded as King George VI.

With the help and support of his wife, known today as England's immensely popular Queen Mother, he embarked on the arduous career of kingship, courageously and calmly bringing his nation through the dark days of World War II. After a reign of fifteen years, his health, never robust, finally broke down, and he died at the early age of fifty-six, to be succeeded by his daughter, Queen Elizabeth II. By then, the monarchy had not only recovered from the traumatic shock of the abdication, but was as strong as ever it had been. That it has remained so was proved in 1977, the year of Queen Elizabeth II's own Silver Jubilee.

Edward VIII

LIECHTENSTEIN
The Valley of Peace

Liechtenstein, the country, is a wedge of territory about one hundred square miles in size "leaning" (in the words of the national anthem, sung to the same tune as England's *God Save The Queen*) "against Alpine heights close to the young Rhine". Just south of Lake Constance, it is bounded by the Swiss canton of St. Gallen and by Austria.

Liechtenstein, the princely dynasty which gave the country its name, had no connection at all with the place until the late seventeenth century, and indeed only in comparatively recent times ceased to be based on its great estates in Austria and the former Bohemia.

Prince Franz Joseph, the principality's present ruler, was educated in Vienna where he studied forestry engineering. He succeeded his great uncle in 1938, arriving in the principality in the spring of 1939, a few weeks after Hitler had annexed Austria. The Third Reich, with its territorial demands, each allegedly the last, was a menacing neighbour for such

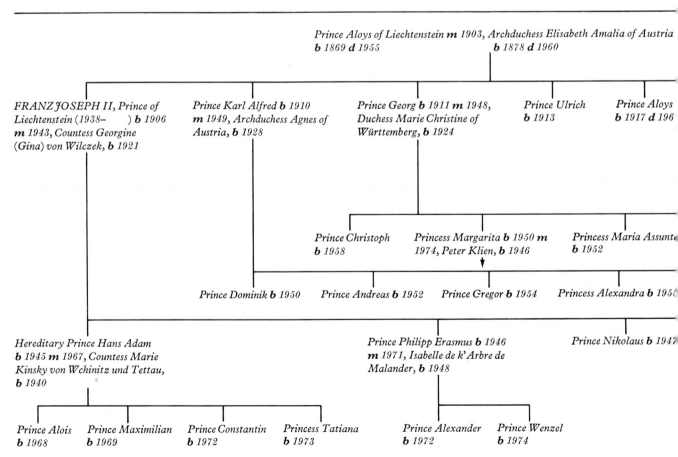

Prince Aloys of Liechtenstein **m** *1903, Archduchess Elisabeth Amalia of Austria*
b *1869* **d** *1955*   **b** *1878* **d** *1960*

FRANZ JOSEPH II, Prince of Liechtenstein (1938–   ) **b** *1906* **m** *1943, Countess Georgine (Gina) von Wilczek,* **b** *1921*

Prince Karl Alfred **b** *1910* **m** *1949, Archduchess Agnes of Austria,* **b** *1928*

Prince Georg **b** *1911* **m** *1948, Duchess Marie Christine of Württemberg,* **b** *1924*

Prince Ulrich **b** *1913*

Prince Aloys **b** *1917* **d** *196*

Prince Christoph **b** *1958*

Princess Margarita **b** *1950* **m** *1974, Peter Klien,* **b** *1946*

Princess Maria Assunta **b** *1952*

Prince Dominik **b** *1950*   *Prince Andreas* **b** *1952*   *Prince Gregor* **b** *1954*   *Princess Alexandra* **b** *195*

Hereditary Prince Hans Adam **b** *1945* **m** *1967, Countess Marie Kinsky von Wchinitz und Tettau,* **b** *1940*

Prince Philipp Erasmus **b** *1946* **m** *1971, Isabelle de k'Arbre de Malander,* **b** *1948*

Prince Nikolaus **b** *194*

Prince Alois **b** *1968*   *Prince Maximilian* **b** *1969*   *Prince Constantin* **b** *1972*   *Princess Tatiana* **b** *1973*

Prince Alexander **b** *1972*   *Prince Wenzel* **b** *1974*

Prince Franz Joseph, with his gentle voice and revealing smile, is so easy to be with that one might be lured into relaxing too much in his presence. A diffident man, he has never taken credit for refusing, alone among European rulers, to repatriate Russians at the end of the Second World War. To save them from almost certain death, he calmly arranged for more than 250 of them to go to South America. He is very knowledgeable about his castle above Vaduz and its contents. In his youth he visited it while his great-uncle was reigning Prince, but it was then not habitable except for a few days at a time during summer. He was brought up partly in Vienna, but mostly in a family castle in the Moravian part of what is now Czechoslovakia. His is the last central European monarchy.

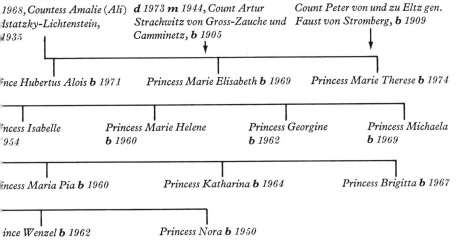

Prince Heinrich **b** 1920 1968, Countess Amalie (Ali) Kotstatzky-Lichtenstein, 1935	Princess Maria Theresia **b** 1908 **d** 1973 **m** 1944, Count Artur Strachwitz von Gross-Zauche und Camminetz, **b** 1905	Princess Henriette **b** 1914 **m** 1943 Count Peter von und zu Eltz gen. Faust von Stromberg, **b** 1909
Prince Hubertus Alois **b** 1971	Princess Marie Elisabeth **b** 1969	Princess Marie Therese **b** 1974
Princess Isabelle 1954	Princess Marie Helene **b** 1960	Princess Georgine **b** 1962	Princess Michaela **b** 1969
Princess Maria Pia **b** 1960	Princess Katharina **b** 1964	Princess Brigitta **b** 1967
Prince Wenzel **b** 1962	Princess Nora **b** 1950

Prince Franz Joseph's wife Gina has the air of a lady who can effortlessly remember every glove or shoe size, birthday, anniversary and telephone number relevant to her rôle—which is precisely how she has to be. Besides being châtelaine of an enormous castle, about 130 of whose rooms are in use, she is the mother and grandmother of a proliferative brood, a number of whom live permanently, or intermittently at Vaduz. She is the sponsor of this, chairman of that and works hand in glove with the Prince in the affairs of their country.

Franz Joseph's eldest son and heir, right, is Prince Hans Adam, who lives with his wife Princess Maria and their four children in a magnificent apartment in the castle at Vaduz. Hans Adam, in his thirties, is serious beyond his years, and understandably content with what life has dealt him. Pope Pius XII was his godfather.

Prince Nikolaus, above, third son of Prince Franz Joseph, lives at Vaduz and is a full-time business assistant to his father. Also based at home is his younger brother Wenzel, whom the family call Wenceslas, the Bohemian version of the name. Both brothers seem to enjoy the opportunities life presents in the Principality. Their elder brother, Philipp, is a merchant banker in Paris—to his father's astonishment, who declares: "He really loves banking. He really does. More than food or drink, even." Prince Franz Joseph's only daughter, Princess Nora, works in London for an environmentalist pressure group.

a tiny country so anxious to preserve its independence. The principality's two political parties therefore entered upon a coalition in order to face any threats in unison, and the Prince quickly became a symbol of national unity. Liechtenstein, like Switzerland, of whose rationing system it became a part, remained inviolate and neutral. The Prince married during the war, and his new wife, Princess Gina, founded the Liechtenstein Red Cross which was to help many refugees and ex-prisoners of war.

Since 1945, Prince Franz Joseph has presided over a period of unprecedented economic boom. Industry flourishes, as does agriculture, comprised essentially of stockbreeding and dairying. There is a tourist trade, and because company taxes are so low, the country is a rendez-vous for international high finance. Frequently changing issues of postage stamps are an additional source of revenue.

For a twentieth-century sovereign, Prince Franz Joseph has comparatively far-reaching powers. The constitution of 1921 recognizes the reigning prince as head of state, with the right to exercise sovereign power in conformity with the constitution. In practice, this means that the prince shares power with the people through the Diet (assembly), which he may convene or close. He is his country's representative to foreign powers; he may appoint certain state officials and remit, mitigate or commute sentences passed by the law. He is the source of honours, conferring titles, orders and decorations. Before receiving the oath of allegiance from his people on accession, a Liechtenstein prince must declare in a written proclamation that he will govern the principality to maintain its integrity and observe the rights of sovereignty.

Franz Joseph's predecessor, Prince Franz I, was the first ruler of Liechtenstein to spend any length of time in his country—indeed, his ancestor Prince Aloys II had made history in 1842 by being first of the line to set foot there at all. Franz Joseph, by contrast, has made Liechtenstein his home. The castle above Vaduz, and the museum in the town below, house part of the dazzling collection of paintings assembled by generations of Liechtenstein princes. Connoisseurship is in fact a family trait, and had Franz Joseph not been born to rule, he would surely have made his career in the fine arts.

Far left: the next-but-one reigning Prince of Liechtenstein is Prince Hans Adam's eldest son, Prince Alois, the namesake of his great-grandfather. Alois and his brothers Prince Constantin centre, and Prince Maximilian, right, have appeared on the stamps of Liechtenstein and looking at their seraphic likenesses one would think that they were well above the cares and woes which plague most children of their age—but not so. They attend the local school in Vaduz and are heirs to the misfortunes which afflict schoolchildren everywhere: grazed cheeks, skinned kneecaps and too much homework.

From the time that the twelfth-century Count Hugo, founder of the line, settled at the castle of Liechtenstein just south of Vienna, the family has produced interesting men. There was the minstrel, Ulrich, Tannhauser's contemporary, and just as famous in his lifetime (except that he was not to have the good fortune of stimulating the imagination of Richard Wagner). Medieval Liechtensteins were warriors too, leading the Austrian army to victory against the Hungarians and aiding the Emperor against the Czechs, Turks or any other foe. From the Emperor, they held a succession of high offices and in time acquired lands and titles, including that of Princes of the Empire.

The first serious Liechtenstein collector was Prince Karl I, Lord High Chancellor to the melancholy Emperor Rudolph II, whose palace in Pragùe resembled a vast museum. Unlike his master, who collected, besides the works of Dürer and other artists, all that was curious and bizarre such as mandrake roots, deformed foetuses and tools of magic, Karl concentrated on precious artefacts: engraved stones, objects of gold and silver, sculptures inlaid with cut gems, pictures and tapestries.

Prince Karl I was not only the first collector, he was also the prince who laid the foundations of the family's riches. In 1620, when the uprising of the Bohemian Protestants was quelled, and when the Winter King was defeated at the Battle of the White Mountain, Karl was in Bohemia as governor general. He was thus able to buy, at bargain prices, several large estates confiscated from the insurgents.

His son, Karl Eusebius, who specialized in paintings above all else, was the real founder of the collection: when his son and successor Johann Adam, called the Rich, housed it in Vienna's Liechtenstein Palace, built for him by an Italian architect, it already included many of the seventeenth-century Flemish pictures that are still its pride. Future princes were to augment the collection, gathering together Botticellis, Leonardos, Rembrandts and Van Dycks, not to speak of Canalettos or the nineteenth-century Germans such as Spitzweg.

Johann Adam also bought two Alpine lordships, Schellenberg (in 1699) and Vaduz (in 1712) from their near-bankrupt owner with a view to becoming a sovereign prince. However, he never enjoyed this glory: it fell

From outside, Schloss Vaduz looks like a cross between a medieval fortress and a granary—but the interior is another story. One could search a lifetime without finding a more quietly lush place, truly fit for a prince. It is certainly the best heated royal residence in Europe. Only about 130 of its rooms are in use, and two of these, both hangar-sized, are the "lumber rooms" where the overspill from the Prince's collection of paintings wait their turn to be on view. A complete change of the pictures is made about every three months. There are some very long corridors, rendered less monotonous than they might have been by the fact that they curve; also because the Prince has installed glazed showcases displaying well-lighted objets d'art in the walls, which are sometimes five feet thick. These, both exterior and interior, are mostly stone, plaster or stucco, but those in the private drawing room are panelled. There are sturdy oak staircases and forbidding shutters, either solid wood or iron, with a diagonal division between the white and red painted sections. Schloss Vaduz must surely be the most luxurious aerie of the century, not even excepting Hitler's chalet at Berchtesgaden.

Prince Anton Florian

instead to his cousin Anton Florian, who exchanged Vaduz and Schellenberg with Joseph Wenzel, Johann Adam's heir, for some other estates.

Anton Florian was tutor to Archduke Charles, the younger son of the Emperor Leopold I. When the Emperor declared Charles rightful King of Spain, tutor and charge went to the Spanish court at Barcelona and here the new King made Anton Florian a grandee of Spain. Later, after Charles ceased to be King of Spain and became instead Emperor Charles VI, he recognized his mentor's pocket lordships as a sovereign state of the Empire.

Anton Florian's successor was Joseph Wenzel, a soldier first and foremost who ruled the new state from a distance. He had ridden into battle against the Turks with Eugene of Savoy and, having reorganized Maria Theresa's artillery at huge personal expense, providing it with light, manoueverable field pieces which he had himself developed, led it in some of the battles of the Seven Years' War.

He died in 1772, to be succeeded by Franz Joseph I (1772-81), Aloys I (1781—1805) and then Johann I, another military hero, who fought Napoleon at Ulm and Austerlitz. Liechtenstein survived the disintegration of the Holy Roman Empire better than most tiny domains. Mediatization —annexation of a small state to a larger—was Napoleon's policy for countries such as Liechtenstein, but Johann I was invited to become a full member of the newly organized Confederation of the Rhine. It has been suggested that Napoleon, who met Johann at the peace negotiations following Austerlitz, had been so impressed by him that inclusion in the Union was intended as a compliment—but this did not stop the Prince

50

fighting Napoleon, and distinguishing himself at the Battle of Aspern.

With Napoleon's fall, the Rhenish Confederation ended. In its place came the German Confederation, the creation of the Congress of Vienna. This lasted until 1866, and Liechtenstein is the only member of both Rhenish and German Confederations that has survived intact to this day. Moreover, it has been called the valley of peace.

The local people were, and are, fiercely patriotic and loyal to their sovereign. For all that, the early Liechtenstein princes had brought them some shocks. Largely of peasant stock, independent and proud, living in the cradle of the sixteenth-century Peasants' Wars, they had not taken kindly to absolute rule. However, serfdom was abolished in 1808 and in 1818 there had been a constitution of sorts. During the revolutionary period of 1848, forced labour and feudal dues ceased, but the constitution for which there was a general clamour only came in 1862.

The Prince who granted it was Johann II. In his seventy years as Liechtenstein's sovereign (he died in 1929), most of the family's Bohemian estates were lost and the castle at Vaduz gradually became the focal point for the family. It was in this period that Liechtenstein's economic attachment to Austria came to an end, as indeed did the Austrian Habsburg Empire. In its place, Liechtenstein entered into a customs union with its other neighbour, Switzerland.

Johann II, a wise ruler, patron of the arts and benefactor of the poor, is remembered as the Good. He was succeeded by his brother Franz I, the first prince to spend long periods in the country. He reigned until 1938, to be succeeded by the present Prince.

Johann II

51

LUXEMBOURG
Jealously Guarded Independence

Grand Duke Jean of Luxembourg was educated in Luxembourg, England and Canada, spending part of the Second World War in the latter after his country had been invaded by Germany in 1940. He helped the war effort from overseas, lecturing and broadcasting, and in 1942, together with his father, Prince Félix, joined the Allied Forces in Britain. Prince Félix was attached to the British Northern Command; Prince Jean joined the Irish Guards. In June 1944, he landed with his regiment at Bayeux. In September, he entered Brussels and a week later crossed the border into the tiny country of his birth to be joyfully greeted by his people, as was his mother, the Grand Duchess Charlotte, when she returned in 1945.

From 1951 until 1961, Prince Jean was a member of the Luxembourg State Council, and then became his mother's *Lieutenant Representant*, a post something like that of regent. When Grand Duchess Charlotte abdicated in 1964 after a reign of forty-five years, he was thoroughly experienced in matters of government.

His country is far from being the musical comedy duchy of *Call Me Madam*. The wooded hills hide highly efficient steel-mills, periodically

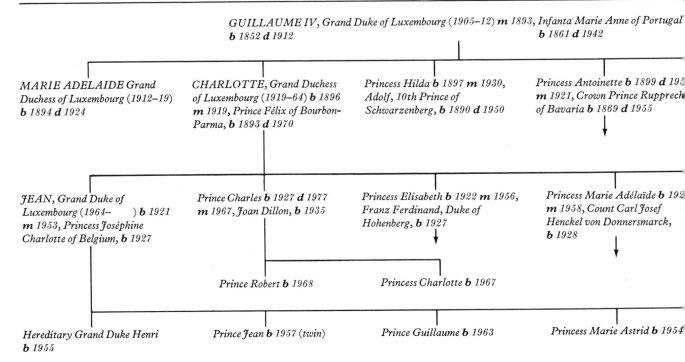

GUILLAUME IV, Grand Duke of Luxembourg (1905–12) *m* 1893, Infanta Marie Anne of Portugal *b* 1852 *d* 1912 — *b* 1861 *d* 1942

MARIE ADELAIDE Grand Duchess of Luxembourg (1912–19) *b* 1894 *d* 1924

CHARLOTTE, Grand Duchess of Luxembourg (1919–64) *b* 1896 *m* 1919, Prince Félix of Bourbon-Parma, *b* 1893 *d* 1970

Princess Hilda *b* 1897 *m* 1930, Adolf, 10th Prince of Schwarzenberg, *b* 1890 *d* 1950

Princess Antoinette *b* 1899 *d* 19[?] *m* 1921, Crown Prince Rupprech[t] of Bavaria *b* 1869 *d* 1955

JEAN, Grand Duke of Luxembourg (1964–   ) *b* 1921 *m* 1953, Princess Joséphine Charlotte of Belgium, *b* 1927

Prince Charles *b* 1927 *d* 1977 *m* 1967, Joan Dillon, *b* 1935

Princess Elisabeth *b* 1922 *m* 1956, Franz Ferdinand, Duke of Hohenberg, *b* 1927

Princess Marie Adélaïde *b* 192[?] *m* 1958, Count Carl Josef Henckel von Donnersmarck, *b* 1928

Prince Robert *b* 1968

Princess Charlotte *b* 1967

Hereditary Grand Duke Henri *b* 1955

Prince Jean *b* 1957 (twin)

Prince Guillaume *b* 1963

Princess Marie Astrid *b* 1954

Jean, Grand Duke of Luxembourg, is sovereign of one of the famous five small countries of Europe, of which his duchy is much the largest, and the only ruler of this exclusive group who is styled royal highness. Jean is spare and sinewy, with an unbending, military bearing. He is conscientious to the extreme and toils untiringly. His wife, Joséphine Charlotte, often looks as if she knew something of which she has no intention of divulging. This disguises a genial whimsicality, of which not a great many people are aware. She is the sister of King Baudouin of the Belgians and the mother of five children, the best known, perhaps, being Princess Marie Astrid, whom the press never seem to tire of marrying off to the Prince of Wales.

modernized, and there is much development in the capital itself. Rich in iron ore, the Duchy is the seat of the European Coal and Steel Authority, the Secretariat of the European Parliament, the European Investment Bank and the European Monetary Fund.

Luxembourg is the *Lux* in Benelux, and when *Be* for Belgium declared its independence from *Ne* for the Netherlands in 1830, there was a period when it was claimed by both. Nine years elapsed before a diminished Grand Duchy was reunited with its Grand Duke, William of Orange-Nassau, the first King of the Netherlands. Belgium grieved over its loss, and for decades referred to it as *la partie cedée*.

Above, heir to the Grand Duke is his eldest son, Henri, Hereditary Grand Duke of Luxembourg, who is incredibly handsome and apparently, completely unflappable. He gratified the military side of his father by passing out of Sandhurst. He seems to be a dedicated loner, who does not mix readily.

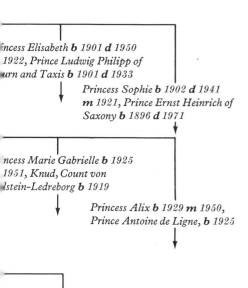

ncess Elisabeth b 1901 d 1950
1922, Prince Ludwig Philipp of
urn and Taxis b 1901 d 1933

Princess Sophie b 1902 d 1941
m 1921, Prince Ernst Heinrich of
Saxony b 1896 d 1971

ncess Marie Gabrielle b 1925
1951, Knud, Count von
lstein-Ledreborg b 1919

Princess Alix b 1929 m 1950,
Prince Antoine de Ligne, b 1925

ncess Marguerite b 1957 (twin)

The Grand Duke's mother, left, is Charlotte, Grand Duchess of Luxembourg, one of the two sisters who abdicated the Luxembourg throne. Charlotte succeeded when Grand Duchess Marie Adelaide abdicated in 1919, and herself abdicated in favour of her son in 1964 after forty-five years. She rarely appears in public, leading a withdrawn life at a small castle near Fischbach. She is in her 80s.

William I's administration was not wildly popular, but on the whole, the people were delighted no longer to be governed from afar. This had been the case for half a millenium: Luxembourg had been governed by Burgundians, Spaniards, Austrians, and French in turn. Earlier, there had been Bavarians, Silesians and Moravians among its rulers, but these, on the whole, were resident sons-in-law of the Luxembourg princes, who aspired, successfully, to the Imperial throne.

The first of these Emperors was Henry VII, who reigned from 1274 to 1313. His arrival on the Imperial throne promised—said Dante, his contemporary—a new Golden Age. Henry VII died before this materialized, but not before he had made his son, John, King of Bohemia. John, who was to lose his sight in 1340, married a Bohemian Princess and it is through this marriage that Luxembourg is connected with that good, saintly Wenceslas who looked out on the feast of Stephen with some satisfaction, having christianized Bohemia in the tenth century. John the Blind perished at Crécy having been led into battle, plumed and armoured, to rescue the King of France from the English troops of Edward II and the Black Prince. Out of admiration, the Black Prince adopted John's plumes and motto (*Ich dien*), which have been held ever since by Princes of Wales. John was succeeded as King of Bohemia by Charles I of Luxembourg who, in 1347, became the Holy Roman Emperor Charles IV. It is to Charles IV that the Empire owes the famous Golden Bull—so-called because its seal (in Latin, *bulla*) shows him enthroned in majesty. This document, the most important in German constitutional history, was designed to end the chaos and private warfare that tended to accompany Imperial elections: Charles IV, building on precedent, specifically nominated seven hereditary elector princes with all but royal prerogatives. Their majority decision in the matter of electing new Emperors was to be absolute. With extra electors appointed from time to time, this system lasted as long as the Holy Roman Empire itself.

While relations governed Luxembourg proper as *stadholders*, two further

Emperor Charles IV

Princess Marie Astrid of Luxembourg is the first-born of the five children of the Grand Duke and Grand Duchesss of Luxembourg. In her mid-twenties, her true beauty is becoming fully apparent. Something of a loner, she tends to wear her feelings on her sleeve. She has attended a language school in Britain and returns to London from time to time to improve her English.

Luxembourg sovereigns were emperors after Charles: his sons Wenceslas and Sigismund. Wenceslas, called the Drunkard, was responsible for the drowning of Prague's vicar-general, Johann Nepomuk, who became a saint. Sigismund is remembered for his failure to protect John Huss, the early religious reformer who was burned at the stake for heresy in spite of Sigismund having promised him safe conduct. It was Sigismund who put Luxembourg in pawn with the Dukes of Burgundy and failed to redeem it. From then on the country was ruled, and exploited, by strangers until, by agreement of all the powers at the Congress of Vienna, Nassau rule began in 1815.

William I's reign proved a disappointment: no constitution; not much personal contact between ruler and ruled; not even native incumbents for official posts and regardless of tradition, French, for years the official language, being replaced by German. Things changed when William I was succeeded by his son, William II, who was known in England as "Young Frog" when he had wooed the Regent's daughter. Now married to the Emperor of Russia's sister, William II made decisive changes: he proclaimed French the official language alongside German and called a deputation of eight Luxembourgeois to the Hague to work on a constitution which was published in October of the same year. Accompanied by his son, Prince Alexander, he visited his Grand Duchy in 1841. The journey became a triumphal progress. He reminded his subjects of their proverbial frankness, begged them to tell him their troubles and when they obliged, he listened. This assured Luxembourg's peace and quiet in 1848, the year of the revolutions. Joining the *Zollverein* assured the country's economic growth, so it is no wonder that the Luxembourgeois call this grand duke the founder of their independence and fortune. They erected an equestrian statue to him in gratitude. A patriotic publication appearing in 1889 so glowingly described the brave military exploits of his youth, when, as Prince of Orange, he fought under Wellington's command, that the reader begins to suspect that "holding high the sword that had been a

Princess Marguerite (left), Prince Jean (second from left) and Prince Guillaume (third from left) are the younger children of the Grand Duke and Duchess of Luxembourg. Guillaume is a teenager; the others are in their twenties. Jean and Marguerite are twins. Jean was at Sandhurst with his brother, Henri. Guillaume is at school in Geneva; Marguerite was enrolled for a time at Cambridge.

Colmar-Berg is where Luxembourg's Grand Ducal family live. It is a rambling structure of Teutonic appearance, whose charm escapes some visitors altogether. One thing to recommend it is the size: it is large enough to accommodate the entire family, complete with entourages and three or four guests for each resident. Architecturally, it is undistinguished, the prison-like appearance relieved only by the central façade in the courtyard. There is a Hanseatic grandeur about the impressive triple-arched entrance and the twin, geometrical turreted towers. The most rewarding feature of the establishment is the gardens, which are scientifically laid out and as carefully nurtured as those at Kew in England.

Grand Duke Adolphe

gift from his mother", he won all but single-handed most of the famous battles he had attended, including that of Waterloo.

William III succeeded in 1849. Although he restricted the liberties granted by his father, Luxembourg, in his reign, experienced undreamt-of happiness and prosperity. The William-railway, opened in 1859, gave a further fillip to trade and it was William who preserved Luxembourg's independence when Prussia threatened to annex it. By a decree in 1867, the country became neutral territory and its capital an open city. The old fortress, a constant bone of contention between Prussia and France, was razed, and as a consequence Luxembourg was left untouched by the Franco-Prussian War of 1870-71.

Although there had been every hope of a succession of Orange-Nassau princes into eternity, William III's three sons by his first marriage, all unmarried, predeceased him. His daughter, Wilhelmina, by his second marriage, the future Queen of Holland, was not eligible to succeed him in

In theory, Luxembourg's Grand Ducal Palace is the ruling family's town residence. However, although guests are often put up there, members of the family only stay the night if caught in town too late to return home. The arched entrance, flanked by sentry boxes with sentries in 'operetta' uniforms, opens directly on to the cobblestoned square. Otherwise there is very little to distinguish the Palace from the surrounding houses. Inside, it takes a turn for the better. The study of Grand Duke William IV, just off the foyer, is precisely as he left it when he died in 1912, and with its Gothic furniture, is thought to be the inspiration for all the machine-made Victoriana of the latter half of the nineteenth century. Most attractive of all are the guest bedrooms, which have elegant, porcelain heating stoves. The walls of these rooms are hung with striped or figured satin damask in such colours as cyclamen, canary yellow or Chartreuse green.

Luxembourg: by a Nassau family compact, Salic law was in operation. Heir to the Grand Duchy was the aged Duke Adolphe of Nassau whose own domains had been grabbed by Prussia in 1866. Like other sovereigns dispossessed by the Prussians, Duke Adolphe had avoided contact with the Prussian court. This was rather a worry for Luxembourg, too small to be able to flourish without good-will all round. So it came as a great relief when, after the death of the last of William III's sons, Duke Adolphe decided on the supreme sacrifice: to shake hands with the Kaiser—on the firm understanding that it was not the Duke of Nassau who was touching the hand that had robbed him of his possessions, but the uninsulted, prospective Grand Duke of Luxembourg. His future subjects were much moved by his noble, truly patriotic gesture.

Grand Duke Adolphe ruled from 1890 to 1905 when he was succeeded by his son William. As this Grand Duke left six daughters but not a single son, a special family law was promulgated to allow the succession in the female line. Accordingly, the eldest girl, Marie Adélaïde, came to the throne and was Luxembourg's sovereign at the outbreak of the First World War. The Germans invaded Luxembourg, as they did the Netherlands, but unlike her neighbours the Grand Duchy could offer no resistance. Marie Adélaïde, aged twenty, gallantly drove to the frontier to order the invaders out of the country. They politely refused. By the end of the war, she was accused of pro-German sympathies. Indeed, France refused to discuss peace terms with her ministers, and Marie Adélaïde was obliged to abdicate. Her sister Charlotte took over, after a referendum eighty per cent. in her favour. During the Second World War, when the family and the government went into exile, the Grand Duchess became the symbol of her people's liberty, "the flame on the altar of Luxembourg's jealously guarded independence".

Grand Duchess Marie Adélaïde

57

MONACO

Gambling, Oceanography, Ballet

Prince Rainier has had an energetic reign in his tiny, 467-acre principality. Since his accession, the economic situation has greatly improved, Monaco now being not only a resort but a business centre. There has been much building, and a plan exists to reclaim land from the sea in order to do more —outward, not upward. And added to such events as the Monte Carlo rally and the Grand Prix there is now the annual T.V. festival. Prince Rainier also intends to improve the facilities of the Societé des Bains and to modernise the casino, from which the Prince, in company with every other Monegasque, is constitutionally barred. (A previous prince of Monaco, officially unaware of its existence, would refer to it only as *ce place là*, vaguely gesturing in its direction).

This Prince of Monaco has a different sort of existence from his pre-

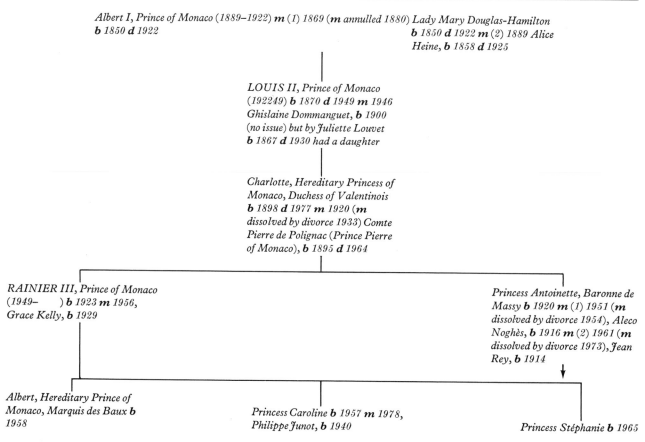

Albert I, Prince of Monaco (1889–1922) **m** *(1) 1869 (***m** *annulled 1880) Lady Mary Douglas-Hamilton*
b *1850* **d** *1922*
b *1850* **d** *1922* **m** *(2) 1889 Alice Heine,* **b** *1858* **d** *1925*

LOUIS II, Prince of Monaco (192249) **b** *1870* **d** *1949* **m** *1946 Ghislaine Dommanguet,* **b** *1900 (no issue) but by Juliette Louvet* **b** *1867* **d** *1930 had a daughter*

Charlotte, Hereditary Princess of Monaco, Duchess of Valentinois **b** *1898* **d** *1977* **m** *1920 (***m** *dissolved by divorce 1933) Comte Pierre de Polignac (Prince Pierre of Monaco),* **b** *1895* **d** *1964*

RAINIER III, Prince of Monaco (1949–   ) **b** *1923* **m** *1956, Grace Kelly,* **b** *1929*

Princess Antoinette, Baronne de Massy **b** *1920* **m** *(1) 1951 (***m** *dissolved by divorce 1954), Aleco Noghès,* **b** *1916* **m** *(2) 1961 (***m** *dissolved by divorce 1973), Jean Rey,* **b** *1914*

Albert, Hereditary Prince of Monaco, Marquis des Baux **b** *1958*

Princess Caroline **b** *1957* **m** *1978, Philippe Junot,* **b** *1940*

Princess Stéphanie **b** *1965*

Prince Rainier of Monaco is frequently in the news, which both pleases and displeases him. "I think people get a false idea of my position," he says. "It is very hard here in Monaco. If I go for a walk, people complain that I am idle; if I don't go out, they complain that I'm aloof." In a country smaller than London's Hyde Park and Kensington Gardens combined, it must be difficult to do anything privately.

decessors in other ways, too, but especially in his happy family life. Although his marriage to the former Grace Kelly, the beautiful and accomplished American actress and movie-star, took place in a positive firework—display of flashbulbs—photographers popped up from behind the very altar—"we try", says the Prince "to live as much as possible like normal people". They have a private retreat, away from the palace, and countless pets (a parrot singing the national anthem was a special favourite). Because the memory of their own wedding ballyhoo still rankles in the minds of Rainier III and Princess Grace, they planned a quiet wedding for their daughter Caroline and Pierre Junot—a family affair with invited guests, controlled publicity and no *paparazzi*. However, there was a walk-about after the wedding.

It is remarkable how Princess Grace seems to have aged so little since her wedding in 1956: some say she grows more beautiful daily. She is not, however, just a beautiful addition to the Principality, but performs her public duties energetically. As Grace Kelly, her acting career took her to Broadway in the late 1940s. Among her most memorable film performances were in *High Noon* and *The Country Girl* (for which she won an Oscar). Bob Hope, in his valedictory toast when she left Hollywood answered the question of how she should be addressed after marriage to a prince by saying "As 'our Grace', of course." To her thousands of admirers, that is how she remains.

Prince Albert, the only son and heir of Prince Rainier and Princess Grace, has inherited his father's *bonhomie* and his mother's chiselled-in-ice features.

59

The principality is small enough to make festive events family affairs for all Monégasques. They were bidden—every single one—to tea at Prince Rainier's twenty-first birthday. The very young and the very old call at the palace each Christmas to receive presents from the family. And many subjects feel that if they disagreed with any proposed legislation, they could drop in to make their views known to their government. Small though Monaco is, there is nothing fusty about it: led by the Grimaldis, the principality is confidently looking towards the twenty-first century.

The Grimaldi family traces its roots to an eleventh-century consul of the Republic of Genoa whose descendants acquired Monaco, Menton and Roquebrune in the fourteenth century. According to legend, the Grimaldi who took over Monaco was Lanfranco, known as The Spiteful. He arrived at the fortress on the rocky promontory disguised as a friar seeking shelter. Once admitted, he drew his sword, murdered his host, opened the gates and let in his own soldiers.

Until recent times, Monaco's princes have been remarkable for the time they spent away from, rather than on their estates, preferring life at the court of France to that in Monaco, once described by an eighteenth-century traveller as "a barren rock and some lemons." Prince Louis I, who succeeded in 1662, was the King of France's godson and accorded the title of a foreign prince at Louis XIV's court. This practically made him a fixture in France. His wife, a daughter of the Duc de Gramont, was certainly right in the centre of court life. As a sister of the Comte de Guiche, the most beloved favourite of Monsieur, the King's brother, she held a job in Monsieur's household. When Monsieur's first wife, the neglected Minette of England, replaced Monsieur in the affections of this beautiful and romantic *Comte*, Monsieur almost died of jealousy. If he

Princess Caroline has been one of the most publicised European princesses of her day. Perhaps the peak of her allure was when it was whispered she might become Princess of Wales. The publicity, the good times in Paris, the choice in Philippe Junot of a much older man for her husband are a contrast to her sheltered education in England at St. Mary's, Ascot, a Catholic boarding school.

rightly suspected Mme de Monaco of having had a hand in this treachery, he was unable to do much about it: Mme de Monaco had for a while been admired by the King, and was, thus, above all reproach. Monsieur was reduced to taking what satisfaction he could from the fact that Mme de Monaco's established lover revenged himself for her unfaithfulness by painfully pirouetting on her hand: even foreign princesses did not rate chairs at court and Mme de Monaco was obliged to sit on the floor, so it was easy for her jealous lover to contrive to grind her hand into the parquet as though by accident.

Mme de Monaco's appointment in Monsieur's household outlasted her mistress: after Minette's death she served the next Madame, but it was not so much fun. Liselotte of the Palatinate refused to respond to her naughty match-making, and remained unmoved by even the handsomest men or the prettiest ladies (for whom Mme de Monaco was known also to have a taste). In spite of all this, the Monacos' marriage was considered to be perfectly *convenable*.

This was more than could be said for that of their eldest son, Antoine. This ill-tempered prince made his wife perfectly miserable. Known as Mlle Grand, she was a daughter of Louis de Lorraine, Comte d'Armagnac and a niece of Monsieur's second great love and evil genius, the Chevalier de Lorraine. As the marriage had taken place under Monsieur's auspices, it could hardly help but fail. During one of Antoine's trips abroad,—a diarist said he had "gone wenching in Genoa" (as though the opera company in Paris did not offer enough scope)—this Princess of Monaco ran away. There had been no sons, only miscarriages and six daughters— the eldest survivor of whom was Louise Hippolyte. Prince Antoine found a husband for her in Normandy: Jacques de Goyon de Matignon, of an old and noble family, who on his marriage to the Grimaldi heiress became a

Above, Princess Stephanie, in her teens, is the baby of the family, with trenchant good looks rarely seen in someone so young. Those who speculate on royal marriages like to think of her, as they did Princess Caroline, marrying into the British royal family: she is a year younger than Prince Edward.

Antoinette, Baronne de Massy, the sister of Prince Rainier, has been twice married and divorced and has three children and three grandchildren. She lives in the medieval village of Eze, perched dramatically on a hilltop along the French Riviera coast from Monaco. She is a dog-lover, devoting her time to the breeding of rare types with impressive pedigrees. Sharing the sofa with her is a Basenji, the breed that does not bark.

Grimaldi himself. However, Prince Antoine's liaisons had yielded several other children, among them a young man who was called the Chevalier de Grimaldi. After Antoine's death, this Chevalier was appointed governor-general of Monaco by Jacques and continued in this post for half a century.

In the French Revolution, Monaco was annexed to France. Jacques's son Honore III was deposed *in absentia* and arrested in his palatial Hôtel de Matignon in Paris (now the presidential residence). His daughter-in-law, made up as for a ball, was taken off to the guillotine. But both his son Honoré IV and his grandson Honoré V survived the Reign of Terror. The latter was to serve with Napoleon's *Grand Armée*, and to become equerry first to the Emperor and then to Joséphine. When the family was restored to Monaco in 1814, it was he who set out to reclaim the principality. Apparently, on the road from Cannes he came upon the Emperor, fresh from Elba. "Where are you going?" asked Napoleon. "Home, sire, to take possession of my estates". "I too", said Napoleon, "to mine".

Honoré V found Monaco in a sorry state. The great Renaissance castle, with its horseshoe staircase like that at Fontainebleau, had been used as a barracks by occupying British forces. The rooms were all looted, including the suite where, in 1767, Honoré III had waited upon Edward, Duke of York as he lay dying.

Now, by the Treaty of Vienna, the French attachment of the principality came to an end, and Italians became the protectors of the lands that had, in fact, once marked the division between Gaul and Rome. In the revolutionary climate of the late 1830's, Menton and Roquebrune were to unfurl the Italian flag, thinking that this would help the lemon trade. Subsequently the Italians tried to make Prince Florestan, the successor of Honoré V, hand over the rest of the principality, but failed, although this prince was in serious financial difficulties.

In order to help his diminished exchequer, Florestan introduced gambling to Monaco. It seemed a good idea, since the ban on gambling which operated in France did not extend to the principality. But the success story of the Casino really began only in the reign of his son Charles III. After Menton and Roquebrune had indicated their willingness to return to France after a plebiscite, he sold them to Napoleon III for four million gold francs. He also allowed the Genoa-Nice railway to run through his territory, and in return France built a proper coastal road through Monaco, now known as the *Corniche*. It had been the lack of communications—the rutted hairpin bends, the hours it took to reach Monaco from France—which had spelt failure for Prince Florestan's Casino. There simply had been too few visitors to his tables.

Now, under the famous entrepreneur, M. Blanc and with easier access, the *Societe des Bains des Mers et du Cercle des Etrangers*, which ran the resort, began to flourish. A new Casino was built, hotels sprang up, visitors flocked, and in 1866, the new complex was named Monte Carlo in honour of Prince Charles. The state, Charles and Blanc all got rich and the Mlles Blanc married well (one landed a Radziwill, another a Bonaparte, while a granddaughter was to marry Prince George of Greece). By 1869, the revenues from these enterprises enabled Prince Charles to exempt his subjects from rates and taxes. He was, as might be expected, a popular ruler and if his subjects missed having a constitution, they made no trouble until 1911, when his son Prince Albert was obliged to grant one.

Prince Albert I succeeded in 1889, by which time his marriage to Lady Mary Douglas-Hamilton had failed. It had been arranged by the Emperor

Albert I

62

Napoleon III whose cousin, Princess Marie of Baden, was the wife of the eleventh Duke of Hamilton, and mother of Lady Mary. It had seemed such a good idea: part of the Hamilton fortune for Monaco; a reigning prince for Mary and an alliance between two great families already connected since the seventeenth century when Hamiltons and Grimaldis had both married Gramonts. Mary, however, had left Albert in less than a year, and gave birth to Prince Albert's son, the future Louis II, at her parent's home in Baden-Baden. The deserted husband comforted himself with study: his great passion was the sea (he was known as The Navigator) and the Oceanic Institute, Aquarium and the Maritime Museum in Monaco are his own creations. He did, in fact, marry again, another heiress, the widow of the Duc de Richelieu who had been Miss Alice Heine of New Orleans. She was one of those elegant, spirited American heiresses, and the first of them to marry a reigning prince.

Prince Albert's son Louis II reigned from 1922 to 1949 and married only once, three years before he died aged seventy-nine. There were no children except a natural daughter, Charlotte, by Marie Juliette Louvet. From 1906 the girl was known as Mlle de Valentinois and in 1919 was created Duchess of Valentinois. In 1920 she married Comte Pierre de Polignac, who became a naturalized Monégasque, assuming the arms and name of Grimaldi by his father-in-law's ordinance. Charlotte renounced her right of succession in favour of her son, the present Prince Rainier, when he reached his majority.

Monaco's Palais Princier is, as the name indicates, a princely rather than a royal residence and its occupants are styled serene, not royal highnesses. Nevertheless, no king, emperor or sultan could ask for a more spectacular site for a home: the view over the Mediterranean is not only south, but east and west as well. Some parts of a thirteenth-century fortress remain, but most of the Palace dates from the seventeenth and eighteenth centuries.

Princess Alice of Monaco

Comte Pierre de Polignac

With these later Grimaldis one enters Proust country. Princess Alice was the partial model for the raffish, fictional Duchesse de Luxembourg and Proust's famous novel also carries allusions to the next generation: Pierre de Polignac had been an old friend of the writer, who said it was quite untrue that Pierre had become a little king—in fact, Proust said, he was even nicer than he had been before his grand marriage. But then came the day when the new Prince Pierre of Monaco refused to subscribe to the *de luxe* edition of Proust's first volume and the friendship was at an end.

A later volume is stiff with allusions to the Grimaldis under the fictional name of Luxembourg. Pierre becomes the Comte de Nassau, who not only insists that the national flag of his adoptive country is flown wherever he happens to be, but insists that everyone rises when his wife passes. "Her grandmother" says a wit "made every man lie down—what a change"

Proust's narrator observes that all this is, of course, quite untrue, that both Duchess and Comte were highly sophisticated people, and that Nassau moreover was a man of taste—as was indeed true of Pierre, as it was of all the Polignacs. The Prince of Polignac, a composer—Bergotte in Proust's novel—and his wife, née Winaretta Singer of the sewing machine fortune, were patrons of the arts, and enthusiastic supporters of Diaghilev, whose company, the Imperial Russian Ballet, had first astonished Paris in 1900.

It was through the Princess de Polignac's offices that in the early 1920s the impressario signed the contract with Pierre that was to make Monte Carlo a centre of the arts, the winter home, in fact of a ballet company which soon became the Monte Carlo Ballet. Monaco's ruling family has taken a helpful interest in ballet ever since: Prince Rainier's sister Antoinette is especially active in its cause and so is Princess Grace.

THE NETHERLANDS
Popular Orange

Queen Juliana's genuine popularity seems to be proved by the fact that few of the historically republican Dutch want to abolish their monarchy. Also, only a truly beloved Queen could have emerged unscathed from the *Greethofmansaffair* of the nineteen fifties, when Greet Hofman, a faith healer, called to court in the hope that she would be able to restore the failing sight of the Queen's youngest daughter, was seen so to dominate the Queen that a crisis arose.

In addition, Prince Bernhard has survived the embarrassing Lockheed scandal. And if the German marriage of Princess Beatrix, Queen Juliana's heir, was originally controversial, there are few Dutch people who do not now accept it. The Princess's husband, Claus von Amsberg, learned Dutch in record time and is a hard-working member of the royal family, of which the succession in the next generation is assured by a trio of his and Princess Beatrix's sons.

Queen Juliana is the longest serving of Europe's three reigning queens having succeeded when her mother, Queen Wilhelmina, abdicated in her favour in 1948. Princess Juliana entered public life on reaching her majority at the age of eighteen, in that year enrolling as a student at the University of Leiden, founded by her ancestor William the Silent. The first two daughters of her marriage to Prince Bernhard were born just before the Second World War.

Soon after, Holland was under German occupation. Queen Wilhelmina and her ministers established a government-in-exile in England, and if her people believed that she had abandoned them, she soon corrected this

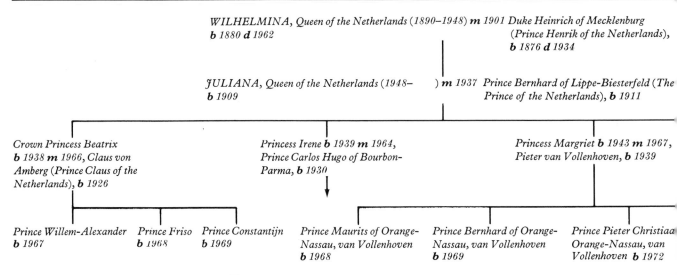

WILHELMINA, *Queen of the Netherlands (1890–1948)* **m** *1901 Duke Heinrich of Mecklenburg* **b** *1880* **d** *1962* *(Prince Henrik of the Netherlands),* **b** *1876* **d** *1934*

JULIANA, *Queen of the Netherlands (1948–*) **m** *1937 Prince Bernhard of Lippe-Biesterfeld (The* **b** *1909 Prince of the Netherlands),* **b** *1911*

Crown Princess Beatrix **b** *1938* **m** *1966, Claus von Amberg (Prince Claus of the Netherlands),* **b** *1926*

Princess Irene **b** *1939* **m** *1964, Prince Carlos Hugo of Bourbon-Parma,* **b** *1930*

Princess Margriet **b** *1943* **m** *1967, Pieter van Vollenhoven,* **b** *1939*

Prince Willem-Alexander **b** *1967*

Prince Friso **b** *1968*

Prince Constantijn **b** *1969*

Prince Maurits of Orange-Nassau, van Vollenhoven **b** *1968*

Prince Bernhard of Orange-Nassau, van Vollenhoven **b** *1969*

Prince Pieter Christiaan Orange-Nassau, van Vollenhoven **b** *1972*

Queen Juliana is so thoroughly human and so solidly Dutch that her people are sentimental about her more or less as an afterthought. She is more like the chairman of the board of a successful corporation than she is a sovereign. Imbued with an innate shyness which makes it almost painful for her to speak, or even appear, in public, and saddled with more than her share of private sorrow, Juliana's over-riding sense of duty has driven her to a pinnacle as one of the most capable monarchs in Europe.

impression by her regular broadcasts with their refrain of "Holland will rise again". Princess Juliana and the children were in Canada, where her cousin, Princess Alice, Countess of Athlone, remembers her as a staunch Red Cross worker and blood-donor. Prince Bernhard's war was spent partly in the air—he trained as a pilot—partly in Canada, and when the Free Dutch Forces were established he became their commander under General Eisenhower. Later Princess Juliana returned to help Queen Wilhelmina work for her people throughout the later war years and they in turn clung to the thought that "hunger will pass, Orange will come back".

In the wake of the liberating allies, the royal family returned to the Netherlands and Queen Wilhelmina reigned until September 4, 1948. Then, in accord with the precept of Charles V (who had said that the office of ruling required enterprise and energy, and was not for people who no

Princess Christina b 1947 m 1975,
Jorge Guillermo, b 1946

Prince Floris of Orange-Nassau,
van Vollenhoven b 1975

Prince Bernhard has been in the prince consort business longer than his two other counterparts for about four years he was the only queen's husband in Europe, after which he was joined by Philip, Duke of Edinburgh and later by Henrik, Prince of Denmark. Bernhard has been much criticised for his repeated deviations from the royal straight and narrow, but it is hoped that in spite of the resignation of his public posts, his many qualities will not be neglected. He is an accomplished businessman, economist, pilot, *bon viveur*, mountaineer and saviour of wildlife.

longer felt in possession of these qualities), she stepped down after fifty years on the throne. At twelve o'clock precisely, as her daughter was acclaimed queen, she once again assumed her childhood title of Princess Wilhelmina.

William the Silent

The decisive moment for the Netherlands, as a state, came in 1544 when the eleven year-old William, son of the Count of Nassau-Dillenburg, inherited from his cousin René the principality of Orange, a sovereign state, which had come to René through his mother together with large stretches of Brabant, Luxembourg and Flanders as well as several hundred other estates. Orange was now a possession of France and the rest part of the Habsburg Empire. William needed an upbringing more princely than his father could provide and so he was taken to Brussels where he joined the household of the Emperor Charles V.

The Emperor made rather a pet of William, who became his private secretary: he was a clever young man, good at languages, including Dutch, which he practised when he stayed at his country house at Breda, where he bred whippets. Then, after Charles V's death, the Netherlands rose against Philip II of Spain and his cruel Inquisition. Feeling that they would not succeed unless they were led by an influential prince, the Dutch people invited William of Orange, also to be known as William the Silent, to become their Captain General, and chief of the semi-piratical "sea-beggars", who took the struggle to the high seas. William became not king but *Stadhouder* of the United Netherland Provinces after they had joined

All the Dutch princesses are "Hons and Rebels", each in her own way, but Crown Princess Beatrix, as heiress to the Dutch crown, naturally attracts comment on her apparent leanings to the left in politics. It is well known that she married a German against popular feeling, but not so often remembered that the last three Dutch consorts have also been of that nationality. Taking a special interest in social and cultural concerns, Beatrix assists her mother with royal duties and has a kind, disarming smile. Indeed, with her husband Prince Claus, she makes one of the most amiable-looking of royal couples: they are hardly ever seen in a non-effervescent mood. Claus's impeccable behaviour, and the fact that he has fathered heirs to the throne, has enhanced his popularity considerably. He undertakes a number of royal duties. His courtship of Beatrix was conducted, as far as possible, in English, neither at the time being adequately fluent in the other's native language.

together in the Union of Utrecht of 1579, and two years later they freed themselves from Spain by signing the Act of Abjuration. The King of Spain, in reply, outlawed William. In 1584, after more than one attempt, he had William assassinated, thus making sure that Orange became a symbol of Dutch liberty for ever. The song *William of Nassau* (now the Dutch national anthem) which was composed in his honour in 1570, became more than ever a hymn of defiance, and the war of independence continued. William's descendants were to govern the United Provinces as hereditary *Stadhouders*, sharing power to a greater or lesser extent at different times with the regents, the republic's select governing group, which essentially represented the merchant classes. By the end of the Thirty Years' War in 1648, the power of Spain was finally broken, and the now officially independant United Provinces of the Netherlands, part republican, partly a monarchy, entered their golden age to become Europe's bastion of free thought and liberty.

The Hague filled with distinguished people, among them the Winter Queen of Bohemia and her husband Frederick V, Elector Palatine, a martyr of the Protestant cause. In gratitude, the Palatines named their second daughter Louise Hollandine. She received an annual christening pension from her sponsors, the governors of the province of Holland, who could hardly have dreamt that she would live into her eighties. Sophie, the mother of George I of England, narrowly escaped being called Frieslandine in honour of her godparents of Friesland. She, too, received a sum of money every year, albeit a more modest one, until she died.

Princess Margriet with her two elder sons, Maurits, left and Bernhard, right. She was born in Ottawa during the Second World War in a hospital room which, for the occasion, was made officially part of Holland: as a possible future sovereign of The Netherlands, Margriet was required to be Dutch by birth. Unlike other members of the family, her taste in dress is not necessarily conventional. She works hard at whatever royal duties are assigned to her and lives at Het Loo, her grandmother's beloved country house near Apeldoorn. Her husband, Pieter van Vollenhoven, son of a Dutch businessman, has quickly acquired the knack of being royal.

William II

Below, Princes Willem-Alexander, Friso and Constantijn, sons of Crown Princess Beatrix and Prince Claus, are the first male heirs to the Dutch throne since the death of Prince Alexander in 1884: the last King of the Netherlands, Willem III, died in 1890. Willem-Alexander, the eldest, follows his mother in the succession. Collectively, they are a handful.

The Winter Queen and her huge family proved exacting and expensive guests, but William the Silent's second son benefited from their stay, since in the entourage of the Queen he met his future wife, Amalie von Solms, with whom he at once fell in love. Amalie's son, William II became the husband of Charles I of England's daughter Mary. Far too grand a wife for the son of "one of my maids" thought the Winter Queen, but Charles I was counting on Orange support and funds for his civil war. Mary duly arrived at The Hague, insisting on being known by her English title of Princess Royal even after her marriage.

William II did not live to see the birth in 1640 of his son William III: he had died eight days earlier, and the baby's first view of the world was black and mournful—even his cradle was hung in black. He always attributed his tendency to "melancholy" to these circumstances. The *stadhoudership* was suspended from William's birth until 1672, when he was called to the post. Four years earlier, at the celebration of the alliance that England, the United Provinces and Sweden had formed against France, William had appeared at one of those state entertainments that were part ballet, part masque and part recital. Alluding to the theme familiar to everyone in the audience, the prince, dressed as an Arcadian shepherd, had sung of "the famous shepherds from whose race I spring" and of their expertise in saving their flock from the wolves. True to his word, when war broke out, he valiantly defended the Netherlands—dykes were broken, polders flooded, and the heroic patriotism of William the Silent's day was reborn. As skilful in diplomacy as in war, he successfully set up an alliance with the Emperor, several German princes and Spain, and at the peace of Nijmegen in 1678, the United Provinces remained intact, while Hainaut, Flanders and Franche Comté fell to Louis XIV.

There was little love lost between William III and his first cousin once removed, Louis XIV, for the French King's aunt Henriette Marie, Charles I's "Popish Queen", was William III's grandmother. Relations had hardly improved when Louis XIV had offered Dutch William his perfectly delightful daughter by Louise de la Vallière as a wife. William had grandly said that Princes of Orange were in the habit of marrying the legitimate daughters of kings and not their bastards—or so the story goes. To Louis XIV's disgust, William married Charles II's niece Mary, thus reinforcing the bond between the United Provinces and Great Britain,

Willem-Alexander

Friso

Constantijn

Irene, Princess of Bourbon-Parma, is the second daughter of Queen Juliana of the Netherlands. Her husband, Prince Carlos Hugo, is the Carlist pretender to the Spanish throne and only recently have the couple been allowed to live in Spain. At the time of her marriage, Irene renounced her rights to the Dutch throne and became a Catholic. Born at the outbreak of World War II, Irene was christened in the Chapel Royal at Buckingham Palace which, for the occasion, was turned into a Dutch Reformed Church. She has the cool assurance and the individual style of a successful high fashion model.

which Louis had done his best to sever. In 1688, after what is known as the Bloodless Revolution, England invited William III to remove his Roman Catholic father-in-law James II, King of England, and to rule in his stead. James Stuart fled to France—it had taken all of Dutch William's diplomatic ingenuity to bring this about—and William combined the offices of *stadhouder* in the Netherlands and King of England. Louis XIV refused to recognise William as King of England and did all he could to help the Stuarts to regain the throne: the Battle of the Boyne, annually remembered by the Orangemen in Ireland, was fought on the first of these occasions.

In 1701, William III died at Hampton Court, after he and his horse had come to grief over a mole-hill, hence the cryptic Jacobite toast "to the gentleman in black velvet". Predeceased by his wife, and childless, William had arranged the Hanoverian Protestant succession of England. For the succession in Holland, he had proposed John William Friso, a direct descendent of William the Silent's brother, and by a series of previous cousinly marriages, also of William the Silent himself. However, the Republic was governed by regents alone until 1747 when John William Friso's son (a son-in-law of George II of England by his marriage to Anne, Princess Royal) became Stadhouder William IV. He was succeeded by his son, William V. This prince had so many differences of opinion with

The fourth and youngest daughter of Queen Juliana is Princess Christina, who lives in New York City. She renounced her rights to the throne when she married Jorge Guillermo Castillo, a Cuban whom she met at the children's hospital at which they both work. Christina is only partially sighted—as is her husband—and for many years was on the tragic verge of total blindness. She devoted all her time to working with others so afflicted. Now raising a family, she is happy and outgoing.

71

the regents that they gradually stripped him of his prerogatives until he virtually retired to Gelderland in 1785.

For about a year, the country was to all intents and purposes without a *stadhouder*, and the regents banned all pro-Orange demonstrations: no orange ribbons, no orange cloth, no oranges or tangerines were allowed on display and carrots could only be put out for sale if their green tops were outermost. By 1786 the various factions—regents, bourgeois, radicals, Orangists were all at daggers drawn, and the regents slowly realized that their best hope of staying in power was to come to terms with William V.

Soestdijk is probably the most roomy of the palaces in which the Dutch royal family live. It is built of white-trimmed brick. There is a very obtrusive widow's walk on top of the highest roof, looking for all the world like the Gloriette on the hill behind Vienna's Schönbrunn. The palace sits somewhat forlornly in a great, flat park which is attractive because of its complete emptiness.

Talks proceeded so slowly that William's wife, a niece of Frederick the Great, set out to the province of Holland to rally support for her husband. She was arrested and the Prussian army goose-stepped into the Netherlands to avenge her. This caused the leaders of the Republic at once to restore William. In 1794, the invading French revolutionary army occupied the Netherlands and transformed the United Provinces into the Batavian Republic. Then came the Napoleonic kingdom under Louis Bonaparte; and finally the Netherlands became part of the French Empire, while William V went into exile, first in England and then to Prussia.

73

It was William V's grandson who, for a very short time, became the fiancé of Princess Charlotte, daughter of England's Prince Regent. It was soon noticed that she was far from enamoured of the young man. Although at first meeting she had apparently seized him by the arm, and said loudly "I like him very much"—this inspite of his far from fine figure, with spindly legs and a thin neck. Then, it had been thought that she had frightened him to death, so fast was his get-away from the Prince Regent's house. She soon jilted him, at first politely, then firmly and in triplicate—copies of her letters to him went to her father and mother. However, he still felt that "the many rejections were not sufficient warrant for despair". He came a-wooing yet again, and became known as "Young Frog". In the end, Princess Charlotte married Prince Leopold of Saxe-Coburg; while "Young Frog" married a daughter of Paul I of Russia.

At the Congress of Vienna, after Napoleon's fall, Young Frog's father was proclaimed King William I of the Netherlands. He became the ruler of all seventeen provinces—the Northern United Republic, Luxembourg (which he ruled as Grand Duke), Limbourg and the southern former Austrian provinces inhabited by Flemings and Walloons. These did not welcome the new state of affairs, and in 1830 they declared their independence. At King William's instigation, a conference of all the nations met in London to deliberate the matter and a new state, Belgium, was in due course recognized. It only remained to elect a king for the new nation, and the choice fell on Leopold of Saxe-Coburg, Princess Charlotte's widower. Young Frog said glumly of Leopold: "First he steals my wife, then my country". King William I, in spite of his horror of bloodshed, promptly made war on the King of the Belgians. The fighting lasted for ten days. Then Louis Philippe of France made warlike noises, which ended the incident. William had gained part of Luxembourg, but this was kept in Belgian pawn until 1839. Two years later he abdicated in favour of his son who was succeeded by William III in 1849.

Queen Emma

Huis ten Bosch, or House in the Wood, situated in the Hague, is, after Soestdijk, Queen Juliana's favourite residence. Conceived by Prince Frederick Hendrik of Orange, it was completed in 1647, but twenty-eight years passed before it was called Huis ten Bosch- the trees were planted after the building was finished. The strict symmetry of the villa's plan is derived from the country houses of Venetian nobility, but there the similarity ends, for the place is unmistakeably Dutch. The justly famous white dining salon must be one of the half dozen most exquisite palace interiors in The Netherlands. The Oranjesaal is also superb, with gloriously flamboyant murals perfectly set off by the restrained beauty of the room's simple architectural details. However the Oriental Suite, with its profusion of gloomy, black lacquer, could be compared with the lying-in-state chamber of an undertaking establishment. Behind the scenes, Huis ten Bosch is thoroughly modern: glistening bathrooms, and kitchens of startling efficiency.

This king was an ultra conservative except in marital affairs. He was married to Sophie of Württemberg, known as *la reine rouge* because of her advanced ideas, from whom he was to live apart, and whose jewels he was to bestow on his mistresses. Sophie had three sons, all to remain bachelors though hardly for want of trying: the Prince of Orange whom the Prince of Wales called *Citron,* and whom to Queen Victoria's disgust had been seen drinking "and goodness knows what else", appeared in England in the guise of a suitor for more than one of her younger daughters. The Queen, requiring sons-in-law of unblemished virtue, would not hear of any such thing. When the German Empress, in an attempt to soften her mother's heart, remarked on this Prince of Orange's good looks and his white teeth, Queen Victoria said in that case they could not be his own, since when last seen they were bad. From "the poor boy, what can you expect with such an example before his eyes" (the Queen meant his father) it became "that odious prince is coming *again*"; indeed, by then, his private life had become the scandal of all Europe.

As all three princes predeceased their father, it was lucky that the sexagenarian William III had remarried after Queen Sophie's death. The new Queen of Holland was Princess Emma of Waldeck and Pyrmont. A cousin of Queen Elisabeth of Roumania (better known as the novelist Carmen Sylva) she was tall, stout, bespectacled and down to earth. After William III's death she became an efficient regent for her daughter Queen Wilhelmina, whose majority was celebrated in 1898 eight years after the death of her father. So enthusiastic were the celebrations that Queen Emma, knowing young Wilhelmina needed peace and quiet for her well-being, begged for less noise—and the celebrants continued their revels in stockinged feet. Queen Wilhelmina's reign lasted for half a century, during which she won the respect of all the world. She lived until 1962, enjoying the satisfaction of seeing her daughter Queen Juliana make as great a success of her reign as she made of her own.

Queen Wilhelmina

75

NORWAY
Two Good Kings

King Olav V of Norway was born a Dane and baptised Alexander Edward Christian Frederik, with no prospects of a crown and not a hint that he would one day be Norwegian. His names, in fact, betrayed his true background, for he was the son of a Danish prince and an English princess, the youngest daughter of Edward VII of Great Britain and of Queen Alexandra. King Olav is thus today the only surviving grandchild of Edward VII and within the first fifty in line to the British throne.

King Olav, or Prince Alexander as he than was, was born at Appleton House on the English royal family's Sandringham estate and it is repeatedly said of him how English he is—but this is not the whole truth. He was two years old when in 1905 his father was offered the throne of Norway and on a grey, November day entered the country for the first time on his father's arm. From then on, he lived as a Norwegian, with a new Norwegian name, Olav, Norwegian friends and Norwegian education.

This began with lessons at the Palace, but later Crown Prince Olav went to Halling School, becoming the first prince in the world to attend a grammar school. He has remained in touch with friends he made there all his life. After spells at the Norwegian military academy and Balliol College, Oxford, he took, on his twenty-first birthday, the oath to the constitution after which he began to perform royal duties.

In 1929 he married his first cousin, Princess Märtha, the second of Prince Carl of Sweden's spectacularly beautiful daughters and sister of Princess Astrid who married Leopold III of Belgium and was tragically killed in a motor accident. The couple went to live in relatively unostentatious style at Skaugum, in Asker, about twelve miles from Oslo, giving the (true) impression, as the King does to this day, of being determined to do an efficient job without unnecessary display.

Crown Princess Märtha

HAAKON VII, *King of Norway (1905–57)* **m** *1896, Princess Maud of Great Britain and Ireland*
b *1872* **d** *1957*   **b** *1869* **d** *1938*

OLAV V, *King of Norway (1957–*) **m** *1929, Princess Märtha of Sweden*
b *1903*   **b** *1901* **d** *1954*

Crown Prince Harald **b** *1937*   Princess Ragnhild **b** *1930* **m** *1953,*   Princess Astrid **b** *1932* **m** *1961,*
m *1968, Sonja Haraldsen,* **b** *1937* Erling Sven Lorantzen, **b** *1923*   Johan Martin Ferner, **b** *1927*

Hereditary Prince Haakon **b** *1973*   Princess Märtha Louise **b** *1971*

When on duty, King Olav is so regal that he appears capable of decapitating with a glance. In private, he is like a reassuring Santa Claus (without the beard and bulbous nose), a jolly, spirited grandfather whom everyone loves. Visitors waiting to be received in audience sometimes fear they have their dates wrong, and that a party is in progress in the King's study when they hear peals of laughter through the walls. Usually, it is the King discussing a matter of protocol with the Court Chamberlain, or a menu with the Housekeeper. One of the things his countrymen appreciate him for most is his passion for sailing and international standing as a yachtsman. He won a gold medal at the 1928 Amsterdam Olympic Games, came second in the World Yachting Championships in 1976 and regularly takes the helm of his 5.5 metre, *Norma*.

Left to right: Princess Astrid, King Olav, Princess Märtha Louise, Prince Haakon Magnus, Crown Prince Harald and Crown Princess Sonja

Harald and Sonja, Crown Prince and Princess of Norway, represent a strong argument in favour of marrying only for love. The unaffected Harald fell for Sonja Haraldsen, an Oslo draper's daughter, when both were in their late teens. They succeeded, after several frustrating years, in obtaining permission to marry and are now going about the business of living happily ever after. Although acclaimed on festive occasions, both are able to go about Oslo unimpeded. Sonja belongs to the purple as if born to it. In 1978, she made a solo state visit to the U.S.A. with pronounced success. When Harald becomes King, Sonja will not be the first draper's daughter to reign as queen consort of Norway. Desirée, who as Queen of Sweden in 1818-44 was also Queen of Norway, was the daughter of Francois Clary, a silk merchant in Marseilles.

Hereditary Prince Haakon Magnus of Norway and Princess Märtha Louise are the royal grandchildren. They live an idyllic life on the farm of their parents, the Crown Prince and Princess, near Oslo. Both attend municipal schools in Oslo and enthusiastically join in school activities. To the obvious delight of their parents, they acquitted themselves admirably when taking part in a school programme in honour of King Olav's seventy-fifth birthday in 1978. They are politely shy, and the world comes as a constantly pleasant surprise to them. The Prince is very like his mother and the Princess is like both her parents.

In the war years, Olav remained based with his father and the government-in-exile in London while the Crown Princess and children went to the safety of the U.S.A. When the war was over he worked closely with his father in Norway, establishing a popular father and son team. Then, in 1954, came the terrible blow of his wife's death after a long illness, followed in 1955 by King Haakon's accident in which he fell, fracturing a thigh bone. From this the King never fully recovered so that the Crown Prince acted as Regent until King Haakon died two years later.

King Olav is sovereign in a country with no aristocracy, but in no sense is he isolated. This must in part be due to what, judged as a public figure, is possibly his chief quality. He is remarkably considerate; punctiliously so, in fact, of the feelings, the wishes, the attitudes and the prejudices of everyone with whom he comes in contact. One example of this was the question of the private dining room of two very old ladies who lodge in the Palace. They were once maids of honour to King Olav's mother, Queen Maud, during whose time it was not thought proper for ladies-in-waiting to sit at table with gentlemen of the household who might be lower in station. A separate dining room was therefore provided, an enormous room equipped at one end with chintz-covered sofas and chairs with writing desks and tables for cards and embroidery. At one time, as many as a dozen gaily chattering young ladies made it their common room. Now, only the two remain, in their eighties and long since pensioned, but the King declared that nothing shall disturb them from their private dining room as long as they both live. To this very select common room the King has added television and other distractions with the result that the ladies often doze happily after lunch and need to be roused when it is time to change for dinner. Neither, incidentally, dreams of dining in day dresses: once when the King went in to deliver a birthday present, he found to his delight that both ladies were dressed as for the opera.

Norway is a constitutional, hereditary monarchy, with executive power held in theory by the King and the Council of State (cabinet) but, as in other Scandinavian countries, the sovereign does no more than assent formally to the decisions and proposals of the Council. The King may closely

Left: King Olav's younger daughter, Princess Astrid, lives in Oslo. She is Mrs. Johan Ferner, having married a non-royal, as did her sister Princess Ragnhild. Mr. Ferner runs his family's business, a clothing store near the Royal Palace, formerly exclusively devoted to menswear, but now selling women's wear as well. Astrid is named after her mother's sister, Queen Astrid of Belgium, King Baudouin of Belgium's mother.

Princess Ragnhild of Norway, King Olav's elder daughter, has been married for more than twenty-five years to Mr. Erling S. Lorentzen, a shipping line owner. They live in Rio de Janeiro and have a son and two daughters. Twice a year—"for state days and bonfire nights"—the family go back to Norway. Ragnhild is a trifle shy, but she is happy, and has the knack of making those around her happy too.

question ministers, but not challenge their decisions. The parliament, called the Storting, is composed of 150 members.

The constitution does not permit the crown to pass to a female heir, but since the present Crown Prince has a son, Norway's monarchy seems secured well into the twenty-first century. For such a new institution, in a country with strong socialist leanings, it is as well-established as it could be. The most cynical find it hard to deny that the royal family have provided useful and at times inspiring service and it can hardly fail to continue to do so providing it preserves its rapport with the people. In this, too, it is hard to imagine failure. Months after King Olav's seventy-fifth birthday celebrations, a visitor remarked on the large number of cardboard boxes stacked against the walls and around the desk in the King's study, saying it was surprising that Olav tolerated such clutter.

"You may call it clutter", replied Olav with the usual smile, "to me it represents 'love'". In the boxes were gifts sent him by children all over Norway, and the King had insisted that the clutter remained until a letter of thanks had been sent to all.

For five centuries prior to 1905, Norway's history is essentially a recital of when the country belonged to Sweden or to Denmark or to both. In the last years of the nineteenth century, however, Norwegians began to grow restless for independence from Sweden and 1905, when King Oscar II vetoed a bill which had been approved by the Storting, the crisis came. Norway's cabinet resigned and the Storting pronounced the union with Sweden dissolved. The Swedish government consented to recognize Norway's independence on the condition that a referendum was held, which duly proved that Norwegians were overwhelmingly in favour of an end to the union.

The throne of the new state was first offered to the second son of Oscar II. Without consulting his son, Oscar rejected it on his behalf with a remark taken to mean that if he was not good enough for it, neither was his son. Oscar remained bitter about the loss of Norway and it is said that this hastened his death, which occurred two and half years later.

King Haakon

Next, the throne was offered to Prince Carl of Denmark, a young man whom the English royal family had considered singularly without prospects when he married Edward VII's daughter Maud. Prince Carl was pleased with the offer and accepted with alacrity. There was some question as to whether the majority of Norwegians would not in fact prefer a republic and this was put to the test by a second referendum which confirmed Carl as the new King by nearly four to one in favour of a monarchy. Prince Carl renounced his Danish nationality and went with his wife and young son to live in Norway, assuming a new name, Haakon, after the early norse kings of the country.

King George V of England and Queen Mary attended their son-in-law's coronation at Trondheim Cathedral, but Queen Mary privately thought the country barbarous and, prompted by her Aunt Augusta, Grand Duchess of Mecklenburg-Strelitz, believed that the new throne had been won by revolution.

In fact, Haakon VII's installation, with the royal guests living aboard their yachts anchored in the nearby fjord, was a dignified, if simple affair and set the tone for the long reign of Norway's first king in six hundred years. Haakon threw himself heart and soul into the job. Before his arrival he had undertaken to learn to speak Norwegian, and claimed to the end of his life that he had succeeded in doing so, fluently. Those who knew him well did not necessarily agree, claiming he spoke it with a machine-gun rapidity that could distress those to whom he might, for all they knew,

The Royal Palace in Oslo sits on the most commanding height in the town's centre and gazes magnificently down the full length of Oslo's principal thoroughfare, Karl Johan Gate, much as the Arc de Triomphe looks down the Champs Elysées in Paris. It is fairly small, built when kings of Sweden were also kings of Norway and only came to Christiania, as Oslo was then called, for short periods each year. Outside, it is stucco on brick and stone; inside it is well-heated, comfortable and the food is good, for the kitchens are modern showpieces. The private apartments are handsome and the Palace boasts two ballrooms, one larger and grander than the other. The interior décor is principally late eighteenth- and early nineteenth-century with French and English influences and the splendour of the State Rooms is dazzling. Kavl, the architect, has restored the chapel to its original, simple Nordic beauty. The grounds, open to the public, can only be described as bleak.

be giving important orders. One of the King's Danish cousins labelled this curious tongue Pure Haakon.

It was in fact not altogether easy for the King to lose his Danish qualities and interests for Norwegian ones. The increasing strength of the strongly anti-monarchist Norwegian Labour Party caused him some embarrassment. Its leaders, for example, snubbed him by refusing the customary invitations to dine at the Palace on the opening of the Storting. For his part, the King never antagonised the Labour Party, which for the first time acquired true power in 1928.

Not until the outbreak of war in 1945 did the King fully capture the imagination of the Norwegians. He refused Hitler's demand to appoint Quisling, as puppet prime minister. For two months after the invasion, the royal family and government remained on Norwegian soil in the far north of the country before escaping, not without drama, to England. There they set up the Free Norwegian Forces and government-in-exile which directed Norway's brave contribution to the defeat of Hitler. In 1945, Haakon returned to a raptuous welcome.

Two years later, his seventy-fifth birthday was celebrated with a real display of public affection. There was a nation-wide subscription to buy King Haakon the present he wanted most, a yacht: appropriately enough for the King of a seafaring people, he loved the sea. Supported by his son (Queen Maud had died just before the war), Haakon reigned another ten years to become the oldest European sovereign of his day.

Queen Maud

SPAIN

Restoration

King Juan Carlos was born in Rome, where his parents were living in exile, but at the suggestion of General Franco, chief of state since 1936, he was educated in Spain, attending military academies and university. Afterwards, he gained first-hand experience in various ministries, and was thus groomed to become Franco's successor as ruler of Spain, which had been declared a monarchy, albeit without a king.

King Juan Carlos is married to Princess Sofia, elder daughter of King Paul of the Hellenes and Queen Frederika. Queen Sofia is a trained nurse, and studied in Greece, then at Salem College (run by her uncle, Prince Georg of Hanover), and took various courses at the University of Madrid. The royal couple are modern in outlook: a godsend to a country where the cry "death to liberty" can still occasionally be heard.

There was some surprise when General Franco made Don Juan Carlos his heir. Legitimists thought that the throne should have gone to the Prince's father, Don Juan. This Prince has, indeed, not renounced it, having been designated the rightful claimant by his own father, King Alfonso XIII.

Apart from the legitimists, there were also the Carlists, whose party had neither favoured King Alfonso XIII, nor his immediate predecessors. Indeed, the royal family of Spain, from the nineteenth century onwards, has been beset by a tragic disunity of which traces linger to this day. There

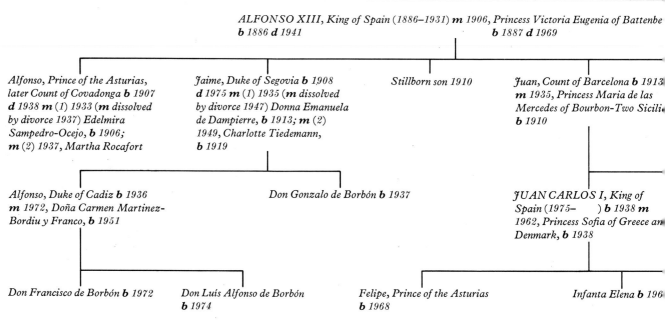

82

King Juan Carlos of Spain with his wife Queen Sofia and three children. Although thoroughly groomed for the Spanish throne from childhood by General Franco, whose methods were not always popular, Juan Carlos has struck out in a direction almost entirely different from what the dictator would have wished. Clearly, the King's plan for Spain is one which he hopes will most benefit people at all levels. Queen Sofia is the elder daughter of King Paul and Queen Frederika of Greece, and sister of King Constantine. She has learned to cope with the problems which confront a consort, and is relaxed, often gay, with a faultless dress sense, looking, if possible, younger than on her wedding day in 1962, and just as pretty.

is still a Carlist claimant to the throne: Prince Carlos Hugo of Bourbon-Parma, the "Duke of Barcelona", who shares ancestors with the King.

King Juan Carlos favours a free and modern society. He sees it as one of the tasks of his government to make participation a matter of priority for all. As Franco's heir, he had enjoyed sweeping powers at the beginning of his reign, but even then his policies were more liberal than those of the dictator. One of his first acts on accession was to begin work on a constitution. As soon as he judged the time ripe, he mounted the referendum which brought Spain into the family of democratic European nations. How the right wing and the Church will take to the new regime still remains to be seen, but they can hardly have been taken by surprise, since the young King's liberal ideas had been apparent ever since he had ascended the throne which has surely been one of the most contended in Europe's history.

Transference of power had been plain sailing in the old days when the Habsburgs had come by the Iberian peninsula in one of their fortunate marriages. But before this, modern Spain's foundations were the several Christian provinces which had been established in what was largely a Moorish country. From these emerged the Kingdoms of Aragon and Castile, which were gathered into a single state in the fifteenth century by Ferdinand of Aragon and Isabella of Castile. It was their daughter Juana's

Don Juan, Count of Barcelona, the father of King Juan Carlos, greets one of his grand-daughters. He lives in exile in Estoril, Portugal, and, although his son is a reigning monarch, is still recognized by legitimists as head of the House of Borbon: something that has never disturbed the affection between father and son. Recently, in a touching gesture, Juan Carlos was pleased to appoint his father Honorary Admiral of the Spanish fleet. Don Juan might have stepped out of the pages of a modern romantic novel, in fact it is said that he was the model for one of Hemingway's heroes. He often visits his son in Spain and both of them are great sportsmen, keen on fishing, shooting, and riding.

nte Gonzalo
14 d 1934

Infanta Beatriz b 1909 m 1935
Don Alessandro Torlonia, 5th
Principe di Civitella-Cesi, b 1911

Infanta Maria Cristina b 1911
m 1940, Enrico Marone-Cinzano,
1st Count Marone, b 1895, d 1968

nte Alfonso b 1941
56

Infanta Maria del Pilar,
Duchess of Badajoz b 1936 m
1967, Don Luis Gómez-Acebo y
Duque de Estrada, Viscount de la
Torre, b 1934

Infanta Margarita b 1939 m
1972, Don Carlos Zurita y
Delgado, b 1943

fanta Cristina b 1965

Maria de las Mercedes, Countess of Barcelona, the mother of King Juan Carlos, was born a princess of Bourbon—Two Sicilies. There have seldom been photographs of her smiling, and this does her a disservice, since although cautious about displaying her feelings, when she does so, her face lights up in the most natural manner. She relaxes by constantly knitting.

Infanta Elena, above, and Infanta Cristina, above right, are the breathtakingly spic-and-span daughters of the King and Queen of Spain. Elena is very like her mother,

while Cristina is hauntingly reminiscent of her great-grandmother, Queen Ena, consort of King Alfonso XIII, the king of Spain whose rule preceded General Franco's.

Felipe, Prince of the Asturias, heir to the throne of Spain, is much taken with the day school he attends, devoted to his friends there, and shows every sign of brightness.

marriage that brought Spain to the Habsburgs, whose rule lasted until the beginning of the eighteenth century.

When in 1700 the last of their line, Carlos II, died, the trouble began. Everyone had known for years that Europe would go to war as soon as he had breathed his last, and indeed had been discussing the partition of Spain for a good many years. In the event it was Louis XIV who shocked the world by presenting his grandson, Philippe, Duc d'Anjou, to his assembled court with the words "Gentlemen, here is the King of Spain". Everyone tried to look suitably stunned, although the arrival of a Spanish suite shortly after Carlos II's death had more than prepared them for this event. The King's sister-in-law had already swept the Duc d'Anjou her lowest curtsey and addressed him as "your Majesty", only to see the boy startled out of his customary lethargy—which however, he soon regained.

It was well known in France that the messengers from Spain also had instructions to make their offer to the court of Vienna in the unlikely case that Louis XIV would refuse the throne for the Duc d'Anjou and feel obliged to honour the partition agreement he had made with the other powers. France was already too powerful for the peace of mind of her neighbours, and the Austrian Habsburgs, of course, would also be intolerably aggrandized by the possession of Spain. Whichever of them accepted the throne, and both families had a claim based on family relationship, the balance of power in Europe would be hopelessly upset. So, soon after the Duc d'Anjou, now known as Philip V of Spain, set off to Madrid, the War of the Spanish Succession started—the war which brought Marlborough and Prince Eugene of Savoy—Castor to the Duke's Pollux—their finest victories. The war ended, more than a decade later, with the recognition of Philip V. The Austrian Emperor's son, the Archduke Charles, who had sped to Barcelona to make good his claim, unexpectedly succeeded as Emperor in 1711, and so became an unsuitable candidate for Spain.

For all that Philip V grew daily more Spanish, the Sun King's hand was felt in Spain. He provided his grandson with a queen politically useful to France and in the Spanish court he planted a spy: the Princess des Ursins. Through her, Paris was informed of every move, however trivial, in the Palace at Madrid—so intimately involved was she with the private lives of

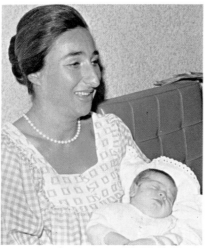

Infanta Maria del Pilar, above, and Infanta Margarita, above right, are the sisters of King Juan Carlos. Both live in Madrid and are married, the former to the Duke of Badajoz, the latter to a doctor, Don Carlos Zurita y Delgado. For many years, the sisters dressed similarly, and they have the effortless elegance characteristic of Iberian women.

the royal couple, that whenever the King meant to spend the night with his wife, it fell to the Princess to carry his sword and his chamber-pot to the Queen's bedchamber.

She did a great deal of carrying: the King, like so many of the Bourbons, was oversexed, and soon wore out his wife. She died at the age of twenty-five after numerous miscarriages and four sons, two of whom survived to succeed to the throne.

The King's grief at his wife's death in no way diminished his physical needs, and he at once instructed the Cardinal Alberoni, his first minister, and Mme. des Ursins to find him a new wife. She was Elisabeth Farnese, niece of the Duke of Parma. Having established a firm grip on her husband on arrival, she was never to relinquish it, and is remembered as the termagent queen whose determination to regain, on behalf of her sons, the Italian territories lost to Spain by the peace treaty of Utrecht, plunged Spain into lengthy wars.

Because there were *infantes* by the King's first marriage, Elisabeth did not believe that any of her three surviving sons would succeed to the throne of Spain: however, she was mistaken.

In 1724, and already showing signs of the strangeness that was to darken his later years, Philip V suddenly abdicated: a crisis of conscience, he said, for was he not in mortal sin for going against the Divine Will that had intended him to be King of France? It is sometimes suggested that he abdicated because of doubting his divine right to the throne of Spain, but these doubts cannot have been too serious, for he bequeathed the throne to the eldest son of his first marriage, Don Luis, who became Luis I.

This luckless young man died in the same year. So Philip V and Elisabeth Farnese came out of retirement and the King reigned on until his death in 1746, when the succession passed to his younger son, Don Fernando, who reigned until 1759.

This monarch was to be described by Horace Walpole as "a man of no abilities and lately of disordered mind." His madness, formerly kept in check by his adored wife, a princess of Portugal, became obvious after her death: Ferdinand could be seen haunting the Palace day and night, now and then snatching a little sleep while sitting in his chair—he was convinced

Alfonso, Duke of Cadiz, is a first cousin of King Juan Carlos. His father was one of the elder brothers of the Count of Barcelona, one of whom was killed in a car accident and the other, Alfonso's father, a deaf mute, renounced all rights of succession for himself and his descendants in 1933. The Duke of Cadiz is a once and future diplomat: he was a successful Ambassador to Stockholm, and although without an embassy at the moment, is one of the best representatives his country could wish for. His wife Carmen provides the genealogical link between the Franco dictatorship and the Spain of Juan Carlos: she is General Franco's grand-daughter. Her mother, from whom she has inherited her beauty, is the Marquesa de Villaverde, first Duchess of Franco, and the daughter of the Caudillo.

Philip V

Queen Marie Louise

Don Manuel Godoy

that death would find him if he went to his bed. However, barely a year after his wife, he died, the last of the children of Philip V's first marriage.

So, in 1759, came the turn of the eldest of Elisabeth's sons. First Don Carlos was called to the throne. He had enjoyed a long apprenticeship as King of Naples and Sicily, and under his enlightened despotism, the backward country had immeasurably progressed. Now, he set about doing the same for Spain, but like so many of her kings, all but imprisoned in the stiff etiquette of the court, he was given to melancholy. His chief release was found not in prayer, but in the fresh air. Hunting was his passion, and the pockets of the grey coat in which Goya painted him were always bulging with hunting and fishing tackle. His wife, a princess of Saxony, died early and he never remarried. There was no real need for King Carlos III to remarry: his Queen had produced six sons—quite enough for the succession to Spain and to Sicily, even though the eldest had to be excluded.

There was no doubt, said Horace Walpole, that the boy was indeed an idiot, for why else should his own father wish to disinherit him? It was settled that the King's second son would become his successor, and, when the reign of Carlos III came to an end in 1788, this prince succeeded as Carlos IV to a Spain improved in almost every aspect—for all that Carlos III had remarked that his subjects were apt to react to his reforms "like children who cry when their faces are washed".

Carlos IV resembled his father in his good nature, in his passion for field sports, and to a certain extent in looks, but he was even plainer, and married an exceedingly plain lady—his cousin Marie Louise, daughter of the Duke of Parma. They had a large number of very plain children. The only handsome face in the whole family belonged to the Queen's lover, and the King's favourite, Manuel Godoy. Apart from a short spell out of power, Godoy was so close to the royal couple that people referred to them as the *Santa Trinita*.

The French Revolution occurred during Carlos IV's reign, but did not much impinge upon Spain until the execution of Louis XVI. Godoy, charged with the task of saving the life of this fellow-Bourbon, made up for his failure by successfully negotiating a separate peace with revolutionary France in 1795. Henceforth, he gloried in the title of Prince of the Peace. In the year 1808, while French troops were in Madrid, ostensibly on a punitive expedition to Portugal (who would keep on trading with Great Britain), a rising in Aranjuez forced Carlos IV to abdicate in favour of his son Ferdinand.

This prince had secretly been negotiating with Napoleon in order to gain the throne. It did not do him much good: the Emperor of the French successfully contrived to lure the royal family to Bayonne, where Ferdinand was made to abdicate in favour of his father. Then, as soon as Carlos IV was once again King of Spain, Napoleon forced him to transfer the crown to his brother Joseph Bonaparte: the documents had already been prepared, all it needed was Carlos IV's signature.

During Joseph's reign, the *Santa Trinita* went first to Chambord and Compiègne, and then to Rome. Ferdinand was at Valençay. Even though he was Napoleon's prisoner, he celebrated his captor's birthday with such over-enthusiastic fireworks that the garden caught fire and was ruined.

Half of the Spanish people, however, did not accept the abdications of Bayonne, and in the absence of their rightful King formed a patriotic government, the Junta, who ruled in the name of Ferdinand VII, the Desired One, by a constitution which was promulgated in 1812. Joseph

Bonaparte—*el rey intruso*—was recognized by the other half of the nation.

An enlighted liberal, he made friends with the liberals of Spain and many Spanish aristocrats accompanied him to France when the Desired One returned to Spain in 1814. The Junta fared no better: Ferdinand VII at once abolished the 1812 constitution and ruled on, ineptly, until 1833.

Not one of his four wives having presented him with a son, he revoked the Salic Law, if law it can be called. At the public outcry which followed, he revoked the revocation, and then changed his mind yet again but begged his *Camarilla* to keep this last decision secret until he was dead.

Accordingly, to the surprise of Spain and of his younger brother Carlos (who gave his name to his supporters, the Carlists) Ferdinand's three year-old daughter Isabella was proclaimed Queen of Spain, and her mother, Maria Christina, became Regent. Don Carlos, regarded as the rightful King of Spain by one half of his niece's subjects, stood for traditionalism, and was recognized by the north of the country. Queen Isabella had the support of the liberal south and centre. This conflict was to involve Spain in two full-scale civil wars and numerous uprisings.

Isabella's reign saw the first of the Carlist wars, and so many risings, insurgencies, and governments that even the Princess Lieven, usually so precise, was to say "Spain is a hopeless mess". Isabella herself grew from an undisciplined girl into a shrewd, good-natured, self-indulgent woman with a great many lovers. Many came to understand this aspect of her character better after the "affair of the Spanish marriages".

Assuring England that he had no intention of drawing the crowns of France and Spain closer together, King Louis Philippe of France married his son to Isabella's younger sister, while the Queen, poor girl, had married her cousin Francis de Asis. (It would have been better to marry Isabella to the son of Don Carlos, so putting an end to the Carlist rift in the

The Oriente Palace in Madrid was built in the late eighteenth century, when Spain was a major European power, and this is reflected in everything about it; no expense was spared in the construction and decoration. The design was one Louis XIV had commissioned from Bernini in connection with modernising the Louvre, but when the French King rejected Bernini's ideas, the artist sold his work to the King of Spain. The Oriente is built round a single, immense courtyard whose inner lining is a massive glass cage on to which the rooms facing the courtyard open. The walls are lined with priceless tapestries and there are sun-filtering shades against the glass. The private apartments are particularly successful, including the Queen's Bedroom, with its ceiling invitingly painted with a wisp of white lace veil blowing wildly against a bright blue sky.

87

next generation; however, this young man refused to act as king-consort, agreeing to marry only if he became king.) Even so, the Queen's marriage to Francis de Asis, son of Francisco de Paula, who had been likened to Manuel Godoy, should have been innocuous enough. In fact, it was a disaster, and was seen as such by all nations anxious to preserve the balance of power in Europe. The reason was that Francisco was thought to be impotent, and known to be effeminate. No children could be expected, and so Louis Philippe's eventual grandchild was likely to inherit Spain.

In the event, Isabella had no less than nine children, though not necessarily by the King-consort. After her unsuccessful wedding night— "What can I say about a man who wore more lace than I did?"—husband and wife did not often share a bed.

Indeed, excessive piety was all that he and his wife had in common: and when, after yet another uprising, Isabella was asked to abdicate, she wrote to the Pope for guidance. He advised her against it, and so, without renouncing the throne, she went into exile with her lover of the day. Her vacant place was filled, for a time, by Prince Amadeo of Savoy, another *rey intruso*. After two years, he left the country in the throes of a second Carlist war, and Spain, for a short time, became a republic: it proved impossible to find an occupant for the vacant throne.

The offer of it went not once, but twice, to a Hohenzollern of the cadet line, whose final conditional acceptance produced such rage in the France of Napoleon III that it led to the Franco-Prussian war of 1870-71. Isabella's son Alfonso, the heir to the crown, was seventeen in 1870, the year that his mother was finally persuaded to relinquish the crown to him. In less than a year, the Carlist war was over. Sadly, Alfonso XII, known as the Pacificador, died at the age of twenty-eight.

Six months after the King's death, his widow, Maria Christina, gave

Isabella II

El Escorial was built during the sixteenth century entirely in one concentrated period of construction lasting twenty-one years and then remained unaltered. It is at once a royal residence, a royal burial place, a museum, a library and monastery and the magnitude of the place may be understood from the fact that there are 1,100 exterior windows; 1,600 interior ones; a dozen courtyards which produce a gridiron effect; 1,200 doorways and eighty-six staircases. The structure is 225 yards long, 175 yards wide and it encloses a basilica which is a scaled-down version of St. Peter's in Rome. The library contains 45,000 volumes and thousands of documents and manuscripts. The bedroom of Philip II, El Escorial's builder, was an alcove with a door opening on to the high altar of the basilica. He died of pediculosis, the condition in which one is literally eaten up by body lice. It took him seven weeks to die, and every day of it, lying in the bedroom, he was enabled to hear mass. After his death, the apartments were sealed for a century.

birth to his son, King Alfonso XIII, who grew up under his mother's wise guardianship, and was to marry Princess Ena of Battenberg, a granddaughter of Queen Victoria. It was on the day of her marriage that the young bride was introduced to the violence still prevalent in Spain. On the way from the church, a bomb was thrown at the wedding coach—and that was only the first of several subsequent attempts on King Alfonso XIII's life. His reign was not an easy one. During the First World War, while credited with being pro-German, he preserved Spain's neutrality.

Meanwhile the "Carlist King", Don Jaime, successor to the latest Don Carlos, had now moved slightly to the left of the King: a reversal of the traditional roles. Don Jaime lived in France, where King Alfonso XIII went in 1931, after an attempt to return to constitutional government in Spain. The country had gone republican, and rather than "having a drop of blood spilt on my behalf", the King had removed himself, fearing that his continued presence in Spain might fan the flames. Nevertheless, the unrest that beset Spain after his move culminated in the Spanish Civil War and ended in 1939, with a complete victory for General Franco, and the right.

On the King's arrival in France, there had been useful talks between Don Jaime and King Alfonso. The old vendetta between the two lines might have been settled at last, had not Don Jaime died without issue before a settlement was reached. His successor as Carlist claimant was his aged uncle, Alfonso Carlos. When this old gentleman died, bringing the direct Carlist succession to an end, Carlist genealogists produced a new candidate, Don Xavier of the House of Bourbon-Parma. It is Don Xavier's son, Prince Carlos Hugo, married to Princess Irene of the Netherlands, who is the Carlist claimant today. King Alfonso died in 1941, having abdicated in favour of his son Don Juan in the same year. His last act was to kiss a crucifix and to say: "*Espana, Dio mio*".

Alfonso XIII

SWEDEN
The Military Choice

When the present King of Sweden, Carl XVI Gustaf, was less than a year old, his father died in a plane crash; so when in 1973, aged twenty-seven, Carl Gustaf became King, he followed his ninety year-old grandfather in the succession. Moreover, Carl Gustaf's great-grandfather, the previous King, had also died a nonagenarian.

Thus, at the time of Carl Gustaf's accession, Sweden was used to much older sovereigns, and there were gloomy forebodings about the future of the monarchy. It was thought by some that the only justification of so progressive a country as Sweden retaining a royal family had been the personality of the old King, and that, rightly or wrongly, people could hardly feel the same about his twenty-seven year-old grandson.

The fears, of course, have been proved unjustified. Swedes retain a natural affection for their sovereigns, and Carl Gustaf's marriage in 1976 to Silvia Sommerlath, a good-looking, German-born career girl, aroused more pro-monarchical feelings than had been seen in the country for many years. Lining the streets was a crowd of 180,000, and more than five million watched the event on television.

In this happy outcome may perhaps be detected the influence of Carl Gustaf's much-loved grandfather, Gustaf VI Adolf. In the last years of his life, he prepared his heir for kingship in an exceptionally imaginative, but also practical way. The Crown Prince's general education began conventionally enough at a co-educational boarding school near Stockholm

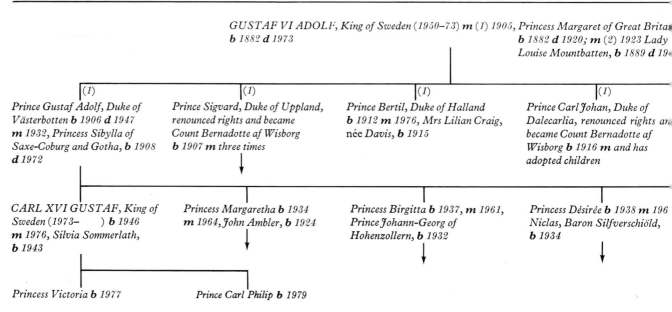

GUSTAF VI ADOLF, King of Sweden (1950–73) **m** (1) 1905, Princess Margaret of Great Britai
b 1882 **d** 1973   **b** 1882 **d** 1920; **m** (2) 1923 Lady
                                                         Louise Mountbatten, **b** 1889 **d** 19

(1)	(1)	(1)	(1)
Prince Gustaf Adolf, Duke of Västerbotten **b** 1906 **d** 1947 **m** 1932, Princess Sibylla of Saxe-Coburg and Gotha, **b** 1908 **d** 1972	Prince Sigvard, Duke of Uppland, renounced rights and became Count Bernadotte af Wisborg **b** 1907 **m** three times	Prince Bertil, Duke of Halland **b** 1912 **m** 1976, Mrs Lilian Craig, née Davis, **b** 1915	Prince Carl Johan, Duke of Dalecarlia, renounced rights an became Count Bernadotte af Wisborg **b** 1916 **m** and has adopted children
CARL XVI GUSTAF, King of Sweden (1973–) **b** 1946 **m** 1976, Silvia Sommerlath, **b** 1943	Princess Margaretha **b** 1934 **m** 1964, John Ambler, **b** 1924	Princess Birgitta **b** 1937, **m** 1961, Prince Johann-Georg of Hohenzollern, **b** 1932	Princess Désirée **b** 1938 **m** 196 Niclas, Baron Silfverschiöld, **b** 1934
Princess Victoria **b** 1977 Prince Carl Philip **b** 1979			

Above, King Carl XVI Gustaf and above right, his first child, Princess Victoria, photographed by the King on her first birthday in 1978. Like any other sovereign, Carl Gustaf became a personage rather than a person when he ascended the Swedish throne in 1973- not always a beneficial change, (but one which he made successfully). As Crown Prince in the shadow of his much-respected grandfather, he tended to keep to the background; as King, he is friendly, energetic and capable. Carl Gustaf is descended twice from Queen Victoria: she was both his maternal and paternal great-great-

grandmother, his father having been a descendant of the Duke of Connaught and his mother of the Duke of Albany. Not unexpectedly, Queen Silvia, below, has taken naturally to her role— there is little that disturbs her composure now. She endeared herself to the Swedes from the beginning by her practicality. On her wedding day, she was determined to have a hand-kerchief readily available, so she folded up a tissue and secured it to a wrist with an elastic band. As she waved to the crowds, the arrangement was revealed beneath the sleeve of her Dior wedding gown.

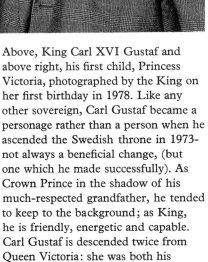

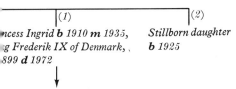

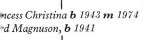

ncess Ingrid **b** *1910* **m** *1935,*
g Frederik IX of Denmark,
899 **d** *1972*

(1)

Stillborn daughter
b *1925*

(2)

ncess Christina **b** *1943* **m** *1974*
d Magnuson, **b** *1941*

Princess Christina, youngest of King Carl Gustaf's four sisters, with her husband Tord Magnuson and two sons Gustaf and Oscar. The family live in a grace and favour house in the park of the Palace of Ulriksdal, Stockholm.

and was followed by training as a naval officer and a course at Uppsala University. But later, he was sent all over Sweden to learn for himself the workings of Swedish industry at every level; and this was supplemented by opportunities to study at first hand the workings of the legal and banking professions and the press, radio, television and Church. Finally, Carl Gustaf had a spell at the Ministry of Foreign Affairs; an economics course at Stockholm University and periods working at the Swedish Embassy in London, the Swiss Chamber of Commerce and at Hambros Bank.

It has been observed, sometimes with regret, that this remarkably comprehensive education will never be put to full use: for of all the European sovereigns, Sweden's King has least constitutional power.

A new constitution, which became effective in March 1975, reduced the sovereign to no more than a figurehead. The lead in forming a new government, usually the most significant contribution a constitutional monarch has to make, passed to the speaker of the parliament, or *Riksdag*. No longer, too, was the sovereign permitted to take part in government meetings, to sign bills or to appoint or dismiss ministers. His duties were reduced to those of a universal ambassador, and although he still enjoys immunity under penal law, the *Riksdag* has the right to decide, if the king fails to fulfil, or is prevented from fulfilling his duties, whether or not he "shall be considered to have abdicated".

Sweden's royal house is unique among reigning European dynasties in having been founded not by an early medieval prince or great lord, but by a sergeant from Gascony who became one of Napoleon's marshals. He was, of course, Jean Baptiste Bernadotte, who in 1810 was chosen by the Swedes as crown prince to the last king of the Holstein-Gottorp dynasty, the elderly and childless Charles XIII. There were various reasons for this highly unconventional choice. The army, which had dethroned Charles's nephew and predecessor, the ineffective Gustaf IV, was anxious to have a "man and a soldier" as king. Bernadotte had proved himself a soldier, and with his rugged looks was certainly a man.

Then the Swedes remembered how conciliatory he had been as Governor of Pomerania and the Hanseatic towns after 1807, and also that when, in 1807, Napoleon had proposed that Bernadotte should invade their country,

Marshal Bernadotte and his wife.

Prince Bertil, Duke of Halland, uncle of King Carl Gustaf, spent holidays during his childhood at Clarence House, one of the English royal family's London residences—his grandfather was the Duke of Connaught, a son of Queen Victoria. A tournament class golfer and a cordon-bleu cook, Prince Bertil has an amiable, easy manner which has made him popular in Scandinavia. His wife, Princess Lilian, is one of the best-dressed royal ladies in Europe and so regal that she could be mistaken for the daughter of a king.

he had successfully side-tracked this plan. In fact, Bernadotte had acquired the reputation of being the most independent-minded of Napoleon's paladins, and when he had defeated the Swedes in Pomerania in 1807, his chivalrous treatment of prisoners had won him admiration.

Bernadotte managed to persuade Napoleon that it would be in the interests of France to accept the Swedish offer. But he refused to give an undertaking never to go to war with France, telling the Emperor that as Swedish Crown Prince he could not be "the vassal of any foreign country". And he had not been in Sweden for more than a few months when he began to move towards an alliance with Russia, as well as with Britain. His objective was to achieve a United Scandinavia by taking Norway from Denmark, and with the collapse of Napoleon, he was able to devote himself to the conclusion of his aims. Norway had fallen to him after a brief campaign in 1814, and in consultation with the Norwegians he worked out a formula for Scandinavian unity which endured until 1905: Norway was allowed to be independent of Sweden in everything except foreign policy.

King Carl Gustaf's eldest sister, Princess Margaretha, with her English husband John Ambler at the christening of their first child in 1965. They have two further children, both boys, and live in a manor house near Oxford. Princess Margaretha is often present at royal occasions in Scandinavia.

Stockholm's Royal Palace is excellently designed: built essentially in the form of a hollow square, its state rooms face outwards while the private rooms face inwards on to the courtyard. The monumental staircases are probably unique: they wind up to the floor above and the direction of the curve is reversed as they rise to the next floor. The decor, in the French style, is generally successful, and the Chapel is as gorgeous as Swedish Baroque can be. The Throne Room is suitably austere and the ballroom has pilasters wonderfully embellished with lapis lazuli.

The constitution he gave Norway survives, to all intents and purposes, as the Norwegian constitution of today.

Charles XIII died in 1818 and Bernadotte, who had been King in fact ever since he arrived in Sweden, now also became King in name, as Charles XIV John. He reigned for twenty-six years, during which he continued to be popular with the army, the middle classes and the peasants; though

however dedicated he might have been to his adopted country, he always remained very much a Frenchman, being hardly able to speak a word of Swedish.

Having been a great soldier, he now showed himself to be a very able economist. He took an interest in every aspect of Swedish life, and set to work to bring the country up to date. While he found it easy to assume a

Drottningholm is prettily situated on a lake about half an hour from Stockholm. It is invariably referred to as "the Versailles of the North" when, actually, it is dissimilar—not even as large as the central block of Versailles and in style like a thousand other Swedish country houses: stucco with white trim, a copper hip-roof and squat turrets here and there. It is, however, unusually attractive. The library is stunning and one state bedroom is like an opera setting. The ballroom has a festive air about it, but the floor is dangerously creaky. There is a well-tailored study with very dark blue walls relieved with thin strips of gold moulding and wall sconces made of bugles. But the masterpiece of Drottningholm is its theatre, which lay shrouded in cobwebs and dust after the death of Gustaf III in 1792 until a student in this century received permission to look into the boarded-up structure for documents. This "lost" theatre, complete with its original scenery, is now in use again, the most perfect example of its kind in the world.

regal dignity, he never tried to forget his humble origins; in fact he was fond of reminding his subjects that he was once a sergeant.

Bernadotte's most remarkable achievement was that in the extremely legitimist post-war Europe, where he was despised as a *parvenu* by fellow monarchs, he should have secured the Swedish throne not just for himself but also for his descendants. Unlike Beauharnais, Jerôme Bonaparte or indeed Napoleon, he did not give his children legitimate royal blood by marrying a king's daughter. His Queen was Napoleon's first love, Desirée, sister of Joseph Bonaparte's wife, Julie, and daughter of a Marseilles silk merchant with Irish connections—Clery's, the Dublin department store founded by the family, flourishes to this day.

Solliden, on the Island of Oland off the east coast of Sweden, is the private summer retreat of the King of Sweden, built by his mother, Princess Sibylla, from whom he inherited it. Completely unencumbered by style, it is a thick-walled, tile-roofed, stucco house with concrete balustrades. Designed to trap the sun, it is set on the side of a hill facing south-east with terraces, ornamental steps and gardens spilling down to the sea.

The chief talent of Bernadotte's son, Oscar I, lay in diplomacy: throughout his reign, he acted as his own foreign minister. His aim was to make Scandinavia a great power by tying Sweden and Norway closely to Denmark, and by moving out of the Russian orbit. About five years before his death, he was threatened with blindness. An eminent Irish eye doctor cured him, but would accept no fee for his services. When the King asked if he could reward him in any other way, the doctor said that he had just heard that his wife, whom he had left behind in Dublin, had given birth to a son and that he would be much honoured if the King would be the child's godfather. Oscar willingly consented, and the child was duly given his name. The godson was destined to be more famous than the godfather, for the doctor was Sir William Wilde, father of the playwright and poet.

Oscar I's son, Charles XV, was genial and artistic, but he lacked his father's political sense. As a result, the monarchy declined in power during his reign, much of the royal prerogative being taken over by the council. He died in 1872 and was succeeded by his brother, Oscar II, who was superior to him in ability and character.

Oscar II

Anxious to restore the monarchy to something of its former influence, he established himself as a mediator in political conflicts, a role which he performed with great success. He had talents in other directions, too, being a writer of both poetry and prose. He also wrote the libretto for at least one opera, which was performed in Stockholm.

In his old age, two years before his death in 1907, Oscar II was faced with the greatest crisis of his reign, the secession of Norway from Sweden, which almost led to war between the two countries. His son, Crown Prince Gustaf, who succeeded as Gustaf V, inherited his grandfather's gift for diplomacy. During the First World War he initiated talks between himself and the two other Scandinavian monarchs, as well as their respective governments, in order to formulate a joint policy of neutrality. In the Second World War, as an octogenarian, King Gustaf was naturally somewhat removed from international politics, and particularly so in view of Sweden's neutrality, which, with Norway and Denmark both under Nazi occupation, made her isolated. A more active part in events was played by the King's nephew, Count Folke Bernadotte, who negotiated for the release of prisoners in the German concentration camps, and then became famous as a peace maker, a role which cost him his life, for he was murdered by Zionist terrorists in 1948 while acting as a mediator in Palestine.

Gustav V

The reign of Gustaf V lasted until 1950, for the old King lived to be ninety-two. His lithe, spare figure was seen on the tennis court well after his eightieth birthday, and even in extreme old age he was a keen swimmer. When he died, his son Gustaf VI Adolf was approaching the age of seventy. But having his father's longevity and splendid constitution, he lived to the age of ninety and enjoyed a highly successful reign. He also found time for scholarly pursuits: he was an archaeologist of world standing. As King in a country where republicanism was strong, he won astonishingly widespread love and respect: whatever their view of the monarchy, Swedes revered King Gustaf as a highly distinguished fellow countryman in his own right.

He had close ties with the British royal family, his second wife, Queen Louise, being a sister of Earl Mountbatten of Burma and an aunt of Prince Philip. His first wife, who died in 1920, was also British: Princess Margaret of Connaught. She was the mother of his children, of whom the eldest was killed in an air crash in 1947, and whose son succeeded as the present King.

Non-Reigning Families

ALBANIA	**Zogu**
AUSTRIA	**Habsburg-Lorraine**
BULGARIA	**Wettin**
FRANCE	**Capet, called Bourbon; Bonaparte**
PRUSSIA	**Hohenzollern**
BAVARIA	**Wittelsbach**
HANOVER	**Guelf**
SAXONY	**Wettin**
WÜRTTEMBERG	**Württemberg**
GREECE	**Oldenburg**
ITALY	**Savoy**
MONTENEGRO	**Petrović-Njegoš**
PORTUGAL	**Braganza**
ROUMANIA	**Hohenzollern**
RUSSIA	**Romanov**
TWO SICILIES	**Bourbon**
YUGOSLAVIA	**Karadjordjević**

ALBANIA

Zog, and his Son

Leka I, King of the Albanians, is in many senses larger than life. Besides being extraordinarily tall, he is rarely seen out of uniform, and habitually goes about armed, usually with two Colt 45s. For a man who spent less than three days of his life in the country of which he was to be sovereign, he knows as much about Albania as his compatriots who have never lived anywhere else. Albania is his obsession: his dreams for it are a lifetime's occupation.

Life for exiled royalty tends to be a compromise with loneliness, but Leka's case is unusual in that more of his fellow countrymen are in exile than *in situ*. While 2.4 million live in Albania, there are three million misplaced Albanians scattered across the globe. Of these the majority recognize and respect King Leka as their sovereign, and his time is spent in their causes. When on the death of his father in 1961 Leka was proclaimed King at the unlikely rendezvous of the Hotel Bristol in Paris, it was in the presence of a hastily convened temporary National Assembly consisting of delegates and exiled court dignitaries from all over the world.

Leka is a well—almost encyclopaedically—informed man from whom the simplest question provokes the most detailed reply: he seems incapable of making an ill-considered statement. In a world of diffident leaders, he is a reflection of the fighting spirit of the Albanians, without question his father's son.

Descended from the earliest recorded Aryan immigrants to the area, the Albanians are the most ancient race in south-eastern Europe. The Albanian name of the country is *Shqipni*. It has long been the home of ancient Mediterranean people who, early on, divided themselves into two groups: Ghegs, in the north, and Tosks in the south, magnificent people often, described as fierce and lawless.

More accurately, they were fearless and obstinately independent: for life in Albania, although the country is rich in deposits of iron, coal, silver, lead and copper, with fruit and olive trees, grain and cattle, has always been hard. For more than two thousand years the country has been repeatedly overrun, which doubtless helped create the national qualities of toughness, resilience, silence and defensiveness. This, and the country's mountainous inaccessibility (Albania is within sight of Italy but the least known area of Europe) are the secrets of its traditional independence, a fact which most of the country's rulers have appreciated.

Christianity made an impact on the Albanians but although the religion is still practised, the majority of the people converted to Islam—this being probably the only lasting influence of all the invasions, occupations, and

*ZOG I, King of the Albanians (1928–39(61)) **b** 1895 **d** 1961 **m** 1938 Countess Geraldine Apponyi de Nagy-Appony, **b** 1915*

*LEKA I, King of the Albanians (1961–   , in exile) **b** 1939 **m** 1975, Susan Cullen-Ward, **b** 1941*

Leka, King of the Albanians, and his wife, who is known as Queen Susan. This is a rare photograph of Leka, who is rarely seen out of uniform. In March 1979, Leka and his entourage left Spain, where he had lived since 1962, at the request of the Spanish authorities: there were reservations about the presence of his heavily guarded, neo-military establishment at Pozuelo on the outskirts of Madrid. His temporary residence is in the Rhodesian capital of Salisbury. To match his height—approaching seven feet—Leka has a towering conviction that he is destined to reign again in Albania. Very wealthy (his father preserved much of the family fortune despite his summary departure from Albania in 1939), Leka can afford to employ a staff of military and other advisers who ensure that he is furnished with first-class information on what happens inside Albania under General Hoxha's regime. If the dictator's grip weakens, Leka seriously intends to step in. His wife, the first Australian Queen of anywhere, was raised in the higher echelons of Australia's landed gentry. Very assured, she is the perfect foil for Leka, who insists that everything is done immediately, if not sooner.

dominating rules. The Albanians were little affected by Greek, Roman or Slavonic penetration. In the fourth and fifth centuries the Goths controlled the country, and in the sixth the Eastern Roman Empire. The Serbs were in and out from the seventh to the fourteenth centuries without much effect. After the fall of the Roman Empire, the Turks began to take an interest in the country and met their match in the glorious Albanian national hero, Skanderbeg, who first defeated them in 1449. Almost every year for a quarter of a century Turkish troops appeared at the border and were regularly annihilated. There were two extended sieges of the country

King Leka's mother, Geraldine, is styled Queen Mother of the Albanians. The daughter of an Hungarian count and an American mother, she married King Zog in 1938, the year before his and her flight from Albania. She lives in Salisbury, Rhodesia when she is not travelling about the world. There is no discernible difference between Geraldine and any other attractive, middle-aged widow of means, except that few actually are as rich as she. She dresses immaculately, in perfect taste, and sometimes has a wistful look.

which the Albanians resisted and survived with accustomed obstinancy. But when Skanderbeg died of a fever in 1468, there was no one to replace him, and Albania became more and more vulnerable to the Turks, eventually falling to them in 1478. They devastated the country and there followed a period of cultural and economic disintegration. For more than four centuries, Albania remained under nominal Turkish rule.

In 1878 a nationalist independence movement began and gained momentum until, in spite of the bitter resentment of other Balkan states, Albania proclaimed its independence on 28th November, 1912. Its autonomy was established in that same year by a European conference which created Albania a new principality, with the German Prince William of Wied as its ruler. The idea of putting him on the throne originated in the romantic but not very practical mind of his aunt, Queen Elisabeth of Roumania, better known as Carmen Sylva. She was ambitious for her favourite nephew, who was married to her protegée Princess Sophie of Schönburg-Waldenburg. The European powers responded favourably: few other candidates put themselves forward for the throne of the most primitive and poverty-stricken country in Europe, renowned for its blood-feuds, absence of railways, few roads and where the largest town was no more than a straggling village.

Prince William arrived in Albania in 1914 to find himself immediately in a maze of trouble and intrigue. Unable to control the situation, he left within six months, Albania remaining a titular principality with the government as a regency for the absent ruler.

It was now that King Leka's father, Ahmed Bey Zogu, appeared. His forebears, the Zogolli, were hereditary governors of Mati in central Albania. At the age of eighteen, in the second year of the principality, he had already attracted notice as a soldier. He was proud of being a warrior, especially of being a warrior with a difference, for he was an intellectual, a keen student of political science, but self-educated, taking his books on campaign. He was active in the movement which proclaimed independence for the country a second time in 1917, and was instrumental in securing the admission of the country to membership of the League of Nations in 1920. That same year, he was briefly minister of the interior. In 1921, at the age of twenty-six, he was appointed commander in chief of the Albanian armed forces. Following this, he was made interior minister again, and in 1922, became prime minister. In 1925, the charade of the principality and its absent ruler having played itself out, Zogu proclaimed the country a republic and himself as its president. In 1928, the National Assembly declared the country a kingdom and Zogu became King Zog I of the Albanians.

The flamboyant Zog was strong, efficient and, when necessary, ruthless. He ruled absolutely, and the ten years, ten months, and ten days of his monarchy formed the only period in modern times when Albania enjoyed political stability under a national government. He created the administration and machinery of a modern state. He organised a police force, trained by British officers, which became a model of its kind. With inspired foresight, he placed the brightest of hundreds of young Albanians in foreign universities and when they had taken degrees and returned to Albania, he found administrative posts for them. He resisted all efforts by Italy, to whom the country was financially beholden, to impose facism in the country. He fostered public education and sponsored native arts and literature; built roads to link the main towns and modernised the harbour

Prince William and Princess Sophie

King Zog

When Zog was President of Albania, he lived in the finest of the several rich merchants' houses in Tirana, the capital. It was not until he became King and contemplated marriage that he decided to build a palace. The family, however, never moved in: they fled into exile just as the building was finished. The new Palace was ransacked, but later restored and it is now the residence of the country's dictator. The merchant house, left, in which King Zog, his sisters, Queen Geraldine and, for a few days, the infant Prince Leka lived, was set on a crowded hillside in the town.

at Durazzo. He even made an attempt to establish a viable railway system. Had not outside events intervened, his reign might have been long and prosperous.

Italy had long considered herself to have a claim on Albania: in return for loans and subsidies, Zog had signed a defensive alliance with Italy and gave her wide business concessions. Now, outraged at Zog's refusal to embrace fascism, Mussolini suddenly presented an ultimatum to the King demanding a monetary and customs union with Italy and the installation of an Italian garrison on Albanian territory, all of which Zog rejected out of hand. So, on Good Friday 1939, Mussolini, backed by his navy and air force and drunk with the success of his Ethiopian campaign, invaded Albania with 100,000 troops. It was the end for Zog: he fled the country with his young Hungarian Queen (they had married a year previously, he at forty-two, she twenty-two) and their son, Leka, less than three days old.

After Zog's departure the National Assembly declared that the crown had passed to the House of Savoy and King Victor Emmanuel III assumed the title of King of Italy and Albania. Albania remained part of the Italian Empire until 1943. During World War II, Greece occupied a part of the country but was forced out by the Nazis who occupied it until 1944. Since that time, the communists have been in control.

Zog was a restless exile, living for a while in Greece before moving on to England, where he lived in a country house in Buckinghamshire. To one observer, it seemed at this time that Zog did nothing but nurse his majesty and take short walks. He also expressed a desire to buy *The Times* newspaper, saying he would give not a penny more than ten million for it. He moved on to the United States before settling and dying in France in 1961.

Princess Ruhijé, fifth of King Zog's six beautiful sisters

AUSTRIA
Europe's Emperors

His Imperial and Royal Highness the Archduke Otto of Austria, who prefers being addressed simply as Dr. Habsburg, without even the *von*, is the eldest son of Charles I, Emperor of Austria and the Empress Zita. Two years after Charles I's coronation as King of Hungary in 1916, for which the Archduke Otto was dressed in ermine and velvet, the Emperor lost his throne, without, however, renouncing his claims. In 1919, the family was sent into exile. First they went to Switzerland, and after the Emperor had twice unsuccessfully attempted to regain his Hungarian kingdom, they were banished to Madeira where the Emperor died in 1922.

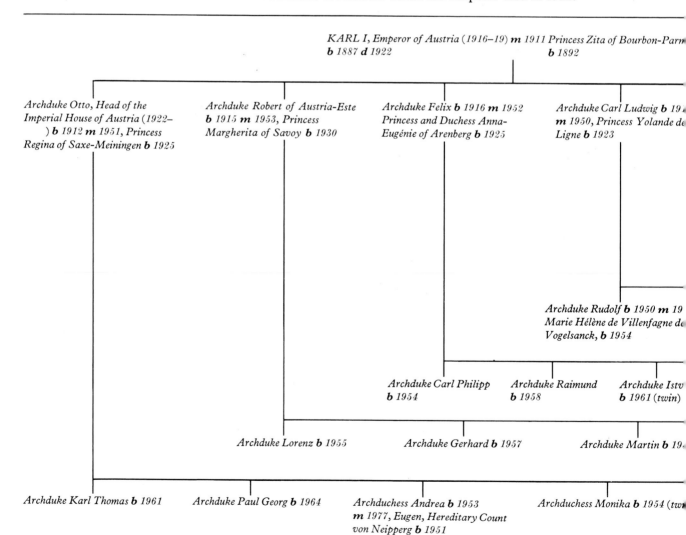

KARL I, Emperor of Austria (1916–19) **m** *1911 Princess Zita of Bourbon-Parm* **b** *1887* **d** *1922*   **b** *1892*

Archduke Otto, Head of the Imperial House of Austria (1922–) b 1912 m 1951, Princess Regina of Saxe-Meiningen b 1925

Archduke Robert of Austria-Este b 1915 m 1953, Princess Margherita of Savoy b 1930

Archduke Felix b 1916 m 1952 Princess and Duchess Anna-Eugénie of Arenberg b 1925

Archduke Carl Ludwig b 19 m 1950, Princess Yolande de Ligne b 1923

Archduke Rudolf b 1950 m 19 Marie Hélène de Villenfagne de Vogelsanck, b 1954

Archduke Carl Philipp b 1954

Archduke Raimund b 1958

Archduke Istv b 1961 (twin)

Archduke Lorenz b 1955

Archduke Gerhard b 1957

Archduke Martin b 19

Archduke Karl Thomas b 1961

Archduke Paul Georg b 1964

Archduchess Andrea b 1953 m 1977, Eugen, Hereditary Count von Neipperg b 1951

Archduchess Monika b 1954 (tw

Since then, Otto von Habsburg, who was educated in Spain, Switzerland, and Belgium, and who gained a PhD. in political and social sciences, has been the head of the House of Habsburg. In 1966, by a decision of the Supreme Court, Otto von Habsburg was allowed to return to Austria, whose cause he had furthered during the Second World War by close cooperation with President Roosevelt and with Washington.

The legitimists, of course, think of him as Emperor Otto I, and King Otto II of Hungary, but he has formally renounced these titles, and with them such panoply as still adheres to many of the out-of-office royal families of Europe. Instead, he is directly engaged in politics.

Thus the descendant of the sixteenth-century Habsburg Emperor Charles V, whose dream had been of one world—or at least of *orbis Europae Christinae*—is an active Pan-European and the Vice-President of the Pan European movement.

Charles V, whose biography took up ten years of Otto von Habsburg's life, was born in 1500. His empire was so immense that the sun literally did not set upon it: at the age of sixteen he had inherited the crown of Spain and the Spanish possessions in the New World from his maternal grandmother, Isabella of Castile, whose marriage to his grandfather, Ferdinand of Aragon, had led to the merging of the two Iberian kingdoms. At the age of nineteen, Charles had inherited his grandfather Maximilian I's possessions

Otto, Archduke of Austria, eldest son of Charles I, last of the Austrian Emperors, prefers to be called Dr. Habsburg. He is internationally known as a frequently published political theoretician, particularly interested in European affairs—some call him Mr. Europe—and is admired for the way he combines brilliance of intellect with a practical approach to life. He lives at Pöcking, West Germany, but is free to reside in Austria if he chooses, and indeed, often makes visits there. In times when the experience of lost sovereignty is an illness from which few families recover, Dr. Habsburg lives a life of enviable contentment. His wife Regina is the daughter of the late Duke of Saxe-Meiningen, whose house gave to Britain William IV's Queen Adelaide. The family are deeply religious and Regina's surviving brother is a Carthusian monk. Regina works in tandem with her husband on his writing, making suggestions, researching and editing.

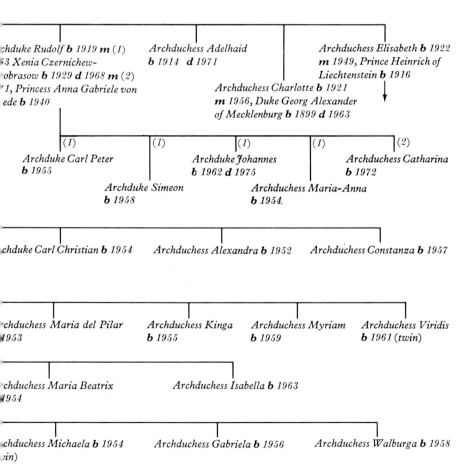

Archduke Rudolf *b 1919 m* (1) 1953 Xenia Czernichew-Obrasow *b 1929 d 1968 m* (2) 1971, Princess Anna Gabriele von *ede b 1940*

Archduchess Adelhaid *b 1914 d 1971*

Archduchess Elisabeth *b 1922 m 1949, Prince Heinrich of Liechtenstein b 1916*

Archduchess Charlotte *b 1921 m 1956, Duke Georg Alexander of Mecklenburg b 1899 d 1963*

(1) Archduke Carl Peter *b 1955*

(1) Archduke Simeon *b 1958*

(1) Archduke Johannes *b 1962 d 1975*

(1) Archduchess Maria-Anna *b 1954*

(2) Archduchess Catharina *b 1972*

Archduke Carl Christian *b 1954*   Archduchess Alexandra *b 1952*   Archduchess Constanza *b 1957*

Archduchess Maria del Pilar *b 1953*   Archduchess Kinga *b 1955*   Archduchess Myriam *b 1959*   Archduchess Viridis *b 1961 (twin)*

Archduchess Maria Beatrix *b 1954*   Archduchess Isabella *b 1963*

Archduchess Michaela *b 1954 (twin)*   Archduchess Gabriela *b 1956*   Archduchess Walburga *b 1958*

Seated: Zita, Empress of Austria, widow of Emperor Charles I, now approaching her nineties. Now based in Switzerland so as to be relatively near her eldest son, Otto, she has been well known as an intrepid traveller—something of a colourful imperial gypsy—spending months on end in hotels and palaces in far-flung parts of the world. She is the tenth daughter and fourteenth child of Roberto I of Bourbon-Parma. After her came ten more brothers and sisters and about half a dozen of the twenty-four are still alive. Zita is herself the mother of eight, with about two dozen grandchildren.

Karl Thomas (aiming rifle), eldest son of Dr. Habsburg, with his father. Karl Thomas, born in 1961 within sight of the lake in which his distant cousin Ludwig II of Bavaria was drowned, is the opposite of his kinsman: proud of his father, and respectful of his views. He, his brother and five sisters (one married) are delightfully resourceful, with interests from riding and shooting to chess, collecting unusual objects and inventing intellectual games.

which stretched from the Netherlands to Austria and in 1520, he became Holy Roman Emperor.

The Habsburg family, which traces its decent back to an eleventh-century knight called Guntram the Rich, and which adopted the name of the Habichtsburg-falcon's castle (situated in present-day Switzerland) was now at the zenith of its power. It had been a mere two hundred years since Rudolph I, the dynasty's founder, had acquired an obscure mountainous region called *Oesterreich* because it was the eastern outpost of the Holy Roman Empire. Having driven out the Bohemian King Ottokar from this region and from Styria, Rudolph I gave these territories to his sons. He married one of them to Ottokar's daughter and his own daughter to Ottokar's son, thus ensuring a Habsburg claim to Bohemia and laying the foundations for the Austrian Empire.

Bellum gerant alii, tu, felix Austria nube ("let others fight wars, you, happy Austria, marry") runs the tag—and that was never so true as in the case of Rudolph's descendant, Frederick, Duke of Styria.

This Duke became the first of a long line of Habsburg Emperors. He was elected to the Imperial throne in 1472 as Frederick III, whose long reign was a disaster, during which parts of the Holy Roman Empire and parts of the Habsburg possessions crumbled away. Weak though he was, he contrived the most splendid match for his son and successor, Maximilian I—marrying him to Mary of Burgundy. It was this Burgundian marriage that brought the Habsburgs the prosperous provinces of Flanders, Franche Comté and the Netherlands.

Maximilian I made Innsbruck his capital, and consolidated the family's Austrian holdings. Besides, he was an energetic Emperor, and responsible for many reforms. He was the first incumbent of the Imperial throne to dispense with the coronation at the hands of the Pope, thus secularizing the hitherto Holy Imperial Office.

Maximilian, married more than once, left two legitimate children: Philip the Fair, whose profile shows hardly a sign of the jutting jaw and pendulous lower lip which characterized his father, and which came to be known as the Habsburg chin, and Margaret, who looked like a true Burgundian. He married both of them into Spain, Philip to Isabella's

Carl Ludwig, Archduke of Austria, a younger brother of Dr. Habsburg, lives in Brussels and is a banker and director of several companies. Like his brother, Otto, he is the author of several politically inspired tracts, one of the most noted being *Social Monarchy*. His wife, Yolande, is a daughter of the Prince of Ligne, and they have two sons and two daughters, all in their twenties.

Geza, Archduke of Austria, usually known as Geza von Habsburg, is a cousin of Dr. Habsburg and descends from the Emperor Leopold II. He is well known in the art world as the head of Christie's, Geneva, and with his wife, Monika, and three children lives at Thonex. Geza's mother, who also had Monika as one of her names, was the youngest daughter of Friedrich August III, the last reigning King of Saxony.

daughter Juana the Mad, and Margaret, whom he had first betrothed to the King of France, to Isabella's son John.

Philip the Fair's marriage turned out to be politically more useful than Maximilian could have dreamt: his daughter-in-law, against all expectation, became the sole heiress to her parents' kingdom, which, with the opening up of the New World, was on the threshold of its Golden Age. It was, of course, unfortunate that she became very strange—apathetic and violent, in turn. After her husband's death in 1506 she became completely deranged. Having adored him, been wildly jealous of him, and having made his life a misery, she granted him no peace even in death. For ever-increasing periods she ordered his coffin to be opened, and then kept vigil over his embalmed corpse (from which the heart had been taken to be buried in Flanders) in case, as in a fairy story that had impressed her, he should return to life. She continued this practise until she died in 1555.

Her son the Duke of Flanders—the future Charles V—was fortunate in not inheriting more than a trace of his mother's unfortunate temperament, but he was burdened with the Habsburg jaw. This, coupled with a stutter, made it difficult for him to make himself understood in any of the many languages he could speak: Latin to the clergy; Spanish to ministers; French to the ladies and German to his horses. Moreover, this malformation made it difficult for him to chew the food that he so inordinately enjoyed, so he suffered agonies of indigestion.

Charles' future wife was discussed from the time that he was six. The roll-call of possible brides included Mary, the daughter of Henry VII of England, Louise, the daughter of François I of France, but in the end he married an Infanta of Portugal. She was not only his first cousin but the result of a long line of previous intermarriages traditional in the houses of Portugal and Spain. All his brothers and sisters married to the glory of the house, especially his brother Ferdinand, who married the daughter of the King of Hungary, so laying the foundation for the future dual monarchy.

With Habsburgs strategically placed all over Europe, it looked indeed as though Charles V was destined to rule over a Christian empire rather larger than that of Charlemagne, especially since he had regained Navarre, France's gateway to Spain. In reality, he left it deeply divided, owing to the growing

Vienna's Schönbrunn is a Rococo
country house in town, so spacious that
it easily contained even the sixteen
children of Empress Maria Theresa. On
a hill nearby, where it was originally
suggested that the Palace should be
built, stands the Gloriette, a monument
to the joys of military victory. From the
house it is an impressive sight, but close
to, it is revealed as a carelessly
constructed pastiche.

rift in the church. Although Charles V thought Luther wrong-headed—"a
single monk going against all Christianity for a thousand years" could
hardly be right—he had quite realized that the malpractices within the
Catholic Church must cease. Sadly, after the sack of Rome, when Imperial
forces held the Pope prisoner, and when Charles could have urged reforms
from within, he failed to act, thus losing an opportunity of uniting the
Christian world.

Charles V left Austria and the eastern lands in the hands of his brother
Ferdinand, while Spain and the Burgundian possessions went to his eldest
son, the tormented, neurotic Philip II.

While the eyes of the world had been on Spain, consecutive Austrian
Habsburgs had improved their holdings and consolidated their position
against the Turks. Ferdinand's marriage to the heiress of Hungary and
Bohemia had left him in possession of both these crowns, thus adding a
sizeable number of Magyar and Czech subjects to his successor Maximilian II's possessions.

Maximilian II left two sons, each to be Emperor in turn; Rudolf II, a
throwback to Frederick III in so far as he, too, concentrated his energies not
on statecraft but in dabblings in the occult, as well as astronomy. It was in
his service that Tycho Brahe, John Kepler and the Elizabethan Sage John
Dee came to Prague, which he had made his capital. There the Emperor
amassed wonders of the applied and fine arts. His paintings included works
by Dürer and Correggio and he also collected anything that was curious or
uncommon, such as deformed foetuses and mandrake roots. He too, was
thought to be a little mad. So, in the end, was his brother Matthias—a
new name in the Habsburg family, and chosen in honour of Matthias,

the last non-Habsburg King of Hungary.

It was in Matthias's reign that the Protestants of Bohemia revolted, because in order to facilitate the imperial election of his nephew, the bigoted Ferdinand, the Emperor had placed him on the throne of Bohemia. This position would automatically give him a vote in the Electoral College. However, Ferdinand, now proposed for the throne, had such a record of stamping out Protestantism in his native Styria that he was unacceptable to the Bohemian Protestants, who called on the Calvinist Frederick V, Elector Palatine, to be their King. Ferdinand of Habsburg in turn called for assistance on his cousin Maximilian of Wittlesbach, who was the head of the Catholic League, the army of the Counter Reformation. Frederick and his English wife, Elizabeth, now known as the Queen of Bohemia or the Winter Queen, were forced to flee Bohemia, and the Empire, after The Battle of the White Mountain outside Prague. The fighting continued long after Ferdinand had become King of Bohemia (and in due course Emperor Ferdinand II) and the disastrously destructive Thirty Years' War was under way.

Neither Ferdinand nor Frederick of Bohemia lived to see its end: it was Ferdinand III, soon to be succeeded by his son Leopold I, who was one of the signatories of the peace treaty of Westphalia in 1648, by which time the balance of power in Europe was weighted in the favour of France, and the Emperor of the Holy Roman Empire was more than ever dependant on the princes. Impoverished as they were by the ruinous war, these liked to play him off against Louis XIV, and to ally themselves to the highest bidder.

Louis XIV left nothing undone to keep the Habsburg Emperor occupied while he made inroads on Habsburg territories and Imperial dominions on his eastern border. This led to the formation of the Grand Alliance against France: England, the United Provinces of the Netherlands and the Empire, as well as Spain, a shadow of its former self, were now friends sworn to preserve the balance of power. All these powers marched to war when Louis XIV accepted the Spanish legacy on behalf of his grandson: they preferred the claim of Leopold's younger son Charles, whose mother was descended from the Habsburgs of Spain. Leopold's death shortly afterwards, followed by that of his heir, obliged the Archduke Charles to return from Barcelona where he had held court as rival King of Spain. In 1711, he was in Vienna to rule as Emperor Charles VI, leaving the Spanish throne to the Bourbon Candidate, the new Philip V of Spain.

The Allies, who had objected to the French crown's acquisition of Spain, could, of course, not countenance one man ruling the combined lands of the Empire and of Spain. The Emperor Charles VI, lately King of Spain, thought it the height of treachery when, by the peace treaty of Utrecht in 1711, Louise XIV's grandson was recognized as the rightful King of Spain after all, on condition that Spain and France were separate inperpetuity. He never quite accepted the decision and vainly hoped to return to Spain. It was not surprising that he had felt so much at ease in Barcelona: his father and all his ancestors since Ferdinand II had observed Spanish etiquette, and had worn Spanish court dress long after it had ceased to be the general fashion. Their very gestures had been Spanish—measured and slow. Indeed, Leopold I had been famous for being so still that people had sometimes wondered if he was still alive.

However, Charles VI was to live in Vienna for the rest of his life, which was much taken up by making arrangements for his elder daughter, Maria Theresa, to become his heir, in spite of her being prevented from so doing by the rule that barred the succession of women.

The Emperor died in 1740, happy to know that his child would succeed to the Austrian possessions, and to become co-ruling Empress with her husband, Francis of Lorraine. His optimism turned out to be unjustified at first. While The War of the Austrian Succession was fought between the Austrian army and that of Bavaria (helped chiefly by Prussia), it was the Elector of Bavaria, and not Maria Theresa and Francis of Lorraine, who was elected to the Imperial throne. Bavaria's chief ally, Prussia, had joined the fight out of self-interest: it coveted Silesia, an Austrian possession on its border.

When her father died, Maria Theresa was a charming girl of twenty-three, with no sign of the unfortunate chin or the madness: new blood had been added to the concentrated Habsburg strain by non-cousinly marriages. By the marriage of the Empress herself to Francis of Lorraine, distantly related to her, the Habsburg line changed into that of Habsburg Lorraine in the next generation: things had come full circle, since Lorraine had been part of the old Burgundian realm that had originally made the Habsburgs great.

With the end of the Seven Years' War and the partition of Poland, Lorraine, part of the lands used as small change in the bartering that went on between the parties, became the possession of the King of Poland, Stanislas Leszczynski, whose daughter Maria of Lorraine was given Tuscany.

Maria Theresa and Francis had sixteen children: Marie Antoinette, their youngest daughter, became the child-bride of Louis XVI of France. Joseph, the eldest son, became his mother's co-ruler after she had been widowed. Both mother and son had a reputation for enlightened despotism, but their characters and methods differed and their combined rule was a period of strain for them both. Finally Maria Theresa died, and Joseph II ruled alone. When he was succeeded by his brother Leopold, the Grand Duke of Tuscany, he had nevertheless achieved much of what he set out to do except in Hungary, where the abolition of serfdom was his only triumph. Typically, his last words were "I have been misunderstood".

Leopold, a reformer in his own right, reigned for only two years. During this time he repaired much of the damage to the monarchy that Joseph had done in his over-enthusiastic, ruthless way. Leopold's son, Francis I, harked back to the old dynastic Habsburg ways. He was a thorough reactionary, who achieved a diplomatic coup by having Austria established, yet again, as the foremost power in Germany—a fact which Prussia found hard to accept. So it was fitting that the Congress to rearrange post-Napoleonic Europe should meet in Vienna. Here then, with the help of the ultra-reactionary Metternich, Francis I's chancellor, the map was redrawn, according to the old model. Almost all Napoleonic innovations were swept away and Europe became ripe for the revolutions a few decades hence, when Francis I had been succeeded by his son Ferdinand I, a much loved, good natured, and somewhat feeble-minded monarch, whom Metternich hoped to manipulate entirely.

The Austrian Empire was badly shaken by the rising of 1848. Metternich departed and the Emperor was forced to resign his post. He was succeeded by his nephew, Franz Joseph, who was to rule for nearly sixty-eight years— a reign surpassed in length by that of only a very few monarchs.

He survived several members of the two generations following him— one of his most often quoted expressions is *mir bleibt nichts erspart*—

The Hofburg was the main residence in Vienna of the Emperors of Austria and the Kings of Hungary, powerfully monumental Austrian Baroque at its peak. For all that, it is inconveniently divided by a street: on one side are the Throne Room, the larger ballroom, some kitchens, the grander state dining room, the chapel which is the home of the Vienna Boys' Choir and the place where the Lippizaner horses strut. In order to reach the private apartments and the less formal of the representation rooms, one must cross the street by a covered gallery. On this side are the bedrooms, a smaller but prettier dining room with its own kitchens below, a suite of drawing rooms, a library, an audience chamber and the Empress Elisabeth's gymnasium.

"nothing is spared me." His wife, the beautiful Empress Elisabeth of the tiny waist and the auburn hair, who had her share of the Wittelsbach neurosis, which made private life at the Hofburg less pleasant than he might have wished, was assassinated. His son, the unfortunate, brooding and possibly mad Crown Prince Rudolf became the victim of the tragedy at Mayerling. His younger brother, Maximilian, Emperor of Mexico, died before a firing squad; the widow, Charlotte of Belgium, went mad. The Emperor's nephew and heir, the Archduke Franz Ferdinand, caused much friction in the Imperial family by his marriage to Sophie Chotek, who was of inferior rank. Their assassination at Sarajevo was the incident which sparked off the First World War. At their lying in state, Habsburg family honour was visibly restated: Sophie's coffin stood on a bier slightly lower than that of the Archduke.

Franz Joseph died in 1916, to be succeeded as Emperor by his grand-nephew, Charles I. Two years later Austria became a republic. The Emperor, highly devout, refused to abdicate a title that had come to him from God, but agreed to retire from public affairs, though planning to remain in Austria. However, when a few months later Austria seemed on the verge of becoming a communist state, he was prevailed upon to go into exile in Switzerland to escape the fate of the Tsar and his family. After making two attempts to regain Hungary, Charles and his wife, the Empress Zita, were banished to Madeira, where the Emperor died in 1922, aged only thirty-four.

Shortly before his death, he had offered his life to God in the service of Austria. The Cause of his Canonisation has since been opened, and he may one day be recognised as a saint if a satisfactory miracle can be attributed to him. It has been suggested that his miracle might be the survival after the Second World War of Austria as a state outside the Soviet bloc.

Vienna's Upper Belvedere Palace, which is separated from the Lower Belvedere by a sloping formal garden. Both were built by Prince Eugene of Savoy, who made the Lower Belvedere his Vienna residence. The Upper Belvedere was never meant to be lived in and few have slept there, an exception being Archduke Franz Ferdinand and his morganatic wife, who left the next day for their rendezvous with an assassin at Sarajevo. The place was, in fact, purely for entertaining.

Charles I and Empress Zita

BULGARIA
Balancing in the Balkans

Simeon II became King of the Bulgarians at the age of six in 1943 and three years later left his country after a communist-rigged plebiscite without having abdicated. This early experience of kingship was not lost on him: a precocious child, who learned to read and write almost immediately after learning to walk and talk, he was to a remarkable extent able to digest the state papers submitted to him by the prime minister and the triumvirite who formed the council of regency. Leaving Bulgaria with his mother, aunt and sister, his first place of exile was Egypt, where the family stayed with Simeon's maternal grandfather, King Victor Emmanuel of Italy.

Simeon's mother, the saintly Queen Giovanna, supervised the completion of her son's education in the United States (where he attended Valley Forge Military Academy in Pennsylvania) and in Europe. At first, the family was poor—they had left Bulgaria with $200 each for expenses. But Simeon married well, his wife being the daughter of a well-known Spanish family, and his business career has since flourished, helping him to finance certain activities: helping Bulgarians who ask his advice, publishing a news bulletin and founding a bureau to deal with various problems.

King Simeon is an actively religious man who prays regularly and discharges the responsibilities of being a father with a dedicated seriousness which involves him in the early hours of each morning with his children before they set off for the French School in Madrid. He gives them a little sermon—a practical exercise designed to encourage them to study, to

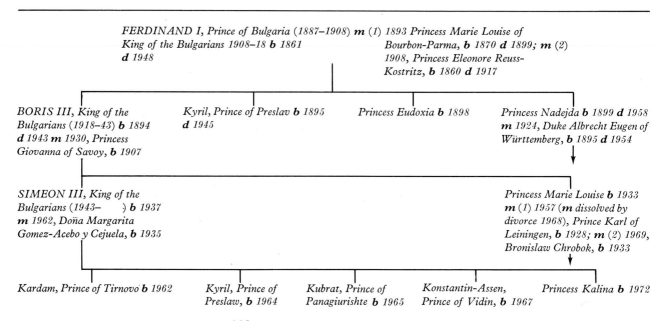

FERDINAND I, Prince of Bulgaria (1887–1908) **m** (1) 1893 Princess Marie Louise of King of the Bulgarians 1908–18 **b** 1861 **d** 1948 — Bourbon-Parma, **b** 1870 **d** 1899; **m** (2) 1908, Princess Eleonore Reuss-Kostritz, **b** 1860 **d** 1917

BORIS III, King of the Bulgarians (1918–43) **b** 1894 **d** 1943 **m** 1930, Princess Giovanna of Savoy, **b** 1907

Kyril, Prince of Preslav **b** 1895 **d** 1945

Princess Eudoxia **b** 1898

Princess Nadejda **b** 1899 **d** 1958 **m** 1924, Duke Albrecht Eugen of Württemberg, **b** 1895 **d** 1954

SIMEON III, King of the Bulgarians (1943–) **b** 1937 **m** 1962, Doña Margarita Gomez-Acebo y Cejuela, **b** 1935

Princess Marie Louise **b** 1933 **m** (1) 1957 (**m** dissolved by divorce 1968), Prince Karl of Leiningen, **b** 1928; **m** (2) 1969, Bronislaw Chrobok, **b** 1933

Kardam, Prince of Tirnovo **b** 1962

Kyril, Prince of Preslaw, **b** 1964

Kubrat, Prince of Panagiurishte **b** 1965

Konstantin-Assen, Prince of Vidin, **b** 1967

Princess Kalina **b** 1972

Simeon, King of the Bulgarians, lives in Madrid with his family. So fully does he recognize his responsibilities as a man, a husband, a father, and a king, that he is plagued with worry about many things which probably will never happen. One matter he does not occupy himself with, however, is the restoration of the monarchy in Bulgaria: he treats it as a *fait accompli*, God and the people willing. Handsome, urbane, witty, and meltingly charming, no one seems to know anyone who does not automatically like him.

King Simeon's wife is Spanish, and this is one reason why the Bulgarian royal family live in Madrid. She is so serenly regal that it is difficult to remember that she is the survivor of an insupportable tragedy: when she was still a child her parents were peremptorily and senselessly "executed" without trial at the beginning of the Spanish Civil War.

Kardam, Crown Prince of Bulgaria is the namesake of an eighth-century Khan (King) of the original Bulgarian State whose prowess on the battlefield secured him a place among the country's heroes. Kardam has the look and manner of a young sultan, not inappropriate for the heir to a throne which was once a vilayet of Turkey. Unusually wise and inscrutable for one so young, he is being thoroughly trained by his father in the profession of kingship and knows as much Bulgarian history as some university experts on the subject.

Kyril, Kubrat, Konstantin-Assen and Kalina are the younger children of King Simeon and Queen Margarita. They all speak at least two languages well and are as well-behaved as people like to believe that all royal children are. They are among the four thousand pupils at the French School in Madrid. Kyril is the namesake of his great uncle, Prince Kyril; Kubrat is named after an eighth-century Khan who ruled an early tribal confederation in Bulgaria and Konstantin-Assen continues a name

which has often appeared in Bulgarian history, there having been an Assen dynasty of which one of the rulers was Konstantin-Assen. Kalina carries on the family practice of names beginning with the letter K. (Her mother refused to allow her to be called Klementina for fear that no one would want to marry her). Her musically pleasing name is the Bulgarian for lady-bird and there is also a pretty, white-flowered bramble of the same name. More fortuitous still, Kalina means victorious.

Giovanna, Queen Mother of the Bulgarians, is the sister of King Umberto of Italy. She lives in Estoril, Portugal, where she is the adored doyenne of its colony of royal exiles. There is a saintliness about her, and she has known great sorrow: Princess Mafalda, her sister, died in Buchenwald. But she is as gracious as a papal blessing, has a complexion perfectly complemented by the superb pearls she frequently wears—and knits without ceasing.

The Royal Palace at Sofia, just off the main square, resembles the casino at some fashionable Bavarian spa. It is a relatively large, chunky block with an entrance spilling on to the pavement. Most of the rooms, some of which are genereously proportioned, are oppressively dark. The exception is the monumental Throne Room on the first floor, which has an excessive window complex in the Palladian style at one end.

behave at school, and to make certain they have done their homework and that they have everything they need for the day.

The region now known as Bulgaria was invaded in the sixth century by the Bulgars, a tribe of wild horsemen who lived between the Don and the Caucasus. They mingled with the native Slav people, gradually adopting their dialect and customs and eventually founding the first organised Slavonic power in the Balkans. Most notable of the early rulers was Boris I, who ended his days in a monastery, having been baptised a Christian in 865, an example then followed by the majority of the people. Boris's son, Simeon I, became the most powerful monarch in eastern Europe and assumed the title of Tsar and Autocrat of all the Bulgars, a style which was recognized by Pope John X. This great emperor was responsible for the introduction of Byzantine culture into the country, an influence which has not greatly dissipated in the past thousand years.

In the late tenth century, Bulgaria was invaded by Byzantine forces and allied tribes. Tsar Boris II was dethroned and the eastern part of the country was lost to Byzantium. In the early eleventh century, Tsar Samuel welded the remaining western part into a new state and even managed to recover some lost territory, but in 1014 was tragically defeated by the vindictive Byzantine Emperor Basil II, who ordered the blinding of 15,000 Bulgarian soldiers. Bulgaria then remained part of the Byzantine Empire for the next 175 years until the brilliant Assen family, who were descended from ancient Bulgarian rulers, took advantage of a general insurrection to establish the so-called Second Bulgarian Empire. This survived for almost two hundred years during which the Assen kings were extolled by the Popes above all other Christian monarchs, and Bulgaria attained a hitherto unknown prosperity. Then, in the last quarter of the fourteenth century, Bulgaria was re-conquered by the Turks and until the nineteenth century was part of the Ottoman Empire.

Presiding over the break-up of the Turkish Empire at the Congress of Berlin in 1876, the European Powers made Bulgaria a state once more, with Prince Alexander of Battenberg, nephew of the Tsar Alexander II of Russia, as its sovereign. The Powers had expected Bulgaria to be no more than a Russian puppet, and indeed Russian officers and officials soon flooded the principality. Alexander was expected to be a faithful servant of St. Petersburg, but having fallen in love with his adopted country and its hardworking, taciturn, orderly people, he began to take a more independent line. This eventually disturbed Russia so much that her agents organised a conspiracy against Alexander among discontented

114

army officers. One night in August 1886, they burst in on the Prince, forced him to abdicate on pain of death, and removed him to Russia.

There followed a short-lived counter-coup during which the Prince made the fatal mistake of trying to compromise with the Tsar. This lost him the support of the Bulgarian leaders, who made no attempt to stop him from abdicating soon after.

A new ruler now had to be found who would be agreeable to Russia, to the Bulgarian national leaders and to the rest of Europe—not an easy task: among Europe's royal families, few of the suitable candidates wanted the job: no one had envied Alexander's position, caught between Bulgarian nationalists and Russia. At last, Prince Ferdinand of Saxe-Coburg-Gotha accepted the offer and was duly elected by the Bulgarian National Assembly, the Grand Sobranie, on the 7th July 1887.

Tsar Ferdinand I

Prince Ferdinand was the most capable of the capable Coburgs, and one of the richest. He looked like a fox and was a brilliant, amusing talker with a passion for precious stones, which he would fondle as if their very touch gave him extreme pleasure. When he arrived in Bulgaria, Russia denounced him as a usurper and tried to bring pressure on the Powers to declare his presence in Bulgaria illegal. Ferdinand knew that his success depended on Russian good will, but that the Bulgarian nationalists, headed by Stambouloff, would reject him if he cultivated it. So for seven years he played a waiting game. In the end, it worked. Stamblouloff went out of popularity, Ferdinand dismissed him and then appointed a prime minister acceptable to the Russians.

So successful was Ferdinand that in 1908 he was able to proclaim Bulgaria an independent kingdom with himself as Tsar Ferdinand I. His achievements had been considerable: reorganisation of the army, the building of railways and great improvements to the capital, Sofia. Ferdinand over-estimated his strength, however, in the second Balkan war of 1913, out of which Bulgaria came disastrously. And when he sided with Germany in the First World War, he lost even more territory. By mid-1918, the army in the field was on the brink of mutiny and, having proclaimed a republic, was marching on Sofia. Loyal troops restored internal order but Ferdinand was blamed for allying Bulgaria with the losing side. On the 3rd October 1918, he abdicated in favour of his son Boris.

Boris III faced a critical situation: the provisional government which took over at the time of the abdication was not favourably inclined towards the continuance of the Coburg monarchy. The new king had to stage a military coup to place himself firmly on the throne. There followed a successful and popular reign of twenty-five years, but at the end of it Boris was unwillingly drawn into the Second World War on the side of Hitler, a marriage fated not to succeed. He died only two days after having paid a visit to Hitler in August 1943, a sudden death which has never been satisfactorily explained. It is known that over a period there had been several stormy sessions between himself and Hitler and during the last visit there had been another strong disagreement, but whether Hitler had him poisoned because he refused to declare war with Russia remains unproved. Six year-old Simeon succeeded him under the regency of Boris's brother Prince Kyril and two others, and in 1945 these three were murdered by the communists who then abolished the monarchy.

Ferdinand died a forgotten figure in Coburg in 1948, having lived to see his two sons meet horrible deaths, his grandson in exile and his work in Bulgaria brought to nothing.

King Boris III

FRANCE

Kings of France and Navarre

The Count of Paris is regarded by legitimists as Henri VI, King of France and Navarre. His childhood was largely spent near Larache in Morocco. When his uncle, then head of the family, died in 1926 and the Count's father succeeded, the family were obliged, by the Law of Exile, to leave French territory. They moved to Brussels where the Count completed his education. In 1931, he married his cousin, Princess Isabelle of Orléans and Braganza, and settled at the Château d'Agimont on the Franco-Belgian border. At the time, the Count was the proprietor and editor of two newspapers—*Ici France* and *Le Courier Royal*.

In World War II, the Count, prevented from serving in the French or British armies, spent a year in the Foreign Legion. Subsequently, he took his family to Pamplona, the capital of Navarre. Afterwards, the family went on to Cintra in Portugal. When the Law of Exile was nullified in 1950, they returned to France where the Count was able to involve himself

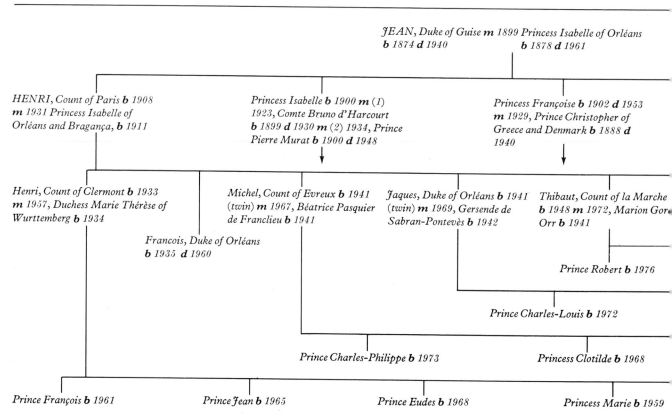

Henri, Count of Paris, lives in the château where he was born at Aisne, in France. Although he now claims to have given up his political career, the Count could never forget how to be a king of France. In a lifetime of self-grooming, he mastered the art and style of sovereignty so completely that De Gaulle favoured Henri as a candidate to succeed him in the presidency. The Count's wife Isabelle is a distinguished, imposing personality, who has always worked closely with him, helping especially in the enormous task of arranging (for presentation to the nation) more than four million Bourbon-Orléans family documents. The mother of eleven children, ten of whom are living, she has found time to write an engrossing autobiography entitled *Tout M'est Bonheur*. It is the tale of a very resourceful woman.

incess Anne b 1906 m 1927,
ince Amedeo of Savoy, 3rd
ke of Aosta b 1898 d 1942

incess Isabelle b 1932 m 1964
iedrich Karl, Count of
hönborn-Buchheim b 1938

Princess Anne b 1938 m 1965,
Prince Carlo of Bourbon-Two
Sicilies b 1938

Princess Claude b 1943 m 1964
Prince Amedeo of Savoy, 5th
Duke of Aosta b 1943

Princess Hélène b 1934 m 1957
Count Evrard van Limburg-
Stirum, b 1927

Princess Diane b 1940 m 1960,
Carl, Duke of Württemberg b 1936

Princess Chantal b 1946 m 1972,
Baron François Xavier de
Sambucy de Sorgue b 1943

ppe

ince Foulques b 1974

Princess Diane b 1970

incess Adélaide b 1971

Princess Blanche b 1962

in politics, and to the surprise of traditional monarchists, his ideas were very democratic. From time to time he spoke in public and, until 1967, published a monthly information bulletin. Then, he gave up his political career, and since has devoted his time to two foundations of which he is president: La Fondation Condé, which cares for old people in Chantilly, and La Fondation de St. Louis, which he established in 1974 to conserve and maintain several historic buildings belonging to the family. Among them is the Château d'Amboise, where the St. Louis foundation plans to institute a museum and a centre for historical research. There could be no more fitting environment for a cultural centre than this castle on the Loire. It is one of the monuments to that patron of the arts, François I, last great king of the Valois dynasty.

France's original royal dynasty, that of the Capetians, failed in the male line in the fourteenth century. It was replaced by a collateral line, the Valois, which was transformed into the line of Valois-Orléans in the fifteenth century, and in turn failed with the last of François I's inadequate grandsons.

The Bourbons, a cadet line of the Capetians, trace their descent to Robert de Clermont—a son of Louis, the Capetian king of France who was canonized, and to Beatrix de Bourbon, heiress to the Seigneurie de Bourbon, which was soon transformed into a duchy. It was a prosperous estate, especially with the purchase of the Viennois, whose counts became vassals of the Bourbons on condition that their custom of calling the heir to the title *dauphin*—after the dolphin in their arms—be retained.

In François I's day, the Bourbon line was represented by Charles, Duc de Vendôme, first prince of the blood in his Bourbon capacity and *duc et pair de France* in his own right. It was Antoine, the son of Charles, who married Jeanne d'Albret, the daughter and heiress of the King of Navarre.

Henri, Count of Clermont, the Count of Paris's eldest son and heir, is married to Marie Thérèse, daughter of Philipp Albrecht, the late Duke of Württemberg and sister of Carl, the present Duke, who happens to be married to a daughter of the Count of Paris. The Count and Countess of Clermont live apart, but it is thought that no divorce is contemplated at present. Second in line of succession as head of the family is their eldest son François, named after his father's younger brother, François, who was killed in the Algerian war in 1960.

Fourth son of the Count of Paris is Prince Thibaut. He and his wife Marion are two of the "beautiful people" of European royalty. They are the authors of a quite accomplished romantic novel entitled *A Castle in Bavaria* and have also turned their talents to operating a successful art gallery. Thibaut is tall with a leonine head; Marion's Chilean ancestry is reflected by her alabaster-white skin and raven hair.

118

Antoine's son, Henri IV, was to change his religion three times in all. Brought up as a Protestant, he became a Catholic after the Massacre of St. Bartholomew. In 1575, having succeeded as King of Navarre, he once again became a Protestant, and leader of the Huguenots. As such he had defeated King Henri III's Catholic troops led by one of the King's famous *mignons*—or minions—whom all Paris called "the Princes of Sodom". The King of Navarre, and his cousin the King of France (whose sister Margot he had married during his Catholic interlude) were later reconciled. Before Henri III was assassinated in 1589, he had appointed the King of Navarre as his heir to France. The religious war continued for another five years; but 1594 saw the last of Henri IV's conversions—*"Paris vaut bien une messe"*—and it was as a Catholic that he was crowned and anointed the first Bourbon king of France.

He restored royal power, united the country, reorganized the economy, and at Nantes he promulgated the Edict guaranteeing Protestants rights and concessions. France, bled white in the religious wars, became prosperous once more.

He came to be called *le Vert Galant*—because of his innumerable mistresses, by whom he had countless bastards. As for wives—Henri IV annulled the marriage with Margot in 1599 and in 1600 he married a Medici lady—Marie, to whom his mistress of the day referred as "your fat Florentine banker". There were two sons: the Dauphin, who became Louis XIII, and Gaston, who became the Duc d'Orléans, prince of plotters. The daughters of the marriage—Elisabeth, Christine and Henrietta Marie, married respectively Philip IV of Spain, Victor Amadeus I of Savoy and Charles I of England.

Louis XIII was not yet nine years old when he succeeded to the throne of France in 1610 after his father had been assassinated, so his Rubenesque mother acted as Regent until 1617. Her chief advisers were the unscrupulous and rapacious Concinis, who became the Marquis and Marquise d'Ancres. Together, they reversed all of Henri IV's wise policies and the Grand Design to make France the master of Europe. One of their first acts was to ban the nobles, which later caused considerable trouble.

Louis XIII, an enigmatic figure, was the image of Henri III—as was Gaston his brother. He was said to be fond of his wife,—Anne of Austria, an Infanta of Spain—but rarely shared her bed. Like Henri III, he had his *mignons*, but he made less of a cult of them.

Louis XIII's real passion was reserved for field sports: and it was a happy day when he bagged no less than six wolves, although it must be admitted that wolves were then still plentiful: the Louvre itself, now a royal palace, had not so long ago been known as *la Louvrerie*—a hunting lodge in the middle of wolf country. Now that the wolves had retreated outside Paris and with them other game, the King enlarged and rebuilt the old hunting box at Versailles. At the Louvre, he passed the time in falconry and it was his falconer, Charles d'Albert de Luynes, who became the first of his favourites. A very different proposition from Henri III's friends with their painted faces "like so many whores", Luynes was a manly figure with no vice in him, truly devoted to Louis. Created a *duc*, and Connetable of France, Luynes was not enough of a statesman to improve France's finances, but matters improved when after his death his place as adviser and first minister was taken by the great Cardinal de Richelieu, who re-adopted the Grand Design, but did not reinstate the nobles.

Numberless revolts later—some staged by the notorious Gaston who

Anne, Duchess of Aosta, the sister of the Count of Paris, bears a marked resemblance to Queen Anne, the last Stuart sovereign of England. The widow of the 3rd Duke of Aosta who was Viceroy of Ethiopia when that country formed part of the abortive Italian Empire, she has two daughters, one of whom is married to a prince of The Two Sicilies and the other to the Archduke Robert of Austria, brother of Dr. Otto Habsburg.

119

The Louvre, France's national museum and gallery, was originally a palace begun by Francis I in 1546. By the time of Louis XIV, who spent his last nights in Paris there before returning to die at Versailles, it was used only intermittently as a royal residence. The Louvre as seen today came into being during the reign of Louis XV, when after comprehensive redesigning, it became a museum.

Louis XIV

invariably escaped retribution—Richelieu and the King had created a strong modern state. It seemed that "Fortune herself accompanied the King, and victory was his very handmaiden". Louis XIII's greatest gift to France arrived in the world at Fontainebleau, where Anne of Austria, against all expectation, gave birth to a Dauphin in 1638. This miraculous infant had been conceived when the King had spent a night with his Queen at the Louvre after a long separation—a chance rainstorm had prevented him from travelling on to his own establishment.

The Cardinal now introduced into the King's household Henri d'Effiat, Marquis de Cinq Mars. He was to be the last of Louis XIII's *mignons*, on whom he doted. Cinq Mars was grasping and disloyal and became the tool of Gaston, plotting as usual. As usual, the conspiracy was discovered; as usual, it was not Gaston who suffered, but Cinq Mars who went to the scaffold in 1642. This was the year that saw the death of Richelieu and in 1643 Louis XIII himself died. It had been his fate to be overshadowed in his lifetime by the great Richelieu, and after death by his son. This child, aged four, paying a deathbed visit, was asked his name by Louis XIII, and anticipated events by replying "Louis XIV, Papa".

When he succeeded, Anne of Austria, now Regent for her son, commanded the services of Cardinal Mazarin, Richelieu's disciple, whom Louis XIII had instructed to continue all his master's policies. Trouble and unrest soon followed. There were two near civil wars. The first was called the Fronde. The second was called the *Fronde des Princes*. Both were directed against Mazarin: he fled, but soon returned to power.

He was said to be a great comfort to Anne of Austria—too great thought some, and it was alleged that they had been secretly married. Married to her or not, the Cardinal's influence on the Regent was enormous and extended to the upbringing of the princes. Louis XIV, deified from the first, and regarded as "the image of God on earth"—albeit in petticoats to begin with—was taught all the manly arts.

Philippe received a very different education. Considered "too pretty for a boy" by the Regent's ladies and a potential danger to the King by Mazarin, Philippe was purposely encouraged to become effeminate. Mazarin himself supplied a nephew as Monsieur's first lover. For all of Philippe's delight in interior design, in gossip and in dressing up, he was to become a brave and gifted soldier. It was said that he minded exposure to gunpowder less than exposure to the sun, which ruined his complexion. After

120

Mazarin's death in 1661, Louis XIV began his personal reign, which saw the Grand Design succeed beyond all dreams.

French manners, dress and food came to be copied all over Europe and etiquette was worked into a fine art. Privileges of seating were graded strictly according to rank: a new duchess was said to have swooned with happiness at now rating "the divine tabouret"—a large, low foot-stool. Privileges of service to the monarch—especially at his *levée*, which resembled a bishop's investment—were jealously guarded: the handers of the royal shirt, the royal gloves and even the holder of the royal candle were happy to be so honoured. It was all part of the scheme: where nobles spent their energies fighting for tiny privileges among each other, they had none left for plotting against the King.

Louis XIV's France, now the greatest power in Europe, was watched with anxious eyes by his cousin William of Orange, *Stadhouder* of the United Provinces of the Netherlands. It was he who became Louis' most implacable enemy.

In the 1670s, the King was at the height of his glory. In the 1680s he moved his court to Versailles, after improving, on a grand scale, his father's improvements. Soon it became the *bon ton* among the Empire's princes to send their sons to the Sun King's court as to a finishing school.

What they learned there, except for vices, was another question: the Sun King's household was a poor model; so was Monsieur's: both were dominated by favourites, female in one case, male in the other. Louis' poor little Spanish Queen, whose only asset was her blonde hair, spent her life in prayer and pregnancy, of which the only lasting result was a single son, the Dauphin. Monsieur's wife, Minette, sister of Charles I of England, died young, convinced that she had been poisoned by her husband's favourite.

Both Louis XIV and Monsieur had become widowers when they were around forty. Monsieur's second wife was the daughter of the Elector Palatine, called Liselotte, whose amusing, outspoken letters are filled with hatred for the King's second, secret wife, the dreaded Mme de Maintenon, whom she called "the eclipse of the Sun". Mme de Maintenon's official position was that of Honorary Mistress of the Household to the Bavarian princess who married the Dauphin. The Dauphine, a melancholy lady, died soon after she had produced three sons: the Ducs de Bourgogne, d'Anjou and de Berry.

It was the Duc d'Anjou to whom the King of Spain left his empire when he died in 1700. Louis XIV's acceptance on behalf of his grandson led to the war that proved the French army not to be invincible after all: Marlborough and Prince Eugene of Savoy inflicted such blows on Louis XIV's army that France was never quite to recover.

At the end of the day, the Duc d'Anjou was recognized as King of Spain after all, but had to renounce any claim to the French throne. This was a matter of the greatest regret to him, since even before the war had ended, a series of illnesses had wiped out almost the entire succession to France: his father, the Grand Dauphin, had died in 1711. He was followed by the Ducs de Berry and Bourgogne, together with his cousin Adelaide of Savoy, wife of the Duc de Bourgogne. When the great King himself died in 1715, there was only one fragile life, that of the future Louis XV, between the King of Spain and his French heritage. This infant life was guarded by Liselotte's son Philippe, Regent of France, who was widely suspected of being the poisoner of the entire succession.

Louis XIV ordered the creation of Versailles, arguably the most splendid palace in the western world, and in the 1680s made it his court. Twenty-eight villages were originally demolished to provide space for the park and its grand canal. The façade, seen from the gardens, looks like one continuous line and extends for 1,902 feet. There are 2,498 rooms, and there were so many clocks that the post of clock winder (once occupied by the father of the writer Beaumarchais), was full-time. Even so, the sanitation was appalling, the fountains and canal were choked with night waste and in hot weather, the place smelled like a sewer.

Mme de Maintenon

Louis XV's childhood was a period of princely intrigues against his guardian whose licentious life made him an easy target. He was, however, gifted, clever, politically astute and devoted to the young King, and when he died in 1723, Louis XV became the master of a fairly stable country. After an illness so severe that his recovery seemed miraculous, it was clear that the wisest course would be to marry Louis as soon as possible to secure the succession. A previous marriage with his Spanish cousin was cancelled and the new bride was imported—Maria Leszczynska, daughter of the King of Poland, who had lost his crown and who lived as a pensioner in Lorraine. It was this Queen, who produced no less than ten children, who complained that her life consisted of *"coucher, grossesse, accoucher"*.

The King's old tutor, Cardinal Fleury, was his adviser and first minister—as powerful in his way as had been the Cardinals Richelieu and Mazarin. It was Fleury's aim to restore the prestige of France and to this end, Louis went to war as frequently as his great-grandfather. The celebrated Mme de Pompadour was soon to rule this King as Mme de Maintenon had ruled Louis XIV. As that lady had "reformed" the Sun King, and had been responsible for the air of hypocrisy that characterized his court in the later part of the reign, so Mme de Pompadour—friend of *les philosophes*—wished to influence her royal lover in the direction of enlightenment, but failed: with his melancholy temperament, the King needed both pleasure and religion.

By the 1750s, when the finances of France were again in a dreadful state, Louis XV had become unpopular and after an assassination attempt, began to brood on his mortality. However, he lived on, and it was Mme de Pompadour, now the most hated woman in the kingdom, who died in 1764, and there were annual deaths thereafter: the Dauphine and finally the patient Queen. Obsessed now by morbid thoughts, Louis XV found comfort in Mme du Barry, to whom his heirs refused to speak. The Dauphin's son, fat and apathetic, a throwback to his grandfather, had an enchanting Austrian wife, as silly as she was haughty: Marie Antoinette.

Louis XVI's reign began well enough. He was all for reform, at least in theory. For all his wish to make his good people happy, the Bastille, on the point of being demolished by order of the King, was stormed in 1789, and the French Revolution was under way: triggered off by the American Revolution with which, in secret, the King had every sympathy.

The Queen, the children (a daughter and a son), and the King left Versailles for the Tuileries, where it dawned on the King that "they want to murder me as they did Henri IV", long before he was forced to mount the guillotine, set up in the Place de la Concorde. He did so with admirable firmness and courage, as did the Queen, for all her former frivolity.

The Dauphin, imprisoned with his parents, survived them for two years as Louis XVII—his mother knelt to acknowledge him immediately after his father's death in 1793. But his gaolers called him Louis Capet, neglecting and ill-treating him until he died aged ten, having spent his entire "reign" in a filthy prison cell.

Louis XVI's next brother succeeded his nephew as Louis XVIII, so proclaimed by French *emigrés* in 1795, while in France the Republic gave way to the Directoire, the Consulate and then Napoleon's Empire, which lasted until 1814. That year, Louis XVIII returned from twenty years' wandering abroad in the wake of the victorious allied armies, only to retire to Ghent when Napoleon returned from Elba. After the Hundred Days,

Louis XVI

Louis XVIII was restored yet again, now called Louis *deux-fois neuf*. By then he was racked by gout, a fat, aged figure in a wheelchair.

His nephew and his heir presumptive, the Duc de Berry, had been stabbed in 1820 and so when Louis XVIII died in 1824, he was succeeded by his brother, Charles X, a king after the heart of the ultra-monarchists, and his reign ended in the revolution of 1830, which forced his abdication and that of his son. Instead of accepting the next in line, the murdered Duc de Berry's posthumous son, the Comte de Chambord as their King the moderate liberals now in power preferred to give the crown to the head of the Orléans line, represented by the son of Philippe Egalité.

To mark the break with the senior line, Egalité's son reigned as Louis Philippe I, King of the French. But more was broken than mere continuity of cypher: even French royalists were now split into factions, which contributed to the eventual fall of the monarchy. Louis Philippe re-established the tricolour flag, dismissed Charles X's ministers and such statesmen of Louis XVIII's reign as had surfaced again to frighten the King, a conservative at heart, with their bourgeois liberalism. The 1840s saw the rise of the radical socialist party and by 1848, popular support for the regime had dwindled. The first revolution of that year brought down Louis Philippe, who was granted asylum in England.

After the fall of the House of Orléans, royalists again turned to Henri V. In 1849, a planned *coup d'état*, however, came to nothing, and it was not until Napoleon III's Empire fell that the Comte de Paris, Louis Philippe's grandson, came to London there to recognize Henri V, Duc de Bordeaux and Comte de Chambord, as the sole representative of the monarchic principle of France. The two gentlemen discussed the restoration and Henri V agreed with the concept of a democratic, constitutional monarchy —a great concession since he was a medievalist at heart. All seemed harmonious, but the stumbling block turned out to be the flag: Henri would have nothing to do with the tricolour—he stood firm by the lilies of France, "the banner of Jeanne d'Arc and Henri IV", and thereby became the first man "to give up a throne for a napkin".

King Louis Philippe

With his death, the senior line became extinct, and legitimists now regarded the Comte de Paris, son of Louis Philippe, as their rightful king. It was his daughter, Princess Hélène, with whom Prince Eddie, Duke of Clarence, the eldest son of Edward, Prince of Wales, fell in love, but there was no marriage: the Comte forbade his daughter to become a Protestant.

Hélène's eldest brother, Philippe, Duc d'Orléans, became head of the House after the Comte de Paris, and was in turn succeeded by his cousin and brother-in-law, the Duc de Guise, father of the present claimant.

FRANCE/BONAPARTE
Genius, and Despair

Prince Louis Napoléon, head of the Imperial House of Bonaparte, was born in Brussels—the law of exile then prevented any Bonaparte from entering France. He was brought up in Belgium and England, where Napoleon III's widow, the Empress Eugénie, and other members of the family lived.

After private tutoring, the Prince went to the Universities of Lausanne and Louvain. During the Second World War, after various requests on his part to join the French army—which remained unanswered—Prince Louis Napoléon joined the Foreign Legion as Monsieur Blanchard; later, under the pseudonym of Monnier, he fought first with the resistance and then with the 17th Infantry Batallion. Twice wounded, and decorated for bravery—now under the family name of Montfort—he was accepted by General de Gaulle. The law of exile was in due course lifted, and Prince Louis, with his family, now has an apartment in Paris as well as the house on the shores of Lake Geneva which is the family home.

He would have liked his marriage to Alix, daughter of an old Italian family, to take place in the chapel of the Invalides, where lies the tomb of Napoleon I, but the government felt unable to grant him this privilege. The Napoleonic legend seemed still too potent.

Although a Bonapartist party exists in France, Prince Louis does not think it very likely that he will ever be called upon to lead the state. He has said that he would be available to serve if popularly desired to do so, but he is careful not to allow his name to be used for political purposes, and takes no active part in politics. He is a businessman with a seat on boards of various European industries and holds many overseas investments. He is a great traveller, and multi-lingual—as is fitting for a

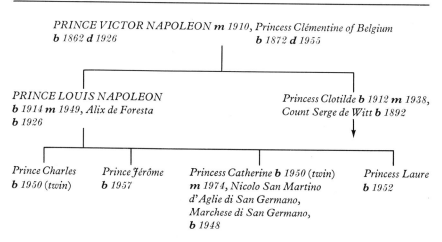

man whose family tree is as international as his, featuring kings of Belgium, Württemberg, Italy and Great Britain. At its root, of course, is the name of Carlo Buonaparte, and of the formidable Madame Mère, Laetitia Ramolino, parents of Joseph, Louis, Lucien, Jérôme, Elisa, Pauline and Caroline Buonaparte, not to speak of Napoleon himself.

There has been much discussion of the descent of the Buonapartes, who were to drop the Italian *u* from their name. Cunerado, Count of Pistoia, who lived in the tenth century, has been mentioned as the family's founder father. In following centuries, various Buonapartes lived in or near Florence, at Sarzana and in Genoa. In the sixteenth century, a Francesco Buonaparte settled in Corsica and it is from this man that Carlo, who did not live to see his children become imperial and royal highnesses, is descended, for all that his most famous son said, with some justification, "Ancestre c'est moi".

Indeed, Napoleon, who had only a single legitimate son, created several supra-national lines of kings and queens. Joseph, his eldest brother, had a spell as King of Naples and Sicily. Louis was King of Holland from 1806 to 1810, and by his wife Hortense had three sons, the third of whom became Napoleon III. For Lucien, the *enfant terrible* of the family, there was admittedly nothing to be had from the Emperor, but he did buy the property of Canino and adopt its princely title by arrangement with the Pope.

As for the sisters, Napoleon made Elisa both Duchess of Lucca and Princess of Piombino. Pauline became the Duchess of Guastalla, and by her second marriage the Princess Borghese, familiar as the model for Canova's Venus. Caroline, married to Joachim Murat, became Queen of Naples after Joseph had moved to Spain.

But in terms of dynastic continuity, Napoleon's youngest brother, Jérôme, was the most significant of all: from him descend the contemporary Prince Louis and his two sons—the only living, legitimate male representatives of Carlo Buonaparte's line. The Emperor, fifteen years older than Jérôme, had high hopes of him, entering him into the navy in the hope that service at sea might strengthen the frivolous youth's character. Jérôme, reaching the West Indies, and learning that as Napoleon's brother he was in some danger from the British fleet, travelled on to Baltimore. There he allowed himself to be extensively feted, and married Miss Elizabeth Patterson, known as Betsey. For Jérôme to remove himself from the dynastic network in this fashion was intolerable to Napoleon. At his insistence, the young man weakly repudiated his wife when Napoleon became Emperor. She returned to Baltimore with Jérôme's son, another Jérôme otherwise known as Bo—thus creating the now extinct American Bonaparte family. To Jérôme came instead the crown of Westphalia in 1807. His extravagance and the fiasco he caused during the Russian campaign are famous. For the Emperor himself, the dynastic preoccupation was consuming. At the very zenith of his power, he divorced the ageing Joséphine, and married instead the eighteen year-old Marie Louise of Austria, daughter of the Emperor Francis I. She was a big, docile creature with a touch of the Habsburg chin, who obligingly gave birth to a son in 1811. This baby was at once created the King of Rome by his father—an echo of the old, defunct Holy Roman Empire which Napoleon had been instrumental in bringing to an end.

Shortly afterwards, the tide began to turn: in 1812 was the retreat from

Prince Louis Napoléon, his wife Alix and 2nd son Jérôme at the memorial service held in 1973 for the centenary of the death of Napoleon III. There is a certain sense of grandeur about everything these Bonapartes do: each move is something of a royal progress and the Prince and his wife frequently use the subsidiary family titles of Count and Countess de Montfort when they travel. They are good hosts, good company and well respected in royal circles.

Napoleon I

Moscow, followed by the defeat at Leipzig, the loss of the Peninsular War, and banishment to Elba. Marie Louise was sent to Austria with her son, while the future of France and Napoleon was discussed, also in Austria.

At Vienna, an international congress was replanning the map of Europe under the leadership of the Austrian Chanceller, Prince Metternich. He, it seemed, would not rest content until every constitution in Europe was swept away, and with them all the Napoleonic reforms.

But first, there was to be another Napoleonic interlude—the Hundred Days. In March 1815, Napoleon escaped from Elba to land in Cannes. He reached Paris after a bloodless march north. Within a few weeks of his return, the French people had been guaranteed civil liberties, a free press, and an extended franchise. Having spent the first fifteen years of his reign in building the Grand Empire, the Emperor said he was now concentrating on the consolidation and the happiness of France. Then in June came Waterloo and the absolute end of Napoleon's career. He abdicated in the Elysée Palace while Parisians outside his window were shouting *Vive l'Empéreur*, "No abdication" and proclaiming his son as Napoleon II.

The four year-old child in Austria knew nothing of this, nor that his reign was to last for only a few days, nor that his mother would shortly cease being the Empress to become the Duchess of Parma instead, while he became the Duke of Reichstadt and only a serene, rather than an imperial highness. Throughout the boy's short life, his Austrian grandfather shielded him from his Napoleonic heritage as much as possible, though not quite successfully. The strain of enduring this mystification is said to have contributed to his early death in 1832.

Napoleon was never to see his second wife or his son again. After the abdication he hesitated too long to reach the ship that was to take him to America, and then found a British warship, the Bellephoron, blocking the harbour at La Rochelle. He surrendered to its commander, Captain Maitland, putting his life in the hands of the Prince Regent as "the most powerful and most generous of my enemies". He hoped to be allowed to settle in England's Kent countryside, where the climate was thought to be mild. However, he was not allowed to set foot there—it was far too close to France. Instead, he was taken to the rocky island of St. Helena, where the conditions of his confinement much shocked post-revolutionary America. So the Napoleonic legend was born, fostered during the years that the great man spent on St. Helena until his death there in 1821.

The law of exile had meanwhile forced all the Bonapartes out of France, scattering them like starlings in the autumn. Jérôme, with his second wife Catherine, daughter of the King of Württemberg moved in 1814 to Trieste, where their three children, Jérôme Napoléon Charles, Napoléon Joseph Charles Paul (called Plon Plon) and Mathilde were born. They were brought up in Rome, where regardless of his straitened circumstances, Jérôme bought a palazzo from his brother Lucien. Soon Jérôme was deeply in debt. In 1816, the King of Württemberg created Jérôme and his wife Prince and Princess de Montfort.

Louis Napoléon did not stay long in his American exile. After his return to Europe, he spent much time in England where, said people who met him, he never doubted that one day he would take over where his adoptive grandfather had left off. After some unsuccessful attempts, his chance finally came in 1848, when the restored Bourbon King Louis

The Duke of Reichstadt

Philippe's government had been toppled by revolution. Louis Napoléon was elected as the First President of the Second French Republic, and in 1852, after a plebiscite, he became the Emperor Napoleon III.

Meanwhile Jérôme's son Plon Plon showed every sign of following in his father's footsteps as far as profligacy was concerned. However, there was more to Plon Plon than there ever had been to the foolish Jérôme. Like his father, he was quarrelsome, like his father, he had charm, but he also had wit and understanding of literature and the arts. He could be seen dining with Flaubert and George Sand, and it was he who organized the first of the International Exhibitions in Paris in 1855. Jérôme died in 1860, and was accorded the grandest funeral Paris had seen in many a year—an occasion exactly after his own heart.

The Archduke Maximilian, in Paris to discuss his forthcoming move to Mexico with the Emperor, was not impressed by the grandeur of Napoleon III's court: all was too *parvenu* for his taste. The Emperor, he thought, was rather ill at ease—"no doubt because he found himself in the company of a prince of more ancient lineage"—but it is doubtful that the Prince was right, for on receiving the Garter from Queen Victoria, the Emperor found it quite easy to make a joke—*"enfin"*, he said, *"je suis gentilhomme"*. If the English ambassador was also astonished at "the freedom at court, their forgetfulness of the *convenances*", Queen Victoria, both as hostess and as guest of the French Imperials, carried away only the most pleasant impressions of Napoleon III and Eugénie, marvelling only, during the couple's state visit to England that she, "a grand-daughter of George III, should be dancing with the nephew of his great enemy in the Waterloo gallery".

Napoleon III

The Second Empire fell in 1870 and the Imperial family went to England, where they found much sympathy. The Emperor died not long after his arrival, and the Bonapartist party now centred their hopes on the Prince Imperial. However, until 1874, when the Prince would reach his majority, it was Plon Plon who acted as the head of the house. His two sons, Victor and Louis, came over for the Emperor's funeral. Victor was found to be tall, intelligent, with the looks of the Italian side of the family, and instantly likeable. So likeable, in fact, that when the Prince Imperial died in the Zulu wars in 1879, the Bonapartists wished to see Victor on the throne. Indeed, the Prince Imperial's will named Victor as his direct successor, and ignored Plon Plon.

The ensuing quarrel between father and son lasted as long as Plon Plon's life. By his deathbed in Rome, in 1891, the family gathered: his wife Clotilde to see that he at least died as a good Christian; his sister Mathilde, to see that he made his peace with Prince Victor to whom he had not spoken for years. Plon Plon remained unforgiving to the end, and motioned his son out of the room. For all his qualities, he had been an impossibly difficult character. He has been called a *César declassé*. His last words were "I fail at everything" but he did make a good death— for which the credit must go to Clotilde: her husband's final repentance was little short of a miracle.

Prince Victor married Princess Clémentine of Belgium after a long courtship—the bride's father, King Leopold II, had felt, as his own match-making father before him, that Bonapartes in the family spelt trouble. So Clémentine waited until he had died, and at once accepted her faithful suitor. It is her son, Louis, who became the present head of the house on Prince Victor's death in 1926.

127

PRUSSIA
All Highest

Prince Louis Ferdinand, head of Prussia's royal family, the Hohenzollerns, would be German Emperor today if Germany had not become a republic at the end of the First World War.

Known as the rebel prince, after the title of his book, he is tall, Prussian, and correctly bred, with a house full of pictures of his royal relations. He lives as a prosperous farmer and looks forward to the day when a united Europe, of which a united Germany must form a part, will be composed of republics and monarchies. He never forgets that both Churchill and Lloyd-George had thought it a mistake to end his family's rule in Germany, has high hopes of reigning one day and frequently reminds people that, in politics, the word "impossible" does not exist.

Prussia and the Hohenzollerns: it is difficult to think of one without the other, but in fact, the Zollerns (who became high, or Hohen Zollerns as they grew in power) came from the south of Germany. Their ancestral castle—

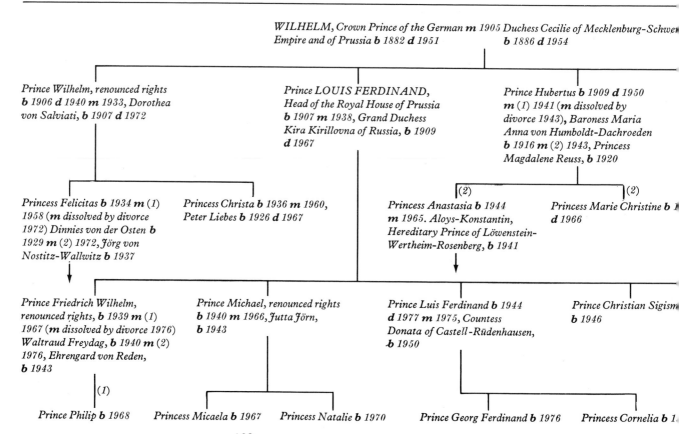

WILHELM, Crown Prince of the German **m** 1905 Duchess Cecilie of Mecklenburg-Schwer
Empire and of Prussia **b** 1882 **d** 1951   **b** 1886 **d** 1954

Prince Wilhelm, renounced rights **b** 1906 **d** 1940 **m** 1933, Dorothea von Salviati, **b** 1907 **d** 1972

Prince LOUIS FERDINAND, Head of the Royal House of Prussia **b** 1907 **m** 1938, Grand Duchess Kira Kirillovna of Russia, **b** 1909 **d** 1967

Prince Hubertus **b** 1909 **d** 1950 **m** (1) 1941 (**m** dissolved by divorce 1943), Baroness Maria Anna von Humboldt-Dachroeden **b** 1916 **m** (2) 1943, Princess Magdalene Reuss, **b** 1920

Princess Felicitas **b** 1934 **m** (1) 1958 (**m** dissolved by divorce 1972) Dinnies von der Osten **b** 1929 **m** (2) 1972, Jörg von Nostitz-Wallwitz **b** 1937

Princess Christa **b** 1936 **m** 1960, Peter Liebes **b** 1926 **d** 1967

(2) Princess Anastasia **b** 1944 **m** 1965. Aloys-Konstantin, Hereditary Prince of Löwenstein-Wertheim-Rosenberg, **b** 1941

(2) Princess Marie Christine **b** 1 **d** 1966

Prince Friedrich Wilhelm, renounced rights, **b** 1939 **m** (1) 1967 (**m** dissolved by divorce 1976) Waltraud Freydag, **b** 1940 **m** (2) 1976, Ehrengard von Reden, **b** 1943

Prince Michael, renounced rights **b** 1940 **m** 1966, Jutta Jörn, **b** 1943

Prince Luis Ferdinand **b** 1944 **d** 1977 **m** 1975, Countess Donata of Castell-Rüdenhausen, **b** 1950

Prince Christian Sigism **b** 1946

(1) Prince Philip **b** 1968

Princess Micaela **b** 1967   Princess Natalie **b** 1970

Prince Georg Ferdinand **b** 1976   Princess Cornelia **b** 1.

though badly shaken by a freak earthquake in 1978—still stands on a hill in the old province of Swabia. In 1227 the family became Burggraves of Nuremburg, and in due course the rulers of a number of southern German territories. In 1417 one of the burggraves acquired the northern province of Brandenburg for 300,000 florins. In the same year he became a Prince Elector, which increased his influence even further, although Brandenburg was a poor, infertile province, called the "sandbox" of the Empire. The senior Hohenzollerns remained in their territories of Ansbach and Bayreuth comforted by the thought that they might inherit sandbox and electorship if and when the northern line died out.

Prussia, on the Baltic coastline of mainland Europe, did not enter the picture for another hundred years. Originally a country where snake-worship and human sacrifice had been the order of the day, it was christ-ianized by the Knights Templar of the Teutonic Order, some of whom settled there, and also colonized by landless younger sons known as Jung-herren or Junkers. Poland figured at this early stage in Prussian history by gaining suzerainty over the eastern part of the territory. In 1512, Margrave Albrecht of Brandenburg was elected Grand High Master of the Teutonic Order, whose headquarters were at Königsberg and in this way the first Hohenzollern came to Prussia. Then in 1525, he joined the Reformation by becoming a Lutheran and as such was no longer a suitable figure-head for the Catholic Knights of the Order. But instead of departing from Prussia he secularized the knights' lands, assumed the title of Duke of Prussia and founded the ducal line which ruled until 1618, when the then Elector of Brandenburg inherited the title.

The next Elector, Friedrich Wilhelm, who is remembered as the Great Elector, secured Prussian independence from Poland. He also saved Brandenburg from the worst ravages of the Thirty Years' War and in 1648

Prince Louis Ferdinand of Prussia was completely shattered by the needless death of his son and heir in 1977 as the result of distressing injuries sustained in a military accident. Nor has he been entirely able to accept the death in 1967 of his wife, Kira, sister of the Grand Duke Vladimir, head of the Romanov family. With all this, he is a thoroughly endearing man who bristles with good humour. Louis Ferdinand lives mainly on his farming estate at Wümmehof near Bremen, but business interests in South America have virtually transformed him into a trans-Atlantic commuter. He speaks English fluently with, surprisingly enough, a Detroit accent.

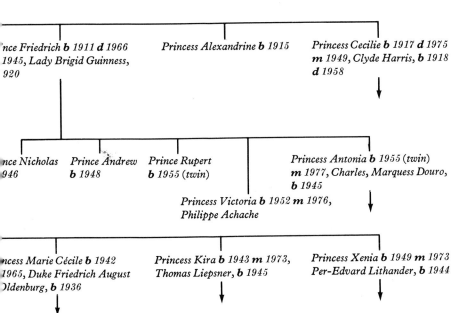

*nce Friedrich **b** 1911 **d** 1966*
1945, Lady Brigid Guinness,
920

*Princess Alexandrine **b** 1915*

*Princess Cecilie **b** 1917 **d** 1975*
***m** 1949, Clyde Harris, **b** 1918*
***d** 1958*

nce Nicholas
946

Prince Andrew
***b** 1948*

Prince Rupert
***b** 1955 (twin)*

*Princess Antonia **b** 1955 (twin)*
***m** 1977, Charles, Marquess Douro,*
***b** 1945*

*Princess Victoria **b** 1952 **m** 1976,*
Philippe Achache

*ncess Marie Cécile **b** 1942*
1965, Duke Friedrich August
*Oldenburg, **b** 1936*

*Princess Kira **b** 1943 **m** 1973,*
*Thomas Liepsner, **b** 1945*

*Princess Xenia **b** 1949 **m** 1973*
*Per-Edvard Lithander, **b** 1944*

gained a number of small but useful territories strung out across the north of Germany.

The Great Elector died in 1688, having laid the foundations of Prussia's industry, administrative bureaucracy, communications system, navy and standing army. The upkeep of all this needed careful budgeting and it was hard on the treasury that the *gloire* of the next Elector, another Friedrich, depended not only on a strong state but also on precious stones with which he studded his crooked shape; *bibelots;* an expensive mistress and expensive palaces. Modelling himself on Louis XIV, Friedrich III went in for pomp and ceremonial, and it was in his reign that court etiquette in Berlin became full of constraint. It became even stiffer in 1701, when the court travelled to Königsberg in Prussia, where Friedrich, with his own hands, placed a crown upon his head. He said "I receive this royal crown from God and no-one else"—true in so far as it had pleased God to arrange for the Emperor in Vienna to respond to pressure from the Kings of France and England, each of whom hoped to use Friedrich for their own purposes, not to mention pressure from Friedrich himself who longed to be a king. He was now known as Friedrich I, King in Prussia (the limiting "in" was to be changed to "of" in 1742).

Friedrich's second wife, Sophie Charlotte, who had described herself as looking like "the Player Queen" at the coronation because all the seams of her dress were picked out in diamonds, found the atmosphere of her husband's court stifling. She spent most of her time at the palace Friedrich had built for her and which, after her early death, came to be called the Charlottenburg. Here she entertained her intellectual friends, and her mother, the Electress Sophie of Hanover. Here also she could receive visits from the philosopher Leibnitz, who admired her enquiring mind,

Prince Georg Friedrich of Prussia, grandson and heir of Prince Louis Ferdinand, stands by his mother, Princess Donata. She is holding her second child, a daughter, born after the tragic death of her husband after a military accident in 1977. He was his father's third son, but replaced his elder brothers in the succession when they renounced their rights after marrying commoners. These two uncles declare that Georg Friedrich, although still so young, is uncannily like his father and that he is clever for his age. Louis Ferdinand himself naturally worships his grandson, and takes a great interest in his education. Stalwart seems an odd term to describe a girl as pretty as Princess Donata, daughter of the 4th Prince of Castell-Rüdenhausen, but it is apt: she was the inspiration of everyone around her at the time of her husband's death. She lives with the children at Fischerhude near Bremen, not far from her father-in-law, in a house he gave her and his son as a wedding present. Active in the local church, she teaches a Sunday school class and reads the lesson at Sunday services.

and here she would quail under the rudeness of her only son whom she adored, and who was a nightmare to his family.

What was one to do with a boy who, at least in the eyes of his Hanoverian grandmother, was "as beautiful as they paint the cupido" (and just as chubby), but who half-murdered his servants, bullied and all but scalped his cousin, the future George II of England, and whose only happiness lay in drilling a company of palace children.

Sophie Charlotte died of a throat ailment while her problem child was still in his teens. She did not live to see him marry her niece Sophie Dorothea of Hanover, whose, mother, of the same name, was never mentioned owing to her indiscretion with the dashing Count Königsmarck. Young Sophie Dorothea was to give birth to Friedrich the Great (and a whole nurseryful of princes and princesses) but in the early years of her marriage she had disappointingly produced only two consecutive Friedrichs too weak to live for long. Her father-in-law, the King, anxious to secure the succession, married again. This was not a success. His third wife, who never did have a baby, went mad. Moreover, she frightened him to death when she entered his presence in her shift, through a glazed door which she had omitted to open. When this vision in white, horribly bespattered with blood, loomed before him, he took it for the ghost of the *Weisse Frau,* said to presage a Hohenzollern death. He shrieked, fell back, and soon afterwards made way for the soldier-king.

Friedrich Wilhelm buried him with all the splendour he would have loved, but that was the end of pomp in Prussia. Out went the jewelled ornaments and the rich collections. Many of the objects were exchanged for *Lange Kerle:* the tallest of tall young men, whom Friedrich Wilhelm made into the famous Prussian grenadiers. Out, fastest of all, went most of the first King's grasping courtiers and ministers. Friedrich Wilhelm became a rather terrifying lord-high-everything. However, far from wishing to strike fear into his subjects, he required adoration: a story relates how he belaboured a cringing fellow with his ever-present cane, furiously shouting (in the customary third person) "He is not to fear me, he is to love me!".

Under Friedrich Wilhelm's rule, Prussia became highly efficient and financially stable. His parsimony was famous, and good dinners were rare. Only the wine bills were high. Sometimes, when strangers came to admire

Princess Viktoria Luise, only daughter of Kaiser Wilhelm II of Prussia, was born a princess of seventeen territories and by marriage to the Duke of Brunswick became a duchess of twenty-three others. Marriage also made her mistress of a palace which is a handsomer version of Buckingham Palace in London and vastly larger. Today, she makes do with a modest flat in Braunschweig, West Germany, managing admirably on a less extravagant scale.

Princess Antonia of Prussia is the niece of Prince Louis Ferdinand who in 1977 married into a famous English family: her husband is the Marquess Douro, heir to the Duke of Wellington.

the grand military reviews that were his pride, "he had fourteen dishes served up all the time; but this," says his daughter Wilhelmina "was no small effort for my father".

The King spent his spare time at his *tabagie*—a smoking club of his creation, that met every morning around a large table. Queen Sophie Dorothea, adept at stuffing his long clay-pipes, was not admitted to these all-male gatherings. Young Friedrich was welcome, but he was so very different from his father that he did not much enjoy these occasions.

Young Friedrich and his friends were elegant, largely homosexual, sophisticated and agnostic. His tendencies "not comfortable to the laws of the universe", infuriated his father. What most shocked the world, however, was not the Prince's taste, but his father's treatment of him, especially after his attempt to run away. This flight was so ineptly planned by the Prince and his companion (a handsome young officer named Katte), that the young men were caught. Both were condemned to death, but only Katte died, while young Friedrich, saved by a handwritten letter from the Emperor, was forced to watch his friend mount the scaffold. Mercifully, Friedrich fainted as the blow fell. Then he was banished.

The Queen did her ineffectual best to help, but had not the slightest influence on the King. Eventually, Friedrich obtained his father's grudging pardon and was ordered to marry a Brunswick princess. However, the only beloved "principessa" of Friedrich's life remained his flute, to which he had given this title because, he said, he "would never be truly in love with any other". His sister had laughed at this witticism — but it was less funny for his wife, from whom he parted with exquisite politeness soon after he succeeded in 1740 to a Prussia that was solvent and stable. Friedrich Wilhelm had lived up to his title, the "plus-maker": nothing had been wasted in his reign. Even the market women had, by his orders, taken to knitting as they sat by their wares.

Amazingly, Friedrich II had been devoted to his tyrant of a father all

Friedrich II

along. As often happens, the old King's mantle — or rather his soldierly great-coat — fell on the son's shoulders: what is more, Friedrich became a military genius. He realized the old King's cherished dream by winning Silesia from Austria. By backing Charles of Bavaria for Emperor against the Habsburg Maria Theresa, and by double-crossing his allies, he made Prussia so important that France and the Empire forgot their rivalry and joined with Russia to fight Prussia. In the Seven Years' War, it came to be touch and go — even Prussia could not indefinitely hold out against the rest of the world. But, just in time, the old Russian Empress died to be followed by her nephew, who was full of worship for the Prussian King. He positively refused to enter the fray against his hero, and made a separate peace. The rest of Europe wanted the war to end—except for Maria Theresa, who still minded about Silesia. So Prussia won the day: she was now truly a premier power and Friedrich had earned his name of Great.

He moved into Sans Souci, the pink palace which he built at Potsdam. In its rococo music room he gave his famous flute concerts. It was here that Johann Sebastian Bach extemporized on a theme provided by the King which was to become the *Musical Offering*. (The *Brandenburg Concertos* were not, incidentally, composed for Friedrich II, but for a Hohenzollern of Ansbach, where Bach had been employed).

Friedrich II was succeeded in 1786 by one of his countless nephews, the dissolute Friedrich Wilhelm II who had eighteen official children — some legitimate, some legitimized — and no one knows how many bastards. However, he is mainly remembered for mysticism and mistresses: alchemists and Rosicrucian monks had haunted his court, while, in the words of a shocked old general, "all Berlin had become a brothel".

His son, the third Friedrich Wilhelm, reintroduced order and austerity into the realm, but his reign was not a glorious one. After his defeat at the battle of Jena, he lost half his lands west of the Elbe to Napoleon, who for a time had Berlin in his possession.

In 1840 the highly-strung Friedrich Wilhelm IV succeeded. He felt it his hallowed destiny to recreate Charlemagne's medieval empire, now that the Holy Roman Empire was no more. (The Emperor had quietly transformed himself, in 1806, into the Emperor of Austria.) There was now, however, a German Confederation with a parliament in Frankfurt. This was not to Friedrich Wilhelm IV's taste at all. Divine right was all that counted, and those who questioned it were guilty of blasphemy.

In the year 1849, the Federal Parliament in Frankfurt sent a delegation actually offering Friedrich Wilhelm IV the Imperial Crown of a new, democratically governed empire. He declined, and had several sharp things to say about legitimacy and revolutionary new practises. His own plans for a feudal empire came to grief in 1850 when the Austrian Habsburgs had their leadership of the German Confederacy confirmed. This was highly humiliating for the Hohenzollerns. The King's instability grew, and by 1858 he had sunk into insanity, giving way to his brother Wilhelm, who became King Wilhelm I in 1861.

Ten years later, thanks to Bismarck, King Wilhelm's Iron Chancellor, Prussia was again on the rise. He wrenched Schleswig-Holstein from the royal family of Denmark; acquired Hanover by dethroning the blind King Georg when he vacillated between supporting Prussia or Austria in 1886; was victoriously at war with France and indeed it was at Versailles, in the Hall of Mirrors, that Prussia's greatest moment of all occurred. On the exact anniversary of Friedrich I's coronation, the Grand Duke of Baden,

Friedrich Wilhelm II

Wilhelm I

Wilhelm's son-in-law, cried "long live His Majesty the Emperor Wilhelm". Just as Bismarck had planned, Prussia had provided the first German Emperor (the other states had balked at "Emperor of Germany" because of its territorial connotations) and Prussia ruled supreme, without parliamentary interference.

Bismarck had the government pretty well to himself. His monarch was kept much in the dark — even the daily papers were censored for him: each morning he found such press-cuttings as were thought fit for his eyes. Within the family he was an autocratic figure whose word was law. His Queen was thought to counteract his extreme Prussianism, especially in religious questions, but her influence on him was small. It was not a love-match: the great romance of Wilhelm's life had been Elise Radziwill — alas, not well-born enough for a Hohenzollern — and he never forgot her. Though terrifying, the Emperor could also be jovial and kind: a young relation recalls him as a good-looking, bewhiskered old man, with a fascinating single lock of white hair swept about his head and fastened over one ear with white cotton. He had allowed her to help feed the deer in his park, while the rouged Empress looked on from a bathchair.

Wilhelm's eldest son, the tall, bearded Crown Prince Friedrich (who was Queen Victoria's son-in-law) and his wife, Princess Vicky, had ideas more idealistic and far more democratic than the Emperor. The Imperial family was not a happy one. At this solemn, reactionary court, Princess Vicky excited suspicion and sometimes ridicule, although she was as proud of being Prussian as she was of being English. Crown Prince Friedrich was regarded by Bismarck as an ineffectual visionary. The Emperor died in 1888, when Crown Prince Friedrich was already mortally ill. "They look on us as a mere shadow", wrote Vicky, "soon to make way for the reality of Willy".

Willy succeeded within three months, making 1888 "the year of the three Emperors". He became Wilhelm II, but is remembered simply as "the Kaiser". He was forceful, vain, bombastic, conceited, unreliable, and, like his forebears, a great believer in divine right. He gloried in formality and in his appellation of "All-Highest". (His grandmama Victoria said that if Willy expected German formality within the family when he came for visits, he must think again).

Of all the Prussian sovereigns, he was probably the most accomplished. He played sports with indefatigable energy, overcoming the handicap of his withered arm, and he had wit and humour. He was given to such frenetic activity that Bismarck said "the Kaiser is like a balloon, if you don't keep a tight grip on the string, you'll never know where he'll be off to next".

Bismarck treated him much as he had the previous King: censored news, edited documents, and marked some reports "rewrite for H.I.M." Then suddenly, amazingly, the Emperor proved to have been an apt pupil in politics: he engineered matters so that Bismarck had no option but to resign. Like his father, the Kaiser found it difficult to be Emperor under Bismarck. *Punch*, the English magazine, called it "dropping the Pilot".

Wilhelm was strong on family feeling, and a great believer in family life. He loved his wife, the Empress Augusta Victoria, and the children, of which there were six boys and a single daughter. Her brilliant wedding at the Schloss was the last to be celebrated with the traditional torch dance, in whom no one below the rank of royal highness took part, each couple, preceded by a torch-bearer, progressing round the ballroom. At that occasion, King George of England, Tsar Nicholas of Russia and the

Berlin's Charlottenburg, begun in 1695, more or less completed in 1712, was bombed to pieces in November 1943, the day after completion of a long photographic session to record the decorative detail. It was thirty years before, with the aid of those timely photographs and fragments found in the ruins, the building was restored. The famous Watteau paintings and other treasures had been in store the glory of what is, after all, architecturally not an exciting palace. It cannot decide whether it is baroque or neo-classical. The gardens are extremely formal in a gracefully mathematical style. The central hall overlooking the gardens was the inspiration for the Music Room at London's Buckingham Palace.

Kaiser all took part, the last time that they were to meet as loving cousins.

Shortly afterwards, the world was at war. When, in 1914, war-declarations came from Russia and England because the frontiers of France had been breached by the German army, and Kaiser said "if my grandmother were still alive, she would not have allowed Georgie and Nicky to do this to me". Soon he was to be called "the mad dog of Europe", although at the beginning at least, the Emperor of Austria was far more belligerent than the All-Highest. Then it did become the Kaiser's war, and it ended in disaster for Germany and in exile for the Kaiser. His final mistake had been not to abdicate in favour of his grandson, when there had still been time. As it was, nothing was saved in the wreckage, and the Hohenzollerns were out of a job.

Wilhelm's exile in Holland lasted for twenty-three years, almost as long as his reign. His wife died soon after it began, and he remarried, much to the disgust of his children, whom he in turn criticized from afar. People who visited Wilhelm in exile—he lived quietly at Doorn—found instead of an old war-horse, a courteous, humorous, friendly old gentleman. The Crown Prince Wilhelm succeeded him in 1941 as head of the family, and his son is the present Louis Ferdinand.

Wilhelm II

BAVARIA
Melancholia and Eccentricity

Duke Albrecht of Bavaria, head of the Royal House of Wittelsbach, is the grandson of the last King of Bavaria, Ludwig III—who was a cousin of the king who built the castles. When he lost his throne after the Spartakus rising in 1918, it meant an end to a thousand years of Wittelsbach rule.

Duke Albrecht is essentially a retiring man who lives privately in the south wing of the Nymphenburg in Munich with his second wife. He has gained real distinction as a forester of international repute, and has no desire to be regarded as a shadow king, a reticence which contrasts with the hope held by many Bavarians for a return of the Wittelsbachs. Moreover, various fringe English Jacobite groups, remembering Duke Albrecht's Stuart blood (and ignoring the Act of Settlement by which no Catholic prince can ascend the throne of Great Britain) refer to Duke Albrecht as King Albert I of England.

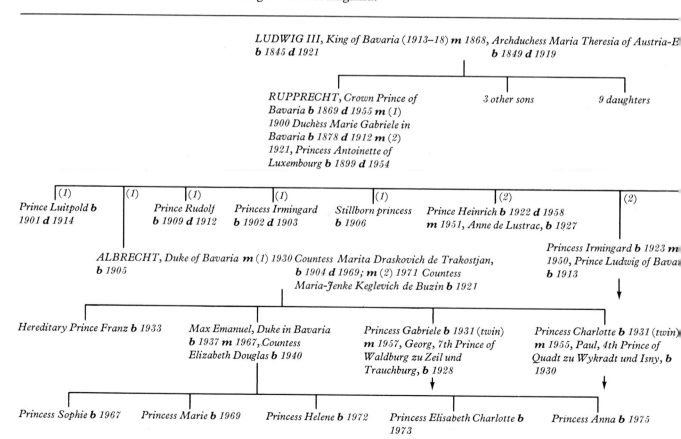

LUDWIG III, King of Bavaria (1913–18) *m* 1868, Archduchess Maria Theresia of Austria-E
b 1845 *d* 1921   *b* 1849 *d* 1919

RUPPRECHT, Crown Prince of Bavaria *b* 1869 *d* 1955 *m* (1) 1900 Duchèss Marie Gabriele in Bavaria *b* 1878 *d* 1912 *m* (2) 1921, Princess Antoinette of Luxembourg *b* 1899 *d* 1954 — 3 other sons — 9 daughters

(1) Prince Luitpold *b* 1901 *d* 1914

(1) Prince Rudolf *b* 1909 *d* 1912

(1) Princess Irmingard *b* 1902 *d* 1903

(1) Stillborn princess *b* 1906

(1) ALBRECHT, Duke of Bavaria *m* (1) 1930 Countess Marita Draskovich de Trakostjan, *b* 1904 *d* 1969; *m* (2) 1971 Countess Maria-Jenke Keglevich de Buzin *b* 1921 — *b* 1905

(2) Prince Heinrich *b* 1922 *d* 1958 *m* 1951, Anne de Lustrac, *b* 1927

(2) Princess Irmingard *b* 1923 *m* 1950, Prince Ludwig of Bavar *b* 1913

Hereditary Prince Franz *b* 1933

Max Emanuel, Duke in Bavaria *b* 1937 *m* 1967, Countess Elizabeth Douglas *b* 1940

Princess Gabriele *b* 1931 (twin) *m* 1957, Georg, 7th Prince of Waldburg zu Zeil und Trauchburg, *b* 1928

Princess Charlotte *b* 1931 (twin) *m* 1955, Paul, 4th Prince of Quadt zu Wykradt und Isny, *b* 1930

Princess Sophie *b* 1967   Princess Marie *b* 1969   Princess Helene *b* 1972   Princess Elisabeth Charlotte *b* 1973   Princess Anna *b* 1975

Albrecht, Duke of Bavaria (second from right), Wittelsbach pretender to the throne of Bavaria and Stuart pretender to the throne of Great Britain, lives at the family showplace, Schloss Nymphenburg, Munich, and looks what he is: a very distinguished, private gentleman in his seventies, the father of four children. Multilingual, he insists whenever possible on speaking the language of whatever guest he has. Maria-Jenke, his second wife (right), is a talented painter under the name Jenke Keglevich.

Franz, Hereditary Prince of Bavaria, pictured here with Princess Maria Gabriella of Italy, is Duke Albrecht's eldest son and heir. Unmarried, he lives in Munich and is a respected art expert, a talent he built into a career, but now enjoys more as a hobby.

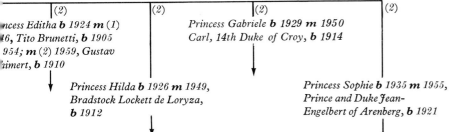

Max Emanuel, Duke in Bavaria and Prince of Bavaria is the second son of Albrecht, Duke of Bavaria and also the adopted heir of the junior branch of the family known as the ducal line, hence the unwieldy titles.

*Many buildings have been inspired by
Versailles, and Herrenchiemsee, above,
built after the French Palace's style
by Ludwig II, deserves the comparison
in many respects. There was no
stinting on the general décor, and the
mirror gallery at Herrenchiemsee, right,
has a slight advantage as a spectacle for
the present day visitor because it is
complete with its thirty-six chandeliers
and its forty-eight candelabra and its
magnificent banquettes along each wall.
Herrenchiemsee also has a show-stopping
entrance and colourful, truly Grand
Staircase inspired by the Ambassador's
Staircase at Versailles, a work of art
in itself. The place is Ludwig's tribute
to the Bourbon kings of France, whom
he so extravagantly admired.*

Indeed, Albrecht of Bavaria, like his father Crown Prince Rupprecht,
traces his Stuart descent twice over: through Charles II of England's
sister Minette; and through Liselotte, the grandchild of Elisabeth, Winter
Queen of Bohemia. Both Minette and Liselotte were married, in turn, to
Louis XIV's brother, called Monsieur. He did not care for his *Mesdames*,
but dutifully fathered children on each. Two of their descendants married,
one of which, a daughter, became the wife of the last Ludwig of Bavaria,
the mother of Crown Prince Rupprecht and the grandmother of Duke
Albrecht.

Prince Rupprecht used to remind the world of his Stuart blood by
dressing his children in Stuart tartan and by laying an annual wreath by the
statue of James I in Munich. Duke Albrecht does not lay wreaths and
neither presses nor denies the Stuart claim—which in any case never
causes Queen Elizabeth of Great Britain loss of sleep: she is on excellent
terms with her Bavarian cousins several times removed.

In one way or another, the Wittelsbachs are linked with almost every
European royal family, but they mostly intermarried with the Habsburgs,
especially when the Reformation reduced the catholic marriage market.
Earlier, in the days when there had been Wittelsbach Emperors, they had
of course had the pick of all Europe's feudal heiresses. Judiciously chosen

brides, as much as conquest and purchase, greatly added to their possessions, which came to include large portions of Austria, Germany and the Netherlands. The Wittelsbachs also became Margraves of Brandenburg, but soon sold this land complete with Berlin: it was a poor sandy place, and a drain on their resources.

Perhaps the dynasty is best remembered for its builders. Ferdinand Maria, a seventeenth-century elector of Bavaria, began the tradition. Determined to keep Bavaria neutral in the struggle for power between the Austrian Habsburgs and the Bourbons of France, he accepted money from both, and invested it in buildings, such as Munich's magnificent Schloss Nymphenburg.

His son Max Emanuel, who succeeded in 1679, another great builder, liked to think of himself as an even greater warrior, although he was thought to overestimate his military talents. He keenly went to all the wars but did not invariably finish them on the side he had first joined. One of his most spectacular exploits of this sort was in the War of the Spanish Succession, in which both the Emperor's grandson the Archduke Charles and Louis XIV's grandson, Philippe, Duke of Anjou claimed the crown of Spain, both being nephews of Spain's late King Carlos II. The crown would, by common consent, have gone to Max Emanuel's son, had that little prince—chosen not because his claim was the strongest but because his house was the weakest of the three—outlived the childless King of Spain. However, the child died in 1699. Carlos, perfectly exasperated by new plans to partition his empire left it entirely to Philippe of Anjou.

Even before Louis XIV had presented his grandson in his new role— "Messieurs, voila le roi d'Espagne"—to his astonished court, the Archduke Charles had rushed off to Spain to stake his claim. France, naturally, supported Philippe, and Europe went to war. Max Emanuel started off on the side of the Emperor, but in 1703 sold his alliance to Louis XIV. The battle of Hochstadt, which saw him victorious, and that of Blenheim, where French and Bavarians were crushingly defeated by Marlborough and Prince Eugene of Savoy, were both fought on Bavarian soil. Max Emanuel was banned from the Empire, and became the governor of the Spanish Netherlands. When the war fizzled out in 1714 because the

Neuschwanstein, in the foothills of the Bavarian Alps, is a monument to Ludwig II's obsession with Wagner: built by him as an imaginary setting for Lohengrin. A celebrated tourist attraction, it is described as fairy-tale, wonderful or humourous. In reality, it is a heavy-handed fake devised in a deadly serious manner. The exterior is all breathtaking Walt Disney, pure fantasy air-brush painting. Inside, it is suffocatingly Methodist chapel— fumed oak pews, reception rooms like registry offices, foyers like waiting rooms in Aberdeen. The guest bedrooms are actually high-class isolation cells, and open on to a corridor the width of the Champs Elysées.

Max Emanuel, Duke and Elector

139

Nymphenburg, on the outskirts of Munich, is the chef-d'oeuvre of the Wittlelsbach real estate. It is still inhabited by the Dukes of Bavaria, money, apparently, being no object. It consists of a massive central block with, as wings, two-storey satellite buildings extending in a line which continues the façade so that the frontage is almost equal to the garden facade of Versailles. The whole of the central block is five and a half storeys high and the great hall in this portion of the building is a full three storeys high.

Nymphenburg's red drawing room is typical of the raffiné *elegance of the interiors. This true stylishness is unusual for a Bavarian palace and the rooms are, therefore, the only ones in any of these palaces which display pictures and furniture to advantage. One can imagine that Ludwig II was bored to distraction in the place.*

Archduke Charles became Emperor Charles VI, things returned to normal. Philippe was officially recognized as the rightful King of Spain, and the Elector of Bavaria was allowed to return home.

During his spell in the north, Max Emanuel had discovered, in the tiny shape of Cuvillies, a positive genius in the decorative arts. This Flemish dwarf, no more than thirteen years old when Max Emanuel had spotted him, now came to Bavaria to create the Amalienburg in the park of the Nymphenburg, the Residenz Theatre, the famous *Ahnengalerie* and the *Reiche Zimmer* in the *Residenz*. All these wonders are tangible memorials to Maximilian Emanuel's beloved *gloire*.

Max Emanuel's son and successor, Karl Albrecht, disputed the Pragmatic Sanctions by which the Emperor Charles VI had hoped to secure the imperial crown for his daughter Maria Theresa. He unsuccessfully went to war, and was bailed out by Frederick the Great of Prussia, the future Emperor. Three years later Karl Albrecht died and the imperial throne reverted to the Habsburgs, with the full consent of his son, the new Elector of Bavaria. This was Maximilian III Joseph, who lived in great style though surrounded by Jesuit priests. He was the last of his line: when he died in 1777, a death hastened by his doctors' insistence that he swallow an image of the virgin to ensure his recovery, the succession went to the Elector Palatine, Karl Theodor.

Karl Theodor died without legitimate sons, and was succeeded by his cousin Maximilian IV Joseph. While this prince had served with the French army in Strasburg, he had met one of those curious, footloose figures who put their talents at the disposal of princely patrons: Maximilian's protegé was an Anglo-American genius, to whom a friend once referred as Mr. Secretary-Colonel-Admiral-Philosopher Thompson. This superman had borne the first three titles in the service of Britain; he was a philosopher throughout his career, and a fellow of the English Royal Society to boot. Maximilian invited him to Bavaria, Thompson accepted, and, already knighted by George III of England, arrived at Munich where he was to be created a count of the Holy Roman Empire. Remembered as Count Rumford (the father of thermo-dynamics) he became the re-or-

ganiser of the army, which was a shambles, and as the social reformer who cleaned up Munich, housing and feeding a multitude of beggars in an institution set up for the purpose—the forerunner of all soup kitchens. He also improved Munich's amenities by transforming the marshland at the bank of the Isar into the famous English garden.

He had left by the time Maximilian IV Joseph became King Maximilian I of a Bavaria which had been handsomely rounded out, thanks to Napoleon, by many square miles. Maximilian appeared at his coronation, having not only signed a treaty of alliance but also having forged a further bond between himself and the Emperor. For Maximilian's daughter Augusta had married Eugene de Beauharnais, Napoleon's adopted son, and although this had looked like a friendship that would last forever, just before the great battle of the nations at Leipzig, which ended Napoleonic rule in Germany, Maximilian deserted Napoleon and returned to the bosom of the allies. This established Bavaria as Germany's most powerful kingdom after Prussia.

Maximilian's son, King Ludwig I, succeeded him in 1825. He was a victim of the famous, brooding Wittelsbach melancholia and eccentricity; a character full of contradiction: romantic in spirit; highly practical, especially in money matters; extravagant but also so parsimonious that the palace cooks had to do without onions when these were dear. The Hellenic age was this prince's passion: it was he who gave his capital the statues of the Glyptothek, and the neo-classical wonders which changed its face.

By one of those curious twists of fate, the Hellenic Ludwig's second son had, in 1832, the offer of the throne of Greece—Russia, England, and France being at last more anxious to see an independent Greece than in earlier days, when Byron, among others, fought for its freedom. The only person to whom no one seriously objected was a Prince of Bavaria. Duly, deaf Prince Otto, aged seventeen, entered the capital of Greece, which had been established in Nauplia by the freedom fighters. He at once determined to move it to Athens. Since only ramshackle cottages nestled at the base of the Acropolis, all the neo-classical architects of Munich were now bidden to transfer their attentions from the "new Athens" to the actual spot that

Schleissheim, near Munich, built between 1701 and 1704, is so unrestrainedly gorgeous that the eye has difficulty navigating the decorative detail. The colour is glistening white, with a red tile roof. The staircase in the Great Hall almost outdoes the classic of its type at the Residenz in Wurzburg. *Yet there is a railway and station almost at the door and structures having little or nothing to do with the Palace obstruct the view of the main façade.*

Ludwig I

141

Linderhof, built in the time of Otto the Magnificent, is the first really sumptuous and striking example of the German neo-Baroque. Nearly everyone goes into raptures over it, but those who do not share such feelings regard it as just a little cage of a villa. They consider that the fine setting disguises the fact that the exterior suggests the presence inside of a casino and dance hall; that it is stylistically perverse and the playfulness usually present in this style is missing. However, the gardens are in the main successful. Particularly charming are the steps like swooping peacocks's tails which ripple gracefully from the carriage drive down to the reflecting pool.

had provided their inspiration, and the Greek capital rose in Germanic neo-classical splendour.

Otto's father Ludwig, alas, had long since also been forced to relinquish his throne, his mistress Lola Montez, née Marie Gilbert, having been his undoing. For all that he had always assured his wife that "of all I know, I find only you worthy of being my wife", he never could resist a pretty face. Indeed, he assured a maximum of temptation for himself by being so rude to ladies wearing fashionable veils, that they became adept at hurriedly sweeping them aside when he was seen approaching in the street: he was in the habit of walking about, quite unregally, in concertina trousers carrying a huge umbrella under the impression that his subjects adored him. However, his government had grown increasingly repressive, alienating Bavaria's liberal elements, while Lola, the latest love of his life, whom he had met about the time that he had reached his sixtieth birthday, alienated his conservative supporters: they thought her a radical and knew that he was putty in her hands. With the 1848 revolution, riots broke out in Munich. Ludwig offered reforms, but it was too late. Outliving his abdication by twenty years, he survived his son King Maximilian II Joseph who died in 1864, leaving a widow, Princess Marie of Prussia, and two sons.

Queen Victoria and her daughter Vicky of Prussia both worried about Ludwig, the nineteen-year old heir: "for that poor boy to have to become king, and always kept like a schoolboy", they exclaimed, but they heard

142

that he was "as amiable as his mother, poor Mariechen . . . left all alone and not of an independent disposition." The Queen Mother of Bavaria, whom Ludwig disliked, was a Hohenzollern. She became a Catholic in order to marry Maximilian of Bavaria, and was, in the opinion of Queen Victoria and her daughter, "not very bright, and always a little cracked on religion". In the opinion of others, it was she who had brought into the Wittelsbach family the fatal gene which drove her sons mad. While it is highly debatable that Ludwig II was ever mad in the sense claimed by the powers anxious to remove him, it cannot be denied that he was exceedingly odd. As for Otto, the younger boy, he was to become hopelessly and clinically insane.

Ludwig is famous for his friendship with Wagner, and for his castles. He had adored Wagner ever since he had been over-excited by hearing Lohengrin as a sixteenth birthday treat. Soon after his accession, the King sent the composer his photograph, a present, and an offer of help in the realization of his work. Wagner's operas were expensive to mount, and musically so revolutionary that there were very few people to appreciate them. The philistines of Munich were shocked at the vast sums put at the composer's disposal. Wagner caricatures abounded: satirists called him Lolus in memory of poor Miss Montez. Decidedly, the composer was not popular and nor was his friendship with the King. Ludwig in turn, proved his dislike of his subjects and his capital by taking to the mountain castle of

Ludwig II, aged twenty-two

143

Hohenschwangau, rebuilt in gingerbread Gothic by his late father. Not far from it, Ludwig was to create Neuschwanstein. It was finished only after Ludwig's passion for Wagner had faded: indeed, the King was never to see its completion. But other building projects were maturing meanwhile: Linderhof, and Herrenchiemsee rose massively, splendidly, ornately and exquisitely gilded.

As has frequently been pointed out, the outcry over the expense of all this building eventually proved absurd. Bavaria itself became the beneficiary of the King's activities, strange though some may seem, as he himself had foreseen when he said "long after the works of statesmen have passed away, the work of artists will continue to gladden the hearts of men."

In affairs of state, Ludwig was more astute than is usually believed. He was all for Bavarian independence, and would have preferred Bavarian neutrality in the wars of his reign, which were all of Bismarck's making, a result of that statesman's grand design for Prussian supremacy in Germany. But it was not always possible to keep out of the general *melée*. In the Prusso-Austrian war of 1860, Bavaria fought on the side of Austria, but victorious Prussia was strangely lenient after the fighting was over.

Bismarck, in fact, had other plans for Bavaria: he had mapped out her King's part as that of "an unprejudiced promoter of German interest". In this role, it fell to Ludwig as the second most powerful king in Germany to write a letter begging King Wilhelm, who was his uncle, to allow himself be be proclaimed German emperor. This was the famous *Kaiserbrief* which led to the creation of the Second Reich in 1871 and its consequence for Bavaria was special privileges, including the promise of the imperial crown should the Prussian line unaccountably die out.

Queen Victoria's daughter, after a visit to Munich—she described the city as "a vast museum"—was surprised that Ludwig felt there should be two emperors, a war-emperor: Kaiser Wilhelm; a peace-emperor: himself. She also observed that he had "a golden cloak made, with white doves, and Charlemagne's crown. His fancies are so childlike" and she reported that Ludwig, shockingly, had "lost all esteem by the company he chooses". Indeed, servants and actors were hardly fit society for a reigning monarch, even if his emotional attachments to them were not generally known. There was, of course, gossip. Very rarely, there was also gossip concerning women, but the only woman at all close to Ludwig was his cousin, Elisabeth, Empress of Austria, of the collateral, ducal Wittelsbach line. She proved a faithful friend and confidante, for all that Ludwig, as a young man, had broken off his engagement to her sister Sophie, having early on decided that marriage was not for him. The Empress herself had her share of Wittelsbach eccentricity, but it was nothing compared to that of Ludwig, who, towards the end of his reign, led an almost exclusively nocturnal existence: Bavarian mountain villagers became used to being woken by the rumble of his gilded coach or the sound of the bells of his swan-shaped sleigh as he went on midnight rides.

Ludwig's brother suffered a total breakdown in 1871—"too sad, he barks like a dog all day long", reported Queen Victoria's daughter. Perhaps the Bavarian ministers, who had decided by 1886 to get rid of Ludwig, really felt that he was going the same way. They appointed a leading alienist, Dr von Gudden, to report on the King's mental condition. He duly pronounced him insane without the formality of an examination. Ludwig's uncle, Prince Luitpold, was appointed regent. When a commission, consisting of Gudden and some other medical men, first appeared

Ludwig II in his thirties

144

at Neuschwanstein to seize Ludwig, peasants armed with scythes and axes repulsed them. The second time, the doctors were successful, and took the King to the castle of Berg. On the day of his arrival, Ludwig and Gudden set out for a walk in the grounds and were never seen alive again. Both their bodies were found in the lake, and no one to this day knows exactly what happened.

The mad Otto succeeded Ludwig but Prince Luitpold reigned for him as regent until dying aged ninety-one in 1912, when his son Ludwig, himself a venerable old gentleman, succeeded him. Although well-liked there was something of an outcry when he assumed the title of king; mad Otto was still alive and indeed lived on until 1916.

In November 1918 came the Spartakus rising, and Ludwig's abdication. He survived this by three years, but his Queen was broken by the hardships endured on the family's flight from the revolutionaries and died a few months later. When the communist reign of terror ended the family returned to Munich. In 1921 Crown Prince Rupprecht became head of the family. In 1933, there was a move to restore him as a means of counteracting Hitler's influence in Bavaria, but nothing came of it. During the Second World War, he was forced to leave Bavaria and he went into hiding in Italy, while the Nazis sent his second wife, Princess Antoinette, a sister of Grand Duchess Charlotte of Luxembourg, to Buchenwald. She never recovered from this experience and died in 1954 at the early age of fifty-four.

Rupprecht, more than thirty years her senior, survived her by a year, and became a legend in his own lifetime. He had the culture and intellectual brilliance of the Wittelsbachs, being in particular an expert on Indian and Chinese art. He was also a man of splendid physique, who swam and climbed mountains until he was eighty. His Bavarians loved him, flocking out to the Nymphenburg on his eighty-fifth birthday to sing the Bavarian national anthem, and to cheer as he acknowledged their congratulations.

Crown Prince Rupprecht

145

HANOVER
Windsor's Cradle

Prince Ernst August of Hanover, Duke of Brunswick and Lüneburg, head of the House of Hanover which became the reigning house of Great Britain in the eighteenth century, is the great-grandson of the last King of Hanover, blind King Georg, who lost his throne in 1866.

Besides being the Duke of Brunswick and Lüneburg, Ernst August, through his English connection, is a Prince of Great Britain and Ireland. Indeed, he set out to establish his historical right to be a British subject in 1955 in a series of legal actions which raised the irrelevant, if curious point that if he was indeed British, had he not committed high treason by serving in the German army in the Second World War? The claim was eventually recognized. He and his wife, the former Princess Ortrud of Schleswig-Holstein-Sonderburg-Glücksburg, are on good terms with the English royal family—a relationship quite unaffected by the fact that a fringe group

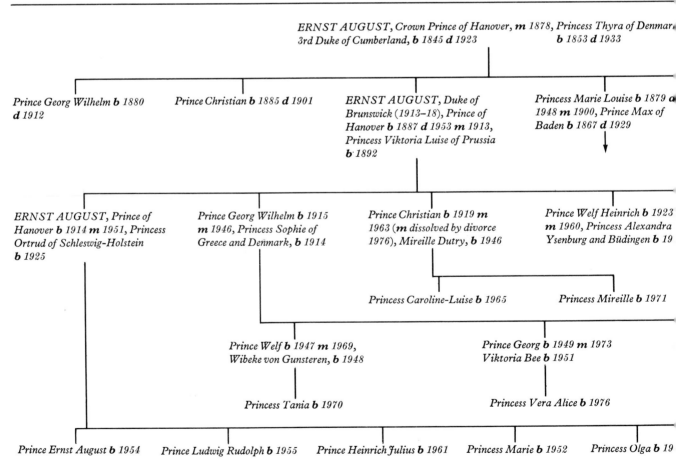

ERNST AUGUST, Crown Prince of Hanover, *m 1878*, Princess Thyra of Denmark, 3rd Duke of Cumberland, *b 1845 d 1923* — *b 1853 d 1933*

Prince Georg Wilhelm *b 1880 d 1912*

Prince Christian *b 1885 d 1901*

ERNST AUGUST, Duke of Brunswick (1913–18), Prince of Hanover *b 1887 d 1953 m 1913*, Princess Viktoria Luise of Prussia *b 1892*

Princess Marie Louise *b 1879 d 1948 m 1900*, Prince Max of Baden *b 1867 d 1929*

ERNST AUGUST, Prince of Hanover *b 1914 m 1951*, Princess Ortrud of Schleswig-Holstein *b 1925*

Prince Georg Wilhelm *b 1915 m 1946*, Princess Sophie of Greece and Denmark, *b 1914*

Prince Christian *b 1919 m 1963 (m dissolved by divorce 1976)*, Mireille Dutry, *b 1946*

Prince Welf Heinrich *b 1923 m 1960*, Princess Alexandra Ysenburg and Büdingen *b 19__*

Princess Caroline-Luise *b 1965*

Princess Mireille *b 1971*

Prince Welf *b 1947 m 1969*, Wibeke von Gunsteren, *b 1948*

Prince Georg *b 1949 m 1973* Viktoria Bee *b 1951*

Princess Tania *b 1970*

Princess Vera Alice *b 1976*

Prince Ernst August *b 1954*

Prince Ludwig Rudolph *b 1955*

Prince Heinrich Julius *b 1961*

Princess Marie *b 1952*

Princess Olga *b 19__*

of Hanoverian legitimists went so far as to recognize him as King Ernst August of England in 1953.

The family's success story began in the early seventeenth century when, in order to avoid endless divisions and subdivisions, a family compact stipulated that only one of the then reigning duke's four sons would inherit land, while the others received appanages instead. Lots were drawn, and the youngest brother won, becoming the inheriting, and marrying duke. Lacking land, the others were in no position to found rival lines of their own, and thus strengthened, the junior line of Brunswick-Lüneburg soon outstripped the senior line of Brunswick in power. In the reign of the marrying duke's son, the duchy became very important indeed.

In the *Rittersaal* of the palace in Hanover, which the marrying duke had first made his residence, his son Ernst August received tangible proof of his state's rise in the world: the electoral bonnet which the Emperor had been persuaded to send from Vienna. An electorship brought privileges which, besides that of electing emperors whenever that post fell vacant, were little short of royal. Although, what with bribes, promises of troops and strings of the cream-coloured Hanoverian horses, Ernst August's new cap of state was to be called the most expensive bonnet in history, it was worth it.

The scene of his installation as an elector was appropriately splendid. All the court was in new clothes, and there was new gilt on the armorial bearings of the Guelfs, ancestors whom the Brunswick-Lüneburgs shared with the Italian House of Este, traceable to the tenth century.

The new elector liked to contemplate his illustrious forebears, who, in the middle ages had ruled over territories stretching from the North Sea to

Ernst August, head of the Royal House of Hanover, uses the title Prince of Hanover, assumed by his father. His ancestor, George I, became the King of Great Britain in 1714 and until the death of William IV in 1837, both countries had the same, Hanoverian monarchs. Then the succession in Britain passed to Queen Victoria. Hanover barred female sovereigns, so William's brother became her king. From then on, the crowns were separated, but had England's constitution, like Hanover's, forbidden female sovereigns Ernst August would today be King of Great Britain.

ncess Alexandra **b** *1882* **d** *1963*
1904, Friedrich Franz IV,
and Duke of Mecklenburg-
werin **b** *1882* **d** *1945*

Princess Olga
b *1884* **d** *1958*

incess Friederike (Frederika)
1917 **m** *1938, Paul I, King of*
e Hellenes **b** *1901* **d** *1964*

incess Friederike **b** *1954*

rincess Alexandra **b** *1959*

Heir to the Prince of Hanover is his eldest son, Ernst August, also styled Prince of Hanover, here photographed dancing with a younger sister. He lives in London, where he toils away in the film world: if will has anything to do with it, Ernst has every chance of becoming a successful film director. One of his achievements has been gaining permission to film inside the palace of Versailles.

The Prince of Hanover's wife Ortrud is famed in royal circles for her outspokenness, and finds the intrusions of the press particularly provoking, especially those of photographers. She and her husband are on good terms with the British royal family and join them on certain occasions. Queen Elizabeth was pleased to allow Ortrud to borrow the Hanoverian wedding crown for her marriage in 1951.

147

Perhaps the most charming, and famed, of this family's dwellings was Herrenhausen, a summer palace near the capital built between 1692 and 1710, with later additions. The inspiration for the uncluttered design of this low, wide building with its evenly spaced windows was Dutch rather than French, probably because the Hanover family had close ties with the House of Orange. Pride of the place were its formal gardens, with their thirteen miles of carefully trimmed hedges. Alas, Herrenhausen was destroyed by bombs in 1943.

the Adriatic. The most splendid of them, Henry the Lion, who first walled and fortified the city of Hanover itself, had long been a legend. And the two men were linked by an interesting historic parallel: the Lion's wife had been Matilda, an English princess; Ernst August's wife was Sophie, the granddaughter of King James I of England. Unlike the Lion, however, Ernst August had unwittingly stumbled into his British connection. Indeed, when he had unenthusiastically married the penniless daughter of Elizabeth Stuart, the Winter Queen, who was to guess that the bride's meagre dowry contained, as it were, the crown of Great Britain? The restoration of her cousin Charles II still lay ahead, and so indeed did the birth of Queen Anne, whose failure to produce heirs ultimately brought the

succession to Sophie and her issue.

In the event, Sophie died, in the famous garden of Herrenhausen, a few weeks before Queen Anne. It was her son, George Louis, who became the first Hanovarian monarch of Great Britain in 1714. He arrived with his son George Augustus; his daughter-in-law Caroline; two favourites, called the Beanpole and the Elephant (one of whom may have been his half-sister) and two granddaughters. His grandson was left in Germany and so was his estranged wife, Sophie Dorothea.

George I, though a hardworking, dutiful monarch of Britain, was Hanover's elector first and foremost. His death occurred in a carriage a few miles out of his native city. In the reign of George II things, from the

Sophie, Electress of Hanover

British point of view, hardly improved. He was absent from England for so often and for so long that a wit felt inspired to post a handbill proclaiming "his Hanoverian Majesty designs to visit his British dominions for three months in the spring." George III, however, glorying in the name of Briton, never visited Hanover at all. He merely sent an assortment of his sons to what Queen Victoria was to call "the cradle of the family": some to the University of Göttingen that George II had founded and some to complete their military training in Hanover's army.

In the absence of their Elector-King, the presence of the princes was welcome proof to the Hanoverians that they had not been abandoned by their ruling family. Nevertheless, they saw with equanimity the departure, in 1803, of the King's representative and youngest son, Adolphus, Duke of Cambridge, who had vainly tried to rouse Hanover against Napoleon when the country preferred to remain neutral. The Hanoverians became willing subjects of Jérôme, the Emperor's brother who was made King of Westphalia, and Adolphus departed to return as governor-general only when Hanover was made a kingdom after the fall of the Bonapartes. In his first speech to the Assembly, he stressed that the House of Guelf was "ever known for its justice and moderation", and promised reforms to the medieval constitution. These, however, had to wait until Adolphus became Viceroy, with full powers of government under his brother King William IV of England.

In 1833, Hanover duly had its new constitution. All the country's officials, including the Professors at the University, swore the required oath of allegiance. It was a step in the right direction as far as the liberal elements were concerned, but short-lived, since all hope of reform ended in 1837 when William IV was succeeded, in England, by Queen Victoria.

Because of Salic law—a code introduced by the Salian Franks in the fifth century, by which women could not succeed as sovereigns—was still in operation in Hanover, Prince Adolphus' elder brother Ernst August became King.

He was thought to be the very wickedest of Queen Victoria's wicked uncles—there were few villainies of which he had not been accused. Deeply loathed in England, even by the members of his own family, he mostly lived abroad: not because he minded about what he called "the general hoot against me", but because no one in the royal family would speak to his wife. The Duke of Cumberland, however, was devoted to her, as he was to the only surviving child of the marriage, Prince Georg, a slender, handsome youth very unlike his terrifying father, who was hideously battle scarred, with only one useful eye. Sadly, an accident in 1832 had also impaired Prince Georg's sight. "To see that lovely creature led about . . . so good, so dear, it is enough to break one's heart", said an aunt. Prince Georg's blindness was a grief to his father, especially since it might make him less die-hard in politics.

The new King of Hanover had no time for liberal ideas. When he left England in 1837 to take up his new post, he prudently first swore allegiance to the Queen of England, and refused to give up his apartments in Kensington Palace or a great many of his mother's jewels—in case his stay among "those damned radicals" should prove to be short.

In the event, his Hanoverian reign was rather a success, though there was unrest when, upon arrival, he rescinded the 1833 constitution. The trouble emanated less from the solid burgers, many of who had regarded Adolphus' government as a *Schlendrianocratie*—a bumbleocracy—than from in-

Ernst August I

tellectuals, especially those at Göttingen. Professor Jacob Grimm of fairy-tale fame and six of his colleagues refused point blank to swear allegiance to the pre-1833 constitution, which Ernst August now revived. The point, the Göttingen Seven explained, was a moral one. It was not that they objected to swearing a new oath, only to breaking the previous one. The King sacked them at once. This led to student demonstrations, riots, arrests, and exile for Grimm and his friends. The King, observing that "dancers, whores and professors are easily bought", found new incumbents for the vacant chairs and soon prided himself on commanding everyone's respect, including that of the radicals—"they know I play no dirty tricks". In fact he did grow quite popular. When, in the revolutionary days of 1848, the disaffected crowd, gathered around the palace, learned that the King would listen to any reasonable complaints, but if demands went too far he would return to England and take his Crown Prince with him, revolution was averted.

In time, even Ernst August had to give a little. He quietly revived the 1833 constitution, but as for the new-fangled Prussian-inspired *Zollverein*—a customs' union—he would have nothing to do with it, a policy which put Hanover at an economic disadvantage. Nevertheless, when King Ernst August died in 1851, Hanover put up a statue to him, inscribed "the father of the country".

Blind King Georg V largely followed in his father's arch-conservative footsteps. In his reign, Hanover did join the *Zollverein*, but when it came to making the choice between Austria and Prussia, struggling for hegemony in northern Germany, he supported the old order, Austria being the traditional leader of the Germanies. In consequence Prussia swallowed up Hanover and its King in 1866. King Georg retired with his wife to Gmunden in Austria, re-assuming the title of Duke of Cumberland, and dying in 1878. His son, Ernst August, lived the life of a country gentleman in Gmunden, and was forced to continue to do so even after inheriting the Duchy of Brunswick on the extinction of the senior line. Bismarck, still iron-willed in spite of the fact that Prussia's supremacy had been sealed in 1871 by the transformation of its King into the German Emperor, had prevented him from taking up the inheritance.

The peace between the Guelfs and the Hohenzollerns was made in the next generation, when the grandson of the blind King married the daughter of the Kaiser. This match came about in amazing circumstances: the groom's elder brother had been despatched, in 1912, to attend the funeral of his grandfather, the King of Denmark. Before setting off, he dreamt that he was attending his own, and spotted two Prussian officers among the mourners. Nothing seemed more far-fetched, but on the journey to Denmark, the Prince's car crashed, he was killed, and as his death occurred on Prussian soil, the Kaiser sent two officers to represent him at the funeral.

This demanded a visit of thanks, and the Cumberlands, who had always driven through northern German without leaving their seats so as not to set foot on Prussian soil, reluctantly sent their surviving son Ernst August to Berlin. Before leaving, he and Princess Viktoria Luise had fallen in love. On marriage, the young man renounced his claim to Hanover, but was allowed by the Kaiser to assume the title of Brunswick, which his father had ceded to him. The couple's children, besides the present Prince of Hanover (which title his father re-assumed in 1931), include Frederika, Queen of Greece and Prince George, who married a sister of the Duke of Edinburgh.

Ernst August, Duke of Brunswick

SAXONY

Inspirers of Dresden

Head of the Royal House of Saxony is Prince Maria Emanuel, Margrave of Meissen, grandson of the last King, Friedrich August III. The Prince had a turbulent early life: he was imprisoned, aged eighteen, for holding anti-Nazi views, but managed to escape both the death sentence and capture by Soviet troops when towards the end of the Second World War they seized the prison where he was being held.

His ancestors acquired the Margraviate of Meissen in the eleventh century, and became Dukes and Electors of Saxony in the fourteenth. The first Elector was Friedrich the Quarrelsome, who was succeeded by his son Friedrich the Gentle, whose sons Ernst and Albert, also great quarrellers, finally divided the country between them, founding the Ernestine and the Albertine lines. The Ernestines ruled over the Electorate and the immediate Saxon possessions; the Albertines over Meissen and the rest.

Ernst's son Friedrich, called the Wise, founded Wittenberg University

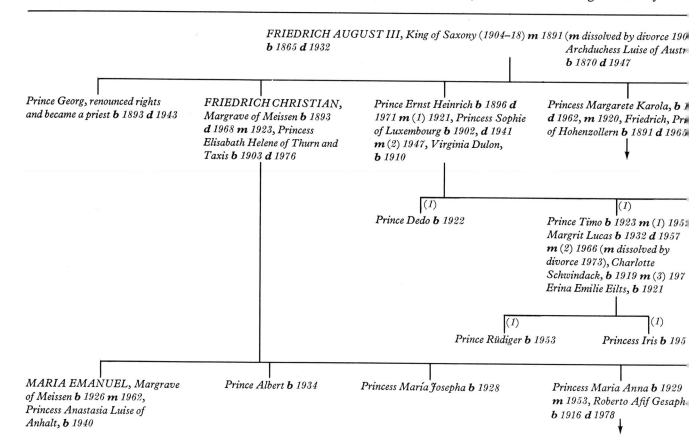

FRIEDRICH AUGUST III, King of Saxony (1904–18) **m** 1891 (**m** dissolved by divorce 190
b 1865 **d** 1932
Archduchess Luise of Austr
b 1870 **d** 1947

Prince Georg, renounced rights and became a priest **b** 1893 **d** 1943

FRIEDRICH CHRISTIAN, Margrave of Meissen **b** 1893 **d** 1968 **m** 1923, Princess Elisabath Helene of Thurn and Taxis **b** 1903 **d** 1976

Prince Ernst Heinrich **b** 1896 **d** 1971 **m** (1) 1921, Princess Sophie of Luxembourg **b** 1902, **d** 1941 **m** (2) 1947, Virginia Dulon, **b** 1910

Princess Margarete Karola, **b** 1962, **m** 1920, Friedrich, Pr of Hohenzollern **b** 1891 **d** 1965

(1)
Prince Dedo **b** 1922

(1)
Prince Timo **b** 1923 **m** (1) 195 Margrit Lucas **b** 1932 **d** 1957 **m** (2) 1966 (**m** dissolved by divorce 1973), Charlotte Schwindack, **b** 1919 **m** (3) 197 Erina Emilie Eilts, **b** 1921

(1)
Prince Rüdiger **b** 1953

(1)
Princess Iris **b** 195

MARIA EMANUEL, Margrave of Meissen **b** 1926 **m** 1962, Princess Anastasia Luise of Anhalt, **b** 1940

Prince Albert **b** 1934

Princess Maria Josepha **b** 1928

Princess Maria Anna **b** 1929 **m** 1953, Roberto Afif Gesaph **b** 1916 **d** 1978

in 1502, and it was here that Martin Luther, who inspired the Reformation, was Professor of Philosophy. He was Friedrich's guest at the Wartburg, high above Eisenach, while he worked on his German translation of the New Testament. Saxony was indeed the cradle of the Reformation: the Electors became Protestants, and when the time came, went to war for their faith. Indeed, the next head of the Ernestine line was defeated by the Imperial catholic troops at the battle of Muhlberg and was forced to cede the electorship to Moritz, head of the Albertine line.

The Albertine line's capital was Dresden, and it was from here that Saxony was henceforth governed. Two electors named Christian and the first of several Johann Georgs took her in to the Thirty Years' War, which ravaged the land and all but decimated the population; however, Johann George came away in 1648 with larger territories than before.

The next and fourth Johann Georg is mostly famous for being unnecessarily devoted to his mistress, and unnecessarily unkind to his wife. That great gossip Count Pöllnitz dined out for years on a quarrel in which the Elector would have murdered his Electress but for the timely arrival of his brother August, justly called the Strong. August wrenched the sword from his brother's hand, then loosened his grasp from the woman's throat and finally carried him struggling to his chamber.

August the Strong enjoyed displaying his strength. His party tricks included straightening horseshoes with his bare hands, but sometimes he varied the entertainment by holding up two of his trumpeters at arm's length for the duration of a fanfare, or by wrestling with the occasional bear. August succeeded his childless brother in 1694. He was married to a princess of Brandenburg-Bayreuth, but a more determined womanizer it would have been hard to find. He produced countless bastards by battalions of mistresses, one of these being Aurora von Königsmarck. She had

Maria Emanuel, head of the Royal House of Saxony, is one of those great rarities, a practising serendipitist for ever discovering things of interest he was not looking for. He has run across dozens of statues and memorials to famous people of Saxony, and besides being a painter, is an authority on military orders and has published works on art and music. His wife, Anastasia Luise, was born a princess of Anhalt and descends from the family that produced Catherine the Great of Russia. She is shy, but a superb hostess and is interested in miniatures and genealogy. They live at Ennetbaden, the elegant residential area near Baden in Switzerland. The family chose to style itself Dukes of Saxony when the throne was lost in 1918, but Maria Emanuel uses his subsidiary title, Margrave of Meissen, to avoid confusion with several kinsmen who may call themselves Dukes of Saxony.

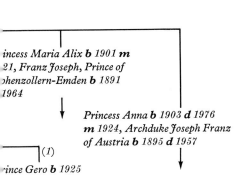

incess Maria Alix b 1901 m
21, Franz Joseph, Prince of
ohenzollern-Emden b 1891
1964

Princess Anna b 1903 d 1976
m 1924, Archduke Joseph Franz
of Austria b 1895 d 1957

(1)
rince Gero b 1925

rincess Mathilde b 1936 m 1968,
rince Johannes Heinrich of
axe-Coburg and Gotha b 1931

August the Strong

arrived in 1695 to ask the Elector's help in her frantic search for her brother, the lover of Sophie Dorothea of Hanover, who had vanished in mysterious circumstances. August was quite unable to help, but promptly fell in love with Aurora. He courted her *a la* Louis XIV.

One day, for instance, she was grandly driven, as if by chance, to the Moritzburg, a palatial hunting lodge. On arrival, the doors were flung open, and a gaggle of courtiers dressed as woodnymphs greeted her in verse. After many allusions to the dawn, Mme Sunrise was bidden to enter and to receive homage from further wood spirits. Chief among these was, of course, the Elector: a tall muscular figure, hung about with hides in his role as Pan. He conducted Aurora to a festive table, where an elegant collation had been set out. During dessert, a stag was seen flying past the window. The party mounted horses and caleches held in readiness, and watched the animal being torn to pieces in the lake. Next, gondolas conveyed the ladies to another bank, where their astonished eyes saw a glittering tent, hung with priceless carpets. Courtiers, dressed in eastern fashion, offered sweetmeats in silver baskets and soon the large figure of the Grand Turk—a vision in jewels—made his entrance. Aurora, alone of all the ladies, was allotted a place on the sofa; the rest settled on the floor to watch the ensuing entertainment provided by suggestive female dancers with jewelled navels. Then it was back to the Moritzburg and so to bed.

In 1697, August the Strong changed his religion. This caused consternation among his Protestant subjects but he reassured them that no persecutions would follow and they soon saw that he had good reason for becoming a Catholic: he put himself in the running for the currently available throne of Poland. Partly by distributing lavish bribes, he was duly elected against strong competition. The new status, and the wars to maintain it, cost a fortune and all but ruined Saxony. When, in 1704, he was deposed in Poland in favour of Stanislas Leszczynski there was a general feeling of despair. In the event, he regained the crown of Poland before his death, which occurred following a drinking-bout in Warsaw: a fitting end for man who had formed an anti-sobriety league.

He left Saxony the richer by Dresden's marvellous Baroque architecture—especially the Zwinger; by the acquisition of pictures; by a vault—the *Grune Gewolbe*—full of priceless *objets d'art* and matching *parures* of every precious stone and by the Meissen Porcelain Manufactory. The reverse of this medal was an immense state debt.

The debts became yet greater in the reign of August III, an even more passionate collector of paintings, and a far less able ruler. It was he who acquired Dresden's pride, the Sistine Madonna, painted by Raphael for the convent of St. Sixtus in Parma. When the painting arrived in Dresden in 1754, legend relates that August pushed away the throne crying "make way for the great Raphael".

August III disastrously left the government of his realm to his favourite, the Count Bruhl, who entered Saxony on the wrong side in the Seven Years War. King and favourite died with a few weeks of each other in 1763. If August III has a claim to fame, besides making Dresden the German Florence and a Mecca for artists, it is that he became the grandfather of no less than seven kings: two Louis and one Charles of France; a Charles and a Ferdinand of The Two Sicilies and Kings Friedrich August I (who also became Grand Duke of Warsaw) and Anton I of Saxony. It was Napoleon who conferred the kingship of Saxony and the Grand Dukedom on Friedrich August, but their association did not work out well for Saxony. At the battle of Leipzig, which ended Napoleon's power in Germany, Friedrich August was captured by the allies, held prisoner, and in 1815 restored to a country diminished by half.

The loss caused the King great dejection: many German princes had also co-operated with Napoleon, but they had been wise enough to desert him in the end. Friedrich August did his best to rebuild the country, ruined yet again by having been a theatre of war. In the process, he instituted a number of reforms which earned him the suffix, the Just. His brother Anton, who succeeded him, took matters further by granting a constitution, but that did not prevent the outbreak of a full-scale revolution in the reign of Anton's heir, Friedrich August II.

Saxony's next King, Johann I, was in his middle fifties when he succeeded, and his successors were his sons Albert and Georg. The latter got on badly with his daughter-in-law, a rebellious Habsburg Archduchess of Tuscany, who claimed Georg had greeted his childless brother's death with the words "at last—I was getting tired of waiting". Crown Princess Luise hated her father-in-law for his bigotry, his bullying ways, his unroyal, knitted stockings and for glaring at her with little cold eyes. He loathed her—for marginally more democratic ways; for laughing at court etiquette; for bicycling in knickerbockers and for general hysteria. Convinced that the incipient madness of the Habsburgs would emerge at full tilt if ever she became Queen of Saxony, he kindly informed her that he had booked her into an expensive *maison de santé*—a euphemism for the lunatic asylum which trouble-making princesses of her generation had learned to dread: too many of them had been quietly removed from too many scenes into these institutions. She ran away, and after her marriage to the good-natured future King Friedrich August III, the last King of Saxony, was annulled, she married an Italian, Signor Toselli. She was forbidden ever to return or to communicate with her husband or her children. Once she did travel to Dresden, incognito, hoping for a family reunion, but was bundled back on to the train by the Chief of Police while loyal Saxons, who had filled her railway carriage with flowers, tearfully begged her to stay. They were, of course, disappointed.

There was disappointment for loyal Saxons, too, when after Friedrich August's forced abdication on the collapse of the German monarchies in 1918, the ex-King was travelling through his former realm by train. It must have been a moving scene when, to loud cheers, he appeared at his carriage window and observed, with the good humour for which he was famous: "I must say, you're a fine bunch of republicans".

Crown Princess Luise of Saxony with Signor Toselli, composer and pianist

WURTTEMBERG
Pomp and Circumstance

Württemberg lies in the south of Germany in the old Province of Swabia. It became a county in the thirteenth century, a duchy in the fifteenth, and a kingdom in 1806. Created, like its neighbour, Bavaria, by Napoleon, it ceased, again like Bavaria, to be a monarchy in the post-war revolutions of 1918. The family now uses its ducal title.

The family fortunes were founded by an eleventh-century warrior knight who settled at the castle of Wirtineberc—also known as Wirtenberg and Wirtemberg—which provided the name for the family and its ever-increasing lands. This castle housed the family until Eberhard, the second count, moved his residence to nearby Stuttgart. From his new seat, he administered territories which had almost doubled in area and included Urach and Teck.

Eberhard the Bearded, the first Duke, also acquired the county of Mömpelgard—which was to be such a useful bargaining counter in the nineteenth century. To save his country from endless divisions, he had it declared indivisible in 1495, and from then on Württemberg passed essentially intact from generation to generation.

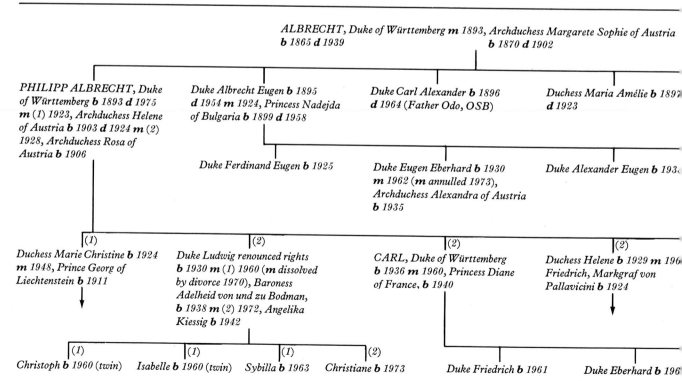

Carl, Duke of Württemberg, is head of the most exclusive of Europe's royal houses. Two branches senior to his, those of Urach and Teck, were disqualified from succession by morganatic marriages. He lives mainly at the family property of Altshausen, near Lake Constance, and his work is operating the estates as a profitable enterprise. Diane, his wife, a daughter of the Count of Paris, is very Gallic, with a finely honed sense of what is *de rigeur*, and what is not.

The Bearded's successor, Duke Ulrich, was one of the princes who protested—hence protestant—against the decision taken by the Diet of Speyer, with its catholic majority, forbidding them to reform their churches and to secularize the belongings of the Roman Catholic Church. In the case of the extravagant Duke Ulrich, it is doubtful that his desire to get his hands on church property were prompted purely by religious zeal: a highly romantic figure (with a *crime de passion* to his credit), he was always in urgent need of funds. Ulrich's reign was long and full of incident: twice expelled from his country, he twice regained it, to introduce reformed doctrines and to endow protestant schools throughout the land.

To these establishments his grandson Duke Christoph added Tubingen's *Collegium Illustre* in 1589. This became the prototype of countless knightly academies designed to raise the tone at German courts by teaching princelings manners and knightly graces. However, in the next century, the court of Stuttgart still failed to meet the exacting standards of its visitors: Electress Sophie of Hanover related that hunting formed the only topic of conversation; that on non-hunting days, meals lasted from morning till night; that the princes engaged in marathon drinking contests

Rosa, Duchess of Württemberg, is the widow of the late Duke Philipp Albrecht. She was his second wife, the first having been Rosa's sister Helene. She is homely and cosy, like a favourite aunt, inviting confidence like an amiable mother confessor.

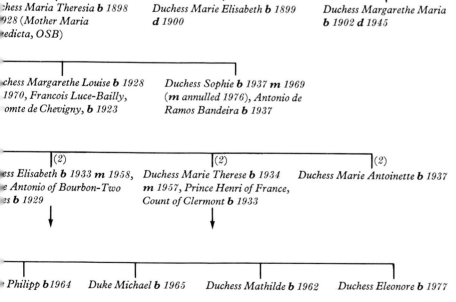

chess Maria Theresia **b** 1898
928 (Mother Maria
edicta, OSB)

Duchess Marie Elisabeth **b** 1899
d 1900

Duchess Margarethe Maria
b 1902 **d** 1945

chess Margarethe Louise **b** 1928
1970, Francois Luce-Bailly,
omte de Chevigny, **b** 1923

Duchess Sophie **b** 1937 **m** 1969
(**m** annulled 1976), Antonio de
Ramos Bandeira **b** 1937

(2)
ess Elisabeth **b** 1933 **m** 1958,
e Antonio of Bourbon-Two
es **b** 1929

(2)
Duchess Marie Therese **b** 1934
m 1957, Prince Henri of France,
Count of Clermont **b** 1933

(2)
Duchess Marie Antoinette **b** 1937

Philipp **b** 1964   Duke Michael **b** 1965   Duchess Mathilde **b** 1962   Duchess Eleonore **b** 1977

The Marquis and Marchioness of Cambridge, who live in England's Cambridgeshire countryside, are members of this royal house, although strictly speaking their German cousins would not recognize them as such. The Marquis descends from Prince Alexander of Württemberg, who in morganatically marrying lost his rights of succession. Through Prince Alexander, the Württembergs are also related to the English royal family: his granddaughter was Queen Mary.

157

Solitude, near Stuttgart, is Württemberg's gross, but nonetheless charming version of Prussia's Sans Souci. The central portion is a heavy, lumbering drum surmounted by a dome which is flat on top. The whole of the round, central portion has elongated windows and above them are prettily conceived round windows, giving the effect of inverted exclamation marks. Separating the windows are gorgeous pilasters. Above, at the roofline, is a top-heavy cornice. The doorway is a variation of the elongated windows, with a great deal of sculptural salad over it.

Karl Eugen, Duke of Württemberg

and that one of them drank her health in one enormous draught, which he spewed up and gallantly downed yet again.

The next Eberhard, called Eberhard Ludwig, in turn earned the criticism of Electress Sophie's niece—she who had become the Duchess of Orléans and lived in France: "A shame that he doesn't defend his country better", she thought when, during his reign, French troops entered Württemberg without resistance. It was the Duke's mother who bought off the invader with 20,000 florins. Informing her son that she had "rid the country of the French scourge" she suggested that he did a little scourging of his own, by delivering the country from his sin. Eberhard Ludwig's sin was called Mme de Gravenitz, whom, in spite of already having a wife, he had married after one of those curious divorces that nobody recognized, least of all his Duchess.

However, in spite of the general disapproval and in spite of his mother's kind offer to furnish proof of the Gravenitz's whoredom, there was no sign of scourging. Eberhard Ludwig remained devoted to the grasping Gravenitz until shortly before he died. When his cousin Karl Alexander succeeded him in 1733, the exchequer was all but empty.

Karl Alexander had three sons, all called Eugen in honour of his hero, the Prince of Savoy. The three Eugens were quickly shipped off to Prussia because the atmosphere at the Regent's court was considered to be too rakish for growing boys by the Margravine of Bayreuth, Frederick the Great's sister, who kept an auntly eye on them. When the first of them, Karl Eugen, returned home to rule it was with a head full of Prussian military ideas. He tripled the army, drilled his soldiers to clockwork perfection, dressed them in Prussian blue and ordered the wearing of moustaches, black, false if necessary. Frederick the Great, no doubt somewhat put out at seeing Württemberg side with Austria in the Seven Years War, called the Duke "my monkey".

The monkey was always highly conscious of his own importance. Refusing to kiss the Pope's slipper in Rome, in spite of the fact that the princes of the church did so without loss of dignity, he explained "there are a great many pontiffs, but only one Duke of Württemberg". He was an autocratic ruler. Despotism was, of course, still the order of the day all over Europe, but benevolence, which characterized it elsewhere, was missing in Württemberg. It was Karl Eugen's proud boast that "when I appear, the country trembles". His pleasures included hunting, buildings and mistresses, but chief amongst them was his army. In order to train officers, he founded the *Karlsschule*. This was a far cry from the old *Collegium Illustre*, and in the words of the poet Schiller, who was a cadet there, "more a barracks than an institution for gentlemen".

Karl Eugen died in 1793 and was succeeded by his two brothers in turn. Each reign was short, so the country had little chance to benefit from their marginally less autocratic ways. In France, they had made enlightened friends: Jean Jacques Rousseau wrote to one of them "were I so unfortunate as to have been a prince . . ." but neither Friedrich Eugen, nor his son Friedrich who succeeded in 1797, saw this exactly as a disadvantage. The court of Württemberg became famous for its pomp and circumstance. The palace in Stuttgart was now very grand indeed. It was also still famous for its conspicuous consumption of food and drink, which made for a number of very ample personages: Duke Friedrich's desk was specially hollowed out so that his pen could reach the state papers placed before him for signature. It was he who signed Mömpelgard—now known

Ludwigsburg, near Stuttgart, is a former Württemberg residence designed by a team of German and Italian architects between 1704 and 1719. It is imposing, well-balanced and set majestically at the top of a series of terraces. Shown here is its charming, small courtyard, embellished by painted and mosaic decorations and some Pompeiian statues.

as Montbeliard—over to Napoleon, receiving a bit of Bavaria in exchange, as well as electoral and royal honours. In return Friedrich I, as he was now styled, became Napoleon's ally against Austria.

Wurttemberg was confirmed as a kingdom by the Congress of Vienna, and both Friedrich I's son, Wilhelm I, and his successor Karl I reigned in comparative tranquillity. In Bismarck's war of 1866, Württemberg marched with Prussia's enemies, but in the Franco-Prussian war she became Prussia's ally.

Queen Victoria was taking an increasing interest in the Württembergs in the hope of finding in that family a husband for her cousin, fat Princess Mary Adelaide of Cambridge ("Her size! it is really a misfortune"). Tired of observing this galumphing granddaughter of George III "valzing with all the gentlemen in a dirty gown", and observing that she was growing embittered, the Queen had begged Vicky to find her a husband. Vicky obliged by producing the Prince Franz von Teck, a great-grandson of Duke Friedrich Eugen, and son of Duke Alexander of Württemberg and a Hungarian countess. According to family law, princes of Württemberg marrying below their station had to renounce all their rights including membership of the royal family. This renunciation had duly been made by Duke Alexander. However, Franz, though he had neither position nor money, was highly welcome in the English royal family. Had not Prince Albert said that it was a blessing when there was a little imperfection in the pure royal descent, so that some fresh blood was infused? Twenty-odd years later, the couple's daughter, May of Teck, was engaged to the Duke of Clarence. Two years later, however, May was in mourning for her fiancée, but it was not long before she married his brother the future George V.

Shortly before the First World War, Queen Mary's eldest son, the future Duke of Windsor, visited his kinsman, the last King of Württemberg. "For a *Konigspaar*", noted the Prince, "Onkel Willie and Tante Charlotte were sympathetic and easy-going. Their ample figures betrayed the justice they did to their four full meals a day. After an enormous lunch the King and Queen took a leisurely drive through the suburbs in an open victoria. Onkel Willie would quickly fall asleep to be constantly aroused by a swift jab of the Queen's elbow to acknowledge the salute of one of his soldiers . . . or to straighten the Homburg hat that kept sliding rakishly to one side of his head". Onkel Willie left no surviving son when he died in 1921, so the succession fell to a catholic kinsman, the Duke Albrecht.

Wilhelm II, last King of Württemberg

159

GREECE
The Exiles

Less than a year after King Constantine was born in 1940 came the unsuccessful Italian invasion of Greece, followed by the successful German one. Prince Constantine's parents were obliged to flee the country, and for the next five years the family were exiles, moving from Crete to Egypt to South Africa, changing their residence more than twenty times.

With the end of the Second World War, and the restoration of the monarchy in 1946, the Prince was able to continue his schooling in Greece. In 1947, when his uncle, George II, died, Constantine became Crown Prince. In 1964, his father became ill with cancer and the Crown Prince was appointed Regent. A month later, King Paul was dead, and his son succeeded as the sixth monarch of his house. The following September, he married Princess Anne-Marie of Denmark in a glittering ceremony in Athens.

Constantine II arrived on the throne of Greece with a fund of goodwill inherited from his father, and there followed an eighteen-month honeymoon during which the throne was stable. Then, in time-honoured Greek fashion, came the crisis. The Defence Minister was threatening to sack all leftish officers, an endeavour in which he had the King's support. The Prime Ministe , Papandreou, whose party stood to the left, dismissed the Defence Minister. The King dismissed Papandreou, although claiming the Prime Minister had resigned.

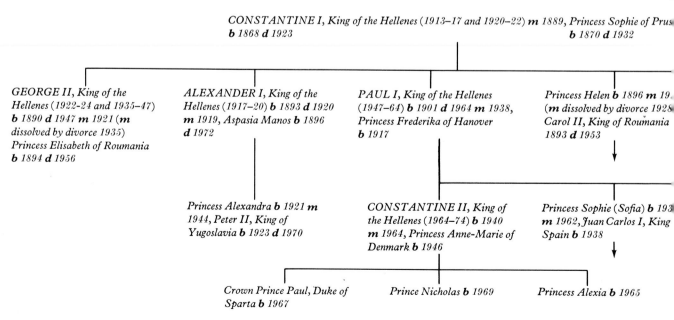

CONSTANTINE I, King of the Hellenes (1913–17 and 1920–22) *m* 1889, Princess Sophie of Prus
b 1868 *d* 1923   *b* 1870 *d* 1932

GEORGE II, King of the Hellenes (1922-24 and 1935–47) *b* 1890 *d* 1947 *m* 1921 (*m* dissolved by divorce 1935) Princess Elisabeth of Roumania *b* 1894 *d* 1956

ALEXANDER I, King of the Hellenes (1917–20) *b* 1893 *d* 1920 *m* 1919, Aspasia Manos *b* 1896 *d* 1972

PAUL I, King of the Hellenes (1947–64) *b* 1901 *d* 1964 *m* 1938, Princess Frederika of Hanover *b* 1917

Princess Helen *b* 1896 *m* 19. (*m* dissolved by divorce 1928 Carol II, King of Roumania 1893 *d* 1953

Princess Alexandra *b* 1921 *m* 1944, Peter II, King of Yugoslavia *b* 1923 *d* 1970

CONSTANTINE II, King of the Hellenes (1964–74) *b* 1940 *m* 1964, Princess Anne-Marie of Denmark *b* 1946

Princess Sophie (Sofia) *b* 193 *m* 1962, Juan Carlos I, King Spain *b* 1938

Crown Prince Paul, Duke of Sparta *b* 1967

Prince Nicholas *b* 1969

Princess Alexia *b* 1965

Left, Constantine, King of the Hellenes, lives with his family in London's Hampstead Garden suburb, encumbered with all the disadvantages of being royal and enjoying few of the advantages. However, he is now free of one anxiety: the government in Athens has agreed not to enforce compulsory purchase of his estates in Greece, which amount to about 80,000 acres. In return for paying substantial property taxes, the King is permitted special facilities to take money out of the country. His wife, Queen Anne-Marie, youngest of the three attractive daughters of the late King Frederik of Denmark, met Constantine at a ball while in her early teens. In 1964, aged eighteen, she was married to him; three years later, she was a queen in exile.

Left, Frederika, Queen Mother of Greece, has for some years lived as a religious recluse under the direction of a guru at Madras in India. Her move towards mysticism seemed to begin in earnest after the fall of the Greek monarchy in 1973, which was nine years after the death of her husband, to whom she was devoted. On the face of it, this life-style is an extraordinary contrast to her *persona* as a busy Queen of Greece. She earned admiration from other royalty when she refused the paltry government allowance offered her on the death of King Paul—and she is not wealthy.

Above: King Constantine and Queen Anne-Marie with their children Paul, Crown Prince of Greece (right), Alexia (centre) and Nicholas. Paul was an infant when the family fled their country and his brother was born almost two years later in Rome. Alexia, styled Crown Princess until the birth of Paul, is very proud of her name, an old Byzantine one: in a family choked with Sophies, Irenes, Olgas and Helens, she is the first royal Greek to be so called. All three are at English schools and could not be more British than if they had been born so.

Above, Princess Katherine of Greece is the grand-daughter of the second king of Greece and the daughter of the third. She is the sister of the next three kings of Greece and the aunt of the present King Constantine II. She is also the sister of Helen, Queen Mother of Roumania, but, in the English Buckinghamshire village where she has lived for more than thirty years, she is known, simply, as Lady Katherine Brandram, wife of a retired British army major.

Prince Peter of Greece is a noted anthropologist and lives at Gentofte in Denmark. He is the grandson of King George I of Greece, nephew of King Constantine I and the son of Princess Marie Bonaparte, the famous psycho-analyst and good friend of Sigmund Freud.

cess Irene b 1904 d 1974
939, Prince Aimone of Savoy,
Duke of Aosta b 1900 d 1948

Princess Katherine b 1913 m
1947, Richard Brandram, b 1911

ncess Irene b 1942

161

Tatoi, outside Athens, was the country residence of the Greek royal family. Its like can be found in many Mediterranean countries, but few of its counterparts can have been as necessary a refuge. With its thick stone walls, loggias, several levels, unruffled quiet, and, above all, its many trees, the house is a retreat from the unrelenting heat and hubbub of Athens. In the grounds are the graves of five kings of Greece.

There followed the Colonels' Coup, and with it authoritarian rule. Constantine attempted to overthrow the junta by trying to rally loyalist support, but when the army failed to respond, he fled the country, remaining officially King until 8th December 1974, when a plebiscite showed 68.8% in favour of a republic, 31.2% for a monarchy and 25% of voters abstaining.

Of the six kings of Constantine's house, one abdicated twice and was restored once and another abdicated twice and was restored twice. Given the country's undecided frame of mind about how it wishes to be governed, it is not inconceivable that some day, Constantine will be voted back.

Having in 1830 won independence in the fight for freedom against Turkey, the Greek leaders began quarrelling. The saying that no Greek likes to be ruled by another Greek was then as pertinent as it is now, and

162

accordingly, the country looked abroad for a king under whom it could un-nite. The crown, having been offered to, and refused by Prince Leopold of Saxe-Coburg (who preferred to become King of the Belgians), was eventually accepted by Prince Otto, second son of the King of Bavaria. His failure to gain the people's sympathy ended in his overthrow in the revolution of 1862.

The Greeks chose a new king by popular vote, the almost unanimous choice being Prince Alfred, second son of Queen Victoria. When Alfred was found to be ineligible (England, as a "Protecting Power" of Greece had agreed to exclude members of its own ruling family from the country's throne), the Greeks chose the seventeen year-old Prince William of Glücksburg, younger son of Prince Christian, heir to the Danish throne.

The young man's father regarded the Greek throne as a doubtful proposition, and hesitated before telling his son of the offer, but the Prince discovered about it for himself: by reading it on the newspaper wrapping around a sardine sandwich in a packed lunch. As Prince Christian expected, William was delighted, and eventually persuaded his father to let him go.

So Prince William was transformed into George I of the Hellenes, adopting the most Hellenic sounding of his christian names. It soon became clear that he regarded the Greek throne as no mere schoolboy adventure. Although often homesick, he never left Greece during his first four years as King, throwing himself into learning the language and getting to know the people. It was a lonely task: he had to rely for advice on Greek politicians, many of whom hoped to exploit him for their own purposes, but the apparently straightforward young Dane turned out to be more astute than they suspected.

He strengthened his position by choosing a Russian bride, the Grand Duchess Olga, niece of the Emperor Alexander II. They led a happy, but simple life with their large family, spending much of their time at Tatoi, a heavily wooded estate in the country. This was their home rather than the great German-Grecian palace Otto had built in Athens, which they regarded as excessively uncomfortable, although its ballroom suited them for roller skating or indoor cycling, favourite pastimes, in which the King, followed by the whole family in order of seniority, would weave in and out of the pillars. The ballroom was also used for balls, but of a relatively informal nature. Indeed, King George kept the formality of his court to a minimum, and this lack of pomp and ceremony has remained a feature of the Greek monarchy.

Although George and his successors were more informal than many European monarchs, they had greater power. The constitution entrusted the monarch with comparatively far-reaching prerogatives, and these made the King's position more difficult than if he had been a mere figurehead. He was continually in danger of being dragged into the maelstrom of Greek politics. During his reign, which lasted for fifty years until 1913, George I had many setbacks, which he survived. In 1913, he was shot by an assassin on a visit to Salonika, recently liberated from the Turks.

At the time of his succession, the new King, Constantine I, was popular enough, an impressive, forceful personality. The first year of the reign was tranquil; then the First World War broke out. The country became seriously divided between supporting the Allies or supporting Germany. Although inclined to support the Allies, Constantine was reluctant to commit the army on their side, for neither it, nor the economy, had properly recovered from the Balkan Wars. The Prime Minister, Venizelos,

George I

As a summer residence, the Greek royal family had Mon Repos, *a villa on Corfu, and it was here that the late Prince Andrew of Greece's only son Philip—now Duke of Edinburgh—was born. Before the island was ceded to Greece by the Powers in 1864,* Mon Repos *was the residence of the British High Commissioner.*

Queen Sophie

was blind to such considerations, motivated by fierce nationalism and determined to join the Allies. In the rift that followed between King and Prime Minister, Britain and France sided with Venizelos. There was a savage campaign against the King, in which it was alleged that Constantine's neutrality was caused by his family relationship with the Kaiser—Constantine's consort, Queen Sophie, was the German Emperor's sister.

The Allies recognized Venizelos's provisional government, and in 1971 the King was forced to abdicate in favour of his second son, Alexander, the elder son being unacceptable because of his alleged German sympathies. While the rest of the family went into exile in Switzerland, the new King was virtually a prisoner in his palace. In the autum of 1920, Alexander was walking in the gardens at Tatoi; his dog was attacked by a pet monkey and, in trying to separate them, Alexander was bitten by the monkey. A month later, he was dead from blood poisoning. Three weeks later, Venizelos lost the general election by a large margin. In December 1920, following a plebiscite, King Constantine was restored.

Two years later, the Greek army was crushingly defeated by the Turks at Smyrna. There followed mutiny in the army, an insurrection at home and, anxious to avoid civil war, Constantine abdicated for a second time. Three months later he died in Sicily.

This time, Constantine was succeeded by his eldest son, George II, who found the country in the grip of a revolutionary committee, which in 1923, the Chief of Staff, General Metaxas, tried unsuccessfully to overthrow. The ruling junta took this as an opportunity to accuse the King of being implicated in the plot, and he was driven into exile. A republic was declared, although the King had not abdicated. King George, now a lonely figure, settled in London at Claridge's Hotel: his marriage to Princess Elizabeth of Roumania had broken up, and there were no children. During

164

the decade of the Republic, Greece was ruled by a series of ineffectual governments; the country twice went bankrupt; there were eleven uprisings and a military coup. Eventually, in 1935, the Greek leaders decided to recall their King, a decision confirmed by the ensuing plebiscite.

Metaxas now became Prime Minister, and under his authoritarian rule Greece recovered somewhat from the preceeding years of chaos. Soon, however, the country was preparing to face an attack from Italy in the imminent European war. The Italian invasion was repulsed, but not the German one which followed. The King and army were obliged to carry on their struggle from Crete, in conjunction with the British until Crete, too, fell to the Axis powers and King George again went into exile.

When the British liberation force entered Greece in 1944, there was a strong communist guerrilla presence in the country, which had joined the resistance movement against the Germans during the years of occupation. Helped by the British, the Papandreou government (which had returned from exile) forced them to withdraw, at least from Athens and the surrounding country. With their departure, there was an upsurge of royalist sentiment and in the plebiscite which followed, the voting was 65% to 35% in favour of the monarchy.

George II as Crown Prince

On his return, the country was still in the throes of a civil war, for the guerrillas were still active in the north. The work and anxiety of the next few months proved too much for the King's health and he died suddenly in April 1947, to be succeeded by his brother, King Paul.

By 1949, the war against the guerrillas had been won, but next, Greece suffered a series of earthquakes and floods. The King and Queen provided leadership and inspiration in the rebuilding of their country, and when King Paul died in 1964, few suspected that in three years' time his son, King Constantine II, would be in exile.

ITALY
Alpine Strategists

King Umberto has been called the May King: his father, Victor Emmanuel III, abdicated in his favour on 9th May 1946, and by the referendum of 2nd June in the same year, Italy, which had been united under one monarchy for just over a century, became a republic.

Umberto was advised to fight by his friends, but refused to do so. He had no desire for a bloodstained throne, and departed to exile in Portugal while his wife, Marie-José of Belgium, moved to Switzerland. Since, the King has kept in touch with his former subjects, and of the two monarchist organisations in Italy, he favours the one that does not aim to involve the crown in politics.

Before its unification, Italy was merely a corner of the Holy Roman Empire where a collection of great families—the Medicis, the Viscontis, the Sforzas and the Savoys—independently ruled over their territories. It was the last of these which, in the eighteenth century, achieved royal status.

The early fortunes of the House of Savoy were founded by an eleventh-century feudal lord, Umberto, called *delle Bianchemani* because of his lily-white hands. These however, wielded the sword to such effect in the service

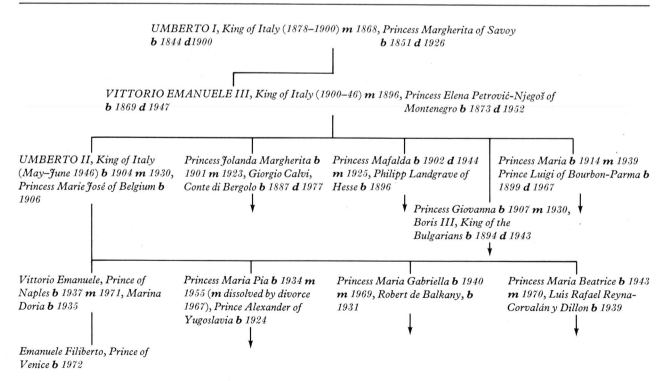

UMBERTO I, *King of Italy (1878–1900)* **m** *1868, Princess Margherita of Savoy*
b *1844* **d***1900*   **b** *1851* **d** *1926*

VITTORIO EMANUELE III, *King of Italy (1900–46)* **m** *1896, Princess Elena Petrović-Njegoš of*
b *1869* **d** *1947*   *Montenegro* **b** *1873* **d** *1952*

UMBERTO II, *King of Italy (May–June 1946)* **b** *1904* **m** *1930, Princess Marie José of Belgium* **b** *1906*

Princess Jolanda Margherita **b** *1901* **m** *1923, Giorgio Calvi, Conte di Bergolo* **b** *1887* **d** *1977*

Princess Mafalda **b** *1902* **d** *1944* **m** *1925, Philipp Landgrave of Hesse* **b** *1896*

Princess Maria **b** *1914* **m** *1939 Prince Luigi of Bourbon-Parma* **b** *1899* **d** *1967*

Princess Giovanna **b** *1907* **m** *1930, Boris III, King of the Bulgarians* **b** *1894* **d** *1943*

Vittorio Emanuele, Prince of Naples **b** *1937* **m** *1971, Marina Doria* **b** *1935*

Princess Maria Pia **b** *1934* **m** *1955 (m dissolved by divorce 1967), Prince Alexander of Yugoslavia* **b** *1924*

Princess Maria Gabriella **b** *1940* **m** *1969, Robert de Balkany,* **b** *1931*

Princess Maria Beatrice **b** *1943* **m** *1970, Luís Rafael Reyna-Corvalán y Dillon* **b** *1939*

Emanuele Filiberto, Prince of Venice **b** *1972*

King Umberto of Italy is a walking *Almanach de Gotha*, with an extraordinary knowledge of the world's royal families. In recent years, he has been plagued by an old arm injury which has necessitated painful operations, but he remains as affable as ever. He lives at Cascais in Portugal. His wife, Maria José, has lived near Geneva since their separation more than three decades ago. Her life, sadly beset by family problems, is lightened by a keen interest in genealogy and music. Among queens, she is unusual for having crossed the Alps on foot.

of the Salic Emperor Conrad II, that he rewarded Umberto with the County of Savoy in lower Burgundy. Umberto's origins are obscure. He seems to have stemmed from Vienne, and to have been a well-connected young man with lands that stretched across the western slopes of the Alps. With the acquisitions made by his successors, which included such counties as Piedmont and Liguria, the House of Savoy came to control both sides of the Alps, including the important passes of Mt. Cenis and St. Bernard: key positions at a time when Holy Roman Emperors were in the habit of quarrelling with the Pope in Rome.

The counts of Savoy exploited their advantage to the full, making alliances now with one, now with another of the opposing powers, and reaped handsome rewards by way of more territories.

A descendant of the white-handed Umberto called Peter often went to England to visit his nieces, one of whom was Henry III's Queen, Eleanor, and the other the wife of Richard of Cornwall, the King's brother. The Queen was proverbial for her generosity to her relations, but it was the King himself who showered Peter of Savoy with honours. He created him Earl of Richmond and installed him handsomely in a London Thames-side palace,

Prince Vittorio Emanuele, only son of King Umberto, with his wife Marina. He inhabits the playboy world of film stars and millionaires, and his exploits are recounted frequently in the press. He is a particular friend of the Shah of Iran.

Amedeo, Duke of Aosta and his wife Claude serve at the counter of a grocer's shop they opened to attract tourists to the village of Borro, near Florence, where they own property. The Duke of Aosta descends from the second son of Vittorio Emanuele II, and in the event of a restoration of the Italian monarchy, has been mentioned as a possible claimant to the throne. Close friends and relatives, however, say he would not be interested.

then known as Savoy House, whose site is now partly occupied by the Savoy Hotel, as well as the Savoy Chapel Royal, where a bronze statue of Peter stands in the courtyard. Peter's brother Boniface, who was his travelling companion, became Archbishop of Canterbury.

One of the early counts, Amadeus VI, wrenched a few cities from the Visconti family and changed the focal point of the House of Savoy from Burgundy to Italy. His grandson, the eighth Amadeus, became the first Duke of Savoy. He was invested (dressed in cloth of gold for the occasion) by the Luxembourg Emperor Sigismund in 1417. He was to gain further distinction: inspite of the fact that he had had a wife and two children and had not taken holy orders (though he was a saintly man) he was elected Pope by the Council of Basle in 1440. He reigned—known as the Anti-Pope Felix V—until 1449. Then he retired to his hermitage on the Lake of Geneva, from where he had already conducted the chief affairs of his state before accepting the anti-papal tiara.

Lesser matters he had left to his son Ludovico, who had succeeded him as Duke of Savoy in 1440. Amadeus, "a second Solomon," had been renowned for his wisdom and his justice. Ludovico was famous for indolence, but his ambitious wife, Anna of Lusignan, daughter of the King of Cyprus, Jerusalem and Armenia, made up for his lack of energy. She induced him to mount an expensive expedition to Cyprus, which gained him nothing except for her father's titles; however, she did bring into the family that most holy of relics: the legendary cloth said to have been wrapped round the body of Christ, with its features inexplicably imprinted, now known as the Turin Shroud.

It was however, from the fortress-castle of Chambéry, in the French-speaking part of their domains, that the dukes of Savoy still ruled, as the counts had done before them. The move to Turin, their subsequent capital, was made by the energetic Emanuele Filiberto, one of the most famous soldiers of the Renaissance, who suceeded to Savoy in 1539.

All through its long history, Savoy had made capital of being the gate-keeper of the Alps, but no one in all its history was to play off the great powers so coldly and so audaciously as the seventeenth-century Duke, Victor Amadeus II, who succeeded aged fourteen in 1675. He spent the first years of his reign under the regency of his mother, Marie-Jeanne Baptiste of Savoy-Nemours, whom he disliked, although she was both fascinating and beautiful. She was so loath to give up the regency that she planned to marry her son off to her Portuguese niece, which would have virtually expatriated him. As soon as Victor Amadeus was in a position to do so, he undid all her plans: what concerned him was the *gloire* of his house. He was a man, it was said, with some good and an infinite number of bad qualities: certainly he was immensely ambitious, and so skilled at playing a double game that he appeared to go along with his mother's French sympathies. He became famous for never finishing a war on the side on which he had started, and outdid even himself when, in the War of the Spanish Succession, he changed sides in mid-campaign.

As a punishment on Victor Amadeus for changing sides, Louis XIV mounted the siege of Turin in 1706, but as the Emperor sent one of his best soldiers, Prince Eugene of Savoy, to Victor Amadeus's aid, the French suffered defeat. Eugene was Victor Amadeus's second cousin, descended from a cadet line. This sole member of the House of Savoy to gain truly international fame had been brought up in Paris. In his youth, he had been much seen about court, a poor relation, destined for the church, grubby,

with lank hair and an upper lip so short that his mouth was never quite closed. No one dreamt that in the little *abbé* there was a great soldier struggling to get out, and no one minded when he rode to the Turkish wars for the Emperor, though there was surprise when he was considered a hero. Only when he inflicted crushing defeats on France in the War of the Spanish Succession did Madame, step-grandmother to Marie Adelaide of Savoy, think he had gone too far: after all, he had eaten Louis XIV's bread throughout his youth. But no one seriously blamed him: the desire to gain *gloire* was only natural. Nor did people blame Victor Amadeus for his double dealing.

The prize that he carried off for backing the winning side was glorious indeed: a royal crown, not hollow like that of Cyprus, but one with land and subjects. In 1713, by the peace treaty of Utrecht, Victor Amadeus gained not only Montferrat, coveted for so long, but also the Kingdom of Sicily, which, now that the power of Spain had finally crumbled, was in the giving of the Austrian Emperor. It hardly mattered that Victor Amadeus was obliged, five years later, to exchange Sicily for the poorer, though more accessible Kingdom of Sardinia: his lust for *gloire* was satisfied by the magic of having become His Majesty. Victor Amadeus's end was less glorious than he might have wished. Having renounced his throne in favour of his son, Charles Emmanuel III, and having married, morganatically, one of his early mistresses, he changed his mind about abdicating. Charles Emmanuel promptly imprisoned him at Moncalieri, where he died in 1732.

Charles Emmanuel III, who reigned for over forty years, had his successes in the Polish wars and in the War of the Austrian Succession. He did not gain Milan, but widened his frontiers a little and died in 1773.

Rome's Quirinale, the town residence of the Italian kings (nowadays inhabited by the President) is a former Papal palace dating from the end of the sixteenth century. Its main glories are the chapel and the Sala Regia, but also very striking is Mascherino's incredible, elliptical spiral staircase. This is a highly refined and astringently simplified interior version of that famous fore-runner of the fire escape, the exterior staircase built during the previous century for the Palazzo Contarini del Bovolo in Venice. The chapel with its grandiose cosmato *floor and its* trompe l'oeil *paintings of St. Peter and St. Paul on either side of the altar, is strangely awe-inspiring in spite of its brazen flamboyance. The Sala Regia, designed by Maderno (who also designed the chapel) is famous for its frescoes of figures leaning from carpet-hung balconies, and non-existent arches which lead the eye into imaginary rooms. The gardens are a sort of amusement arcade with tricky water devices to divert guests: the most complicated is an organ, still in use, played by water.*

Stupinigi, near Turin, in spite of being a blatant gallimaufry of all the wrong styles carelessly put together is, nevertheless, a fascinating example of how exciting such things can accidentally be. The ground plan resembles a simplified drawing of a lobster with some claws missing. It is said that the architect, Juvara, believed that here he had perfected the principle of spatial organisation. The central core, which houses a single, three-and-a-half storey room with eight fireplaces, one chandelier, and a mezzanine gallery, rises a good two-and-a-half storeys above the rest. Much of the furniture is purely architectural, resembling built-in kitchen cupboards. The staircases, inexplicably, are all mean and niggling. It is perhaps the scenic quality of the whole charade which lends the charm.

It was his son, Victor Amadeus III, who dealt harshly with such revolutionary elements as made themselves felt in Turin, and who formed an alliance with Austria to support the French royalists. He died in 1796. When Napoleon appeared on the scene, demanding Savoy and Nice for France, and in due course, annexed the whole of Piedmont, the family, led by King Charles Emmanuel IV, was obliged to retire to Sardinia. Charles Emmanuel abdicated in 1802 and became a Jesuit, to be succeeded when the Napoleonic interlude was over by his brother, Victor Emmanuel I.

Time had stood still for the royals of Sardinia. At court, powdered hair and military pigtails, long since out of style, made a strange sight, as did the elderliness of the pages who were restored to the positions they had held more than a decade before. The enlightened Napoleonic Code was swept away, and the Kingdom of Sardinia returned to the eighteenth century. This led to mutiny, causing Victor Emmanuel to abdicate in favour of his absent brother, Charles Felix, who appointed his cousin Charles Albert of Carignan as Regent.

In 1831, Charles Albert succeeded his childless cousin. In the pre-revolutionary climate of the 1840s, the question of a constitution came up, and he granted one in 1848, which gained him the suffix Magnanimous. Amazingly ambitious, and longing for glory, Charles Albert was obsessed with the idea of creating a northern Italian empire. His aims could only be achieved with the aid of the liberals and the federalists, who themselves wished to see Italy free of Austria. So in 1848, Charles Albert joined the liberal and republican insurgents in their struggle against Austria, if only to acquire the liberated lands himself. The plans, however, misfired. He was routed by the Austrians under the ancient Marshal Radetzky at Custozza and Novara, and, faced with the stringent terms which Austria imposed, abdicated in favour of his son Victor Emmanuel II in 1849. He died, an exile, in Portugal, a few months later.

Victor Emmanuel was a burly figure, very unlike his elegant father, but it fell to him, with the help of Cavour, who became his prime minister in 1852, to realize his father's cherished dreams. Cavour successfully harnessed the forces of the *Risorgimento* for the aggrandisement of the House.

By the marriage of the King's daughter Clotilde to Plon Plon, the cousin of Napoleon III, an alliance was sealed in the war against Austria which started in 1859. In a matter of months, Victor Emmanuel had taken Milan and all other Austrian possessions except for Venice, and had annexed the dominions of the liberal-minded Grand Duke of Tuscany together with those of the Dukes of Parma and Modena. As Cavour had intended, nationalist revolutionaries rallied to the House of Savoy, and with his and the King's blessing, Garibaldi and his Thousand Heroes went to aid the Sicilians in their revolt against their Bourbon King. So that in 1861, Victor Emmanuel II was able to proclaim himself King of a United Italy by the "Will of the Nation", instead of the Will of God, as was suitable for a monarch who owed his position to the forces of the revolution.

He was succeeded in 1878 by his son Umberto I, who was far from being the right young man for the throne. On his accession, he said "King of Italy—the very thought is aging". Admittedly he did his duty, but his politics were not admired. In 1882, he entered into a triple alliance with Germany and Austria in the hope of gaining stability. He also dreamt of empire, but the first Italian expedition to Ethiopia was a disaster. The monarchy lost prestige; there was gossip about the King's *amours* and his private expenditure. In July 1900 Umberto I died by an anarchist's bullet.

He was succeeded by Victor Emmanuel III, the tiny king with the large wife. She had been a Princess of Montenegro, who was welcomed by those who wished to see Italy expand towards the Balkans, but who was referred to by a more snobbish member of the royal family as "my cousin the shepherdess". Soon after his accession, the King seemed to favour a liberal, even a socialist monarchy. There was less pomp at court, there were reforms, there was harmony between the King and his prime minister who had been regarded as a liberal threat in the previous reign. This harmony ended with the beginning of the First World War. The prime minister advocated Italian neutrality, the King intervention. In order to win over the parliament, the King sided with the element of the population which had been whipped into a warlike mood by d'Annunzio and Mussolini.

After the war came Mussolini's rise. He reduced the King to a cypher, in spite of creating him Emperor of Ethiopia and King of Albania. The King remained passive while the Duce pursued his policies, rousing himself only when his prerogative seemed threatened. He did engineer Mussolini's downfall in 1943, but failed to make a clean break with Hitler, planning to withdraw slowly, thus escaping German wrath. These delaying tactics meant heavy Allied bombing while he was inactive, and German vengeance when he acted after all. When, after the war, the Italian people turned against Fascism, it was inevitable that they should demand his abdication.

Umberto I

MONTENEGRO
Melancholy Sleep

King Danilo

The mystery figure of European royalty is King Michael of Montenegro. He was a boy of ten when his grandfather, King Nikola, was driven from his mountainous Balkan country towards the end of the First World War by Crown Prince Alexander of Serbia. In the peace treaties of 1919, Montenegro was annexed to the new Serbo-Croat-Slovene Kingdom, later to be called Yugoslavia—a union which Nikola refused to recognize.

He set up a government-in-exile in Antibes, in France, and on his death in 1921 was succeeded by his eldest son Danilo, who, unwilling to pursue a lost cause, abdicated after six days in favour of his nephew. This was King Michael, now twelve years old, and until the following year, he ruled under the Regency of his grandmother, Queen Milena. It was then that the Conference of Ambassadors formally recognized the union with the Serbo-Croat-Slovene Kingdom. This naturally led to the renunciation of the throne in favour of the Karadjordjević family, which was ruling in the future Yugoslavia.

King Michael eventually settled in Paris, where he embarked on a career in the French civil service as a trade inspector. His only further connection with Balkan politics came in the Second World War when Mussolini invited him to become the puppet King of Montenegro under German and

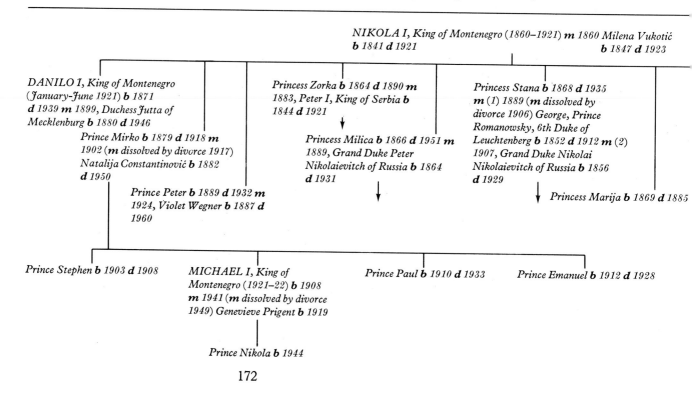

NIKOLA I, *King of Montenegro (1860–1921)* **m** *1860 Milena Vukotić*
b *1841* **d** *1921*   **b** *1847* **d** *1923*

DANILO I, *King of Montenegro (January–June 1921)* **b** *1871* **d** *1939* **m** *1899, Duchess Jutta of Mecklenburg* **b** *1880* **d** *1946*

Prince Mirko **b** *1879* **d** *1918* **m** *1902 (**m** dissolved by divorce 1917) Natalija Constantinović* **b** *1882* **d** *1950*

Prince Peter **b** *1889* **d** *1932* **m** *1924, Violet Wegner* **b** *1887* **d** *1960*

Princess Zorka **b** *1864* **d** *1890* **m** *1883, Peter I, King of Serbia* **b** *1844* **d** *1921*
↓
Princess Milica **b** *1866* **d** *1951* **m** *1889, Grand Duke Peter Nikolaievitch of Russia* **b** *1864* **d** *1931*
↓

Princess Stana **b** *1868* **d** *1935* **m** (1) *1889 (**m** dissolved by divorce 1906) George, Prince Romanowsky, 6th Duke of Leuchtenberg* **b** *1852* **d** *1912* **m** (2) *1907, Grand Duke Nikolai Nikolaievitch of Russia* **b** *1856* **d** *1929*

Princess Marija **b** *1869* **d** *1885*
↓

Prince Stephen **b** *1903* **d** *1908*

MICHAEL I, *King of Montenegro (1921–22)* **b** *1908* **m** *1941 (**m** dissolved by divorce 1949) Genevieve Prigent* **b** *1919*

Prince Paul **b** *1910* **d** *1933*

Prince Emanuel **b** *1912* **d** *1928*

Prince Nikola **b** *1944*

172

Italian control—an offer which King Michael refused.

All his life in Paris, King Michael has preserved the strictest anonymity, never using his titles and living modestly as a private citizen. None of the people with whom he has come into contact know that he was once a king whose rule would have been absolute: although Montenegro had a constitution, and the sovereign was supported by a state council and six ministers, his will decided everything.

Montenegro, an area of 3,255 square miles (about half the size of Wales) was situated in the Balkan peninsular to the north of Albania. In Roman times it was part of the province of Illyria and later it was overrun by the Ostrogoths. In the mid-sixth century A.D. its inhabitants adopted the Orthodox Christianity of the Eastern Church at Constantinople. In the seventh century the region was occupied by the Serbs, the people who inhabit it today being essentially the same race. They simultaneously conquered large surrounding areas and Montenegro duly became part of a confederacy of Serbian states.

It was in 1389, after the Battle of Kossovo, when the Serbs were decisively defeated by the Turks, that Montenegro became a place to be reckoned with. The most stubborn of the defeated Serbs refused to accept Islam, the Turkish faith, and sought refuge in the inaccessible area around the Black Mountain, from which the country takes its name. A protracted struggle for survival against Turkish supremacy in eastern Europe now began.

These early Montenegrins established a theocracy: their rulers were prince-bishops, or Vladikas, who for three centuries were elected. Then, from 1690, the Prince-bishop was empowered to select his successor from his own family in order to ensure continuity of government. The family which in this way became dynastic was called Petrović-Njegoš.

The most remarkable of the dynasty was Petar I, who reigned from 1782 to 1830. He led many campaigns against the Turks, gaining a great victory over them at Krusa in 1796, when 30,000 Turkish soldiers were killed.

Below: King Michael of Montenegro at the time of his accession in 1921, when he was thirteen. Today, he is a wilfully anonymous gentleman, who prefers not to be photographed. During exile in Paris, which has lasted almost all his adult life, he has gone about under a pseudonym, prefixed by plain *Monsieur*. Few, if any, of those with whom he came into contact in his work as a trade inspector knew he was once a king. He is immensely dignified, with pronounced Slavonic features. Since his recent retirement, he has lived simply on an altogether inadequate pension. His days pass as they do for other pensioners: he walks slowly, several times each week, across Paris; plays (but more often nowadays watches) *boule;* sits in the park or at a pavement restaurant when the days are fine and reads and dozes in the library when they are inclement. Sundays he spends at the Louvre after he has attended mass. He enjoys occasional letters from such relations as Giovanna, Queen Mother of the Bulgarians, her son King Simeon and Prince Nicholas Romanoff, all of who remember him with affection. He nevers sees his ex-wife or their only son, Nikola, remaining, as he wants to be, alone.

*ss Elena **b** 1873 **d** 1952*
6, Vittorio Emanuele III,
*of Italy **b** 1869 **d** 1947*

*Princess Anna **b** 1874 **d** 1971 **m***
1897, Prince Franz Joseph of
*Battenberg **b** 1861 **d** 1924*

*Princess Sophia **b** 1876 **d** 1876*

*Princess Xenia **b** 1881 **d** 1960*

*Princess Vera **b** 1887 **d** 1927*

When the town of Cetinje was the capital of Montenegro, the Royal Palace there was this two-storey rectangular house with two short wings extending to the rear and a red tile roof. Privacy was given, in theory, by a low stone wall which enclosed a garden with a few trees and some flowers. The ground was hard-packed, like that of a school playground, because the royal children used it as their playground. Across the road from the Palace still stands a huge tree under which King Nikola used to sit in mid-morning and late afternoon to gossip, hold reunions, and to judge criminal and civil cases. His people entirely approved of this method of spreading news, greeting old friends and dealing with wrong-doers. Today the building is a museum.

Besides being a warrior, Petar was a skillful diplomat, who saved his country from the political storms which overwhelmed Venice and Ragusa, Montenegro's neighbours each side of the Adriatic, at this time. He was also a poet, and a tough ruler who made his wild subjects obey the law. Despite his strictness, he was loved by his people, to whom he was a personal friend. When he died, his nephew and successor, Petar II, canonized him, which shocked the more meticulous priests of the Russian Church.

Petar II, the national poet was almost as legendary: six feet eight inches tall, with long hair and an ecclesiastical beard, he was admired as a superb rifle shot, capable of hitting a lemon thrown into the air by an attendant. "A singular accomplishment for a bishop," noted an English visitor in 1844.

His nephew and successor Danilo wished to marry and so ended the theocracy, proclaiming himself Prince of Montenegro. In his reign, Montenegro was recognized by the major European powers as an independent principality. He was assassinated in 1860 and succeeded by his nephew, Nikola, who became his country's link with the twentieth century.

Nikola I was surely the most picturesque monarch of his day. Tall, powerfully built (as most of the family were), he often wore the colourful national dress, as did his wife, Princess Milena, later to be Queen Consort, for in 1910 Nikola assumed the title of King Nikola I.

He brought his country up to date. On his accession, illiteracy was widespread to the extent that the President of the Council could neither read nor write. Nikola set about building schools and encouraging literacy: indeed ten years after his reign began the first newspaper appeared, while ten years after that the first Montenegrin book shop opened. Nikola also built roads and a short railway and, in 1905, granted a constitution.

King Nikola

His colourful personality made him something of a figure in European politics. His capital, Cetinje, little more than a village, pervaded (as now) by the smell of wood smoke and with cattle strolling in the main street, gave over almost every other house to a foreign delegation or to official use. This was Montenegro in its heyday. The large royal family was happy and exuberant, younger members leaping from tables to chairs to sofas around the Palace in competition to see who could go farthest without touching the floor, the older girls accomplished at playing piano duets. They possessed one of the earliest gramophones and a small collection of records, and they sang to their own guitar accompaniment.

As a result of King Nikola's new diplomatic importance, his children made some splendid matches—with the exception of his third son, Petar, who married the daughter of a tram conductor from London's East End. But this was a lucky match for the family compared with that of his eldest daughter. She married Peter Karadjordjevic, who after the murder of King Alexander Obrenovic became King of Serbia in 1903. When Serbia was invaded by Austria in 1914, King Nikola went to the assistance of his son-in-law, only to be driven from his kingdom at the end of the First World War by his grandson, Crown Prince Alexander, in the interest of Serb unity.

The royal family went into exile, and Montenegro lapsed into a melancholy sleep, from which it has never been aroused. To this day it remains relatively untouched by the twentieth century. Giovanna, the Queen Mother of the Bulgarians, is the daughter of one of those exuberant Montenegrin princesses and made a nostalgic pilgrimage to Cetinje in 1977. She described it as idyllic.

PORTUGAL
The Brazilian Connection

Dom Duarte Pio, Duke of Braganza, has been recognized by Portuguese monarchists as the rightful King of Portugal since the death of his father, Dom Duarte Nuno, in December 1976.

Duarte Pio was born in Switzerland, where his parents were living: since 1834, a law had banned this branch of the royal family from entering Portugal on pain of death. The law was, however, abolished in 1950, and the family returned to Portugal, where Dom Duarte grew up. After a university course in agriculture, he attended a military college, later becoming a lieutenant (pilot) in the Portuguese Air Force.

The Braganzas provided Portugal with an unbroken succession of rulers from 1640 to 1901, but trace their descent much further back, through their kinsmen, the monarchs of the Aviz dynasty, who occupied the throne from 1385 to 1580, and beyond, to Count Henry of Burgundy, who in the late eleventh century started the work of making Portugal an independent state.

His medieval descendants of the Aviz dynasty were occupied in maintaining independence from the Kingdom of Castile, in which one Portuguese King, John I, was helped by John of Gaunt. He was himself a claimant to the throne of Castile in the name of his second wife, Infanta Constance, and the alliance marked the start of the long friendship between Great Britain and Portugal.

In the late Middle Ages, Portugal began to emerge as one of Europe's great seafaring and trading nations. King Afonso V mounted African campaigns in the late fifteenth century, and King Manoel I, his grandson, was styled Lord of the Conquest, Navigation and Commerce of India by special papal confirmation in 1501. In his reign, too, Cabral landed in Brazil, Corte Real voyaged to Labrador and Vasco da Gama opened the sea routes to India. It was the period which marked the beginning of Portugal's Golden Age.

King Manoel's cousin and contemporary, the 4th Duke of Braganza, is remembered for less fortunate events: more than a little mad, he was given to fits of passion, in one of which he murdered his wife. The next generation, however, produced model Braganzas. The 5th Duke was highly

Dom DUARTE Nuno, Duke of Braganza **m** *1942 Princess Maria Francisca*
b *1907* **d** *1976*   *of Orléans and Braganza* **b** *1914* **d** *1968*

Dom DUARTE Pio, Duke of   *Infante Dom Miguel* **b** *1946*   *Infante Dom Henrique* **b** *1949*
Braganza **b** *1945*

176

cultured and a great patron of the arts, while his brother earned the crown's gratitude as Portugal's Ambassador to France, and as Governor of India.

It was the marriage of John, the 6th Duke, into the reigning family that put the Braganzas within reach of the crown itself. After the male line of Aviz died out in 1580, the claim of the Duchess of Braganza, Infanta of Portugal, was recognized by the country's governing body, the *cortes*. On this occasion, however, it was Philip II of Spain (Castile had long since been united with Aragon) who took the prize, paying off the Braganzas to waive their claim. Spain ruled Portugal for the next sixty years.

Then, John, the 8th Duke of Braganza, was called to be king in 1640 by a nation in revolt against Spain. He spent his reign in fighting wars to consolidate Portugal's independence: while victory hung in the balance, he had dedicated his crown to the Virgin Mary by placing it on the head of her statue, an act commemorated by custom ever since—no successor of John was ever to wear the virgin-dedicated crown. The Spanish threat was far from removed by the time he died in 1656, and it was not until the next reign that Spain was obliged to forget her Portuguese ambitions.

John's son, Afonso VI, aged thirteen on his accession, was a miserable figure of a king: his body had been partially paralysed and his mind enfeebled by childhood illness, and he grew up to be a vicious, unpleasant man. He kept low company, barely learned to read or write, and was a great problem to his mother, who acted as Regent before his brother Pedro took charge of him.

It was Afonso's sister Catherine who was sent to England to marry the newly restored Charles II in 1662, taking Tangiers, Bombay and two million cruzados as her dowry. Less acceptable was the little Princess herself: dressed in the Spanish fashion, her sweeping skirts supported by a wide farthingale that made her legs look even shorter than they indeed were, she

Right, Dom Duarte Pio, Duke of Braganza, and his brothers Dom Miguel, centre, and Dom Henrique. Dom Duarte rotates with his brothers as overseer of a farm he owns in northern Portugal, and, with Dom Miguel, is much occupied in restoring a palatial old house in Sintra to its former grandeur. An authority on African affairs, especially of former Portuguese colonies, Dom Duarte is politically active, being the backbone of several Portuguese monarchist parties.

177

advanced to meet her husband for the first time. He had believed her to be seated, and said "My God, they have sent me a bat, not a woman".

After Charles II died, and his brother James II had gone to France in 1689, Catherine returned home and twice ably acted as Regent for her brother Pedro, who had become King of Portugal in 1683 on the death of Afonso VI, whom he had imprisoned in Sintra. Catherine herself survived until 1705, but did not live to see the accession of her nephew John V, who was a baroque king on the model of Louis XIV. Like that monarch, he spent much passion in making love and building magnificent edifices.

In the reign of his son Don José occurred the dreadful Lisbon earthquake of 1755. Had it not been for the strong-handed government of the Marquise of Pombal, there might have been anarchy. The King left the affairs of state to this able minister, himself preferring riding, shooting, cards, the theatre and music, for the last of which all the Braganzas had a special passion. After the devastation of his capital, he never liked to spend time in his palaces, preferring to live under canvas or in wooden buildings.

José's successor was his daughter Maria, who married her uncle Pedro. Maria I and Pedro II ruled jointly, a weak couple dominated by the Queen Mother, who was a daughter of the first Bourbon king of Spain and of Elizabeth Farnese. Queen Maria lost her mother in 1781, her husband in 1786 and her eldest son in 1788, followed by her confessor. This was too much for her, and she became uncurably mad, remaining so for twenty-four years until she died in Brazil in 1816, whence the royal family had sailed when Napoleon overran Portugal.

Because the Queen had been in no fit state to rule, her only surviving son John had assumed the government of the country, and he was proclaimed King John VI in Brazil. While he was anxious to become a father to his people, his terrible wife, Carlota Joaquina, a daughter of Charles IV of Spain, was so desperate to win absolute power for herself that she tried to have her husband declared incapable of ruling. This ploy failed, and when the royal family at last returned from Brazil, the King, liberal in outlook, accepted the radical constitution. The Queen would have nothing to do with it, refusing to swear the required oath. Her penalty was loss of citizenship and exile, but since she produced a certificate signed by ten doctors declaring her unfit for travel, she moved to the palace at the outskirts of Sintra. There, with her son Miguel, she whipped up the absolutist faction, which prevented John from making his constitutional government work.

When the King died in 1826, the crown went to his elder son, Dom Pedro, who had since been proclaimed Emperor of Brazil. Having no intention of returning home, Dom Pedro, after drawing up a moderate constitution, renounced the crown in favour of his seven year-old daughter Dona Maria da Gloria, on condition that she would marry her uncle Miguel the plotter, sixteen years her senior. Dom Miguel was appointed Regent, and told to abide by the new constitution.

Dom Miguel, his mother's son, did no such thing. He at once usurped his niece's throne, being hailed by his friends as "*Il rei absoluto*". His little fiancée, shipped off from Brazil to her kingdom, heard of this coup when she landed at Gibraltar and sailed straight on to England.

In 1831, Dom Pedro abdicated as Emperor of Brazil in favour of his son Pedro II and the following year returned to Portugal, taking up arms against his brother to regain the throne for his daughter. The bloody War of the Brothers, known also as the Miguelite War, lasted until 1834 and ended in victory for Dom Pedro. Dom Miguel went into exile in Germany

*The palace at Mafra, built by the
German architect Frederic Ludwig
during the first quarter of the
eighteenth century, incorporates a small
monastery originally built on the site.
The massive front façade is dominated by
the church, which is reminiscent of some
of Bernini's best work. This is successfully
matched by the interiors, which
are marbled with magnificent
abandon. Many of the Palace's windows
are dramatically exaggerated in size,
heightening the majestic effect of the
exterior, but tending to spoil some of the
otherwise flawless interiors. The library
has a Baroque beauty, but is inferior to
the celebrated one at Coimbra.*

179

Queleuz has been called "the finest expression of aristocratic society of the second half of the eighteenth century", and few have disagreed. This ineffably pretty confection on the outskirts of Lisbon is pink, and that colour characterizes almost everything about the place, for it is a sweet, delicate, even feminine building. About the size of the Grand Trianon at Versailles, it is set on several levels. There have been repeated alterations, one of the most significant being that the northeastern corner is now one-storeyed again after the fire of 1934, which fortunately destroyed the ill-conceived upper floor added in 1790 as an attempt to provide extra space. In 1940, much of the interior was built to a new design and the rest faithfully restored. Queleuz illustrates the Portuguese version of the Rococo style by its intimacy, privacy and by its dainty scale, which successfully disguises a comparatively large fabric. Each façade is varied to match the distance from which it is most often viewed, so that the inner courtyards are small units, with suitably sized windows. The park façade, illustrated here, is much grander, with Doric columns. Everywhere, there are picturesque departures from symmetry and changes of rhythm. The spell of Queleuz is not easily broken.

and raised a family so late in life that one of his daughters survived until 1959, and some of his grandchildren, who included Dom Duarte, the late claimant to the throne, as well as the Empress Zita of Austria, are still alive: interesting when one thinks that Dom Miguel was very much a figure of the Napoleonic period.

Dom Pedro died only a few months after Dom Miguel's capitulation, having declared his fifteen year-old daughter to be of age. Since Maria da Gloria's first marriage to her uncle, celebrated by proxy when she was seven, had been repudiated by Dom Miguel, it was dissolved in 1834. She then married the son of Eugène de Beauharnais, but this young man died two months later. Her next husband was Ferdinand of Saxe-Coburg, who was allowed an official role in matters of state and became his Queen's co-Regent. When Maria da Gloria died giving birth to her eleventh child in 1853, the King-consort acted as Regent for his eldest son Pedro until the boy came of age two years later.

King Pedro V inherited a pronounced sense of duty from his father, but he never got over the early death of his young wife, Stephanie of Hohenzollern-Sigmaringen, fourteen months after her arrival in Portugal. He survived her by just over two years.

Dom Luis, his brother and successor, was surpised to learn that he was king on landing at Lisbon after a visit to England. Queen Victoria had called him "a good, kind, amiable boy", and his reign proved to be a period of prosperity and stability.

Dom Luis's Queen was Maria Pia of Savoy, the daughter of Italy's first king, who shared her husband's interests in every field including that of literature. He has the translation of four of Shakespeare's plays to his credit and it was in his reign that poets, writers and other intellectuals first actively participated in Portuguese politics.

King Luis's son and successor, Dom Carlos, proclaimed in 1889, appreciated art, was a *bon viveur*, an excellent shot, and had a shrewd grasp of politics, domestic and international. His Queen, Amélie of Orléans, was extremely intelligent, and the royal couple were highly popular. Unfortunately, the stability and prosperity the country had enjoyed in the previous reign did not last. Crisis followed crisis and in 1908, an assassin killed the King and the Crown Prince, and wounded a younger prince, Dom Manoel, who became Portugal's next monarch.

When, in 1901, a naval mutiny led to rioting in Lisbon, King Manoel felt that his continued presence in the country might provoke civil war. He therefore left Portugal and settled in England, where he pursued his scholarly interests and, with his wife August Viktoria of Hohenzollern-Sigmaringen, became popular in society. There were no children, so the right of succession went to Dom Duarte Nuno, grandson of Miguel the usurper-king.

He married a great grand-daughter of the Emperor Pedro II of Brazil, thus uniting the two surviving branches of the Portuguese royal house. She died in 1968, after which Dom Duarte lived on alone in the echoing Coimbra Palace on a modest sum which he received from the government. He had firm views about the monarchy, seeing it as the best of all systems of government because it provided continuity, and an economical means of maintaining a head of state. A father-figure to loyalists, he did not, however, actively press his claim, although it would have been the fulfillment of his life to see the restoration of the House of Braganza. His son, Dom Duarte Pio, is the present claimant.

King Carlos

Dom Duarte Nuno

181

ROUMANIA
Romance

King Michael of Roumania was a sovereign twice over.

He was nearly six years old when his father, Crown Prince Carol, renounced the throne of Yugoslavia in order to pursue his mistress, Madame Lupescu. Michael became heir apparent, and when King Ferdinand died the following year, Michael succeeded, with a Regency to govern for him.

Two years elapsed before the Prime Minister, finding the prospect of a lengthy regency unsatisfactory, invited Carol back—so that the father became King in place of the son.

After a controversial period of ten years, the Second World War came to the Balkans. King Carol was already unpopular with various factions in the country; now under Soviet and Nazi pressure, he gave up enormous territories. On September 6th, 1940, he abdicated in favour of Michael, now a serious-minded youth of nineteen, and fled the country. Yugoslavia's real ruler, however, was to be General Ion Antonescu. Pro-Nazi, he assumed dictatorial powers and indeed had regal aspirations.

For Michael it was a nightmarish, nerve-racking situation, with Nazis in control of his country and the communists, inside and abroad, greedy for it and gaining power. He did not stand by idly: in 1944, he brought off

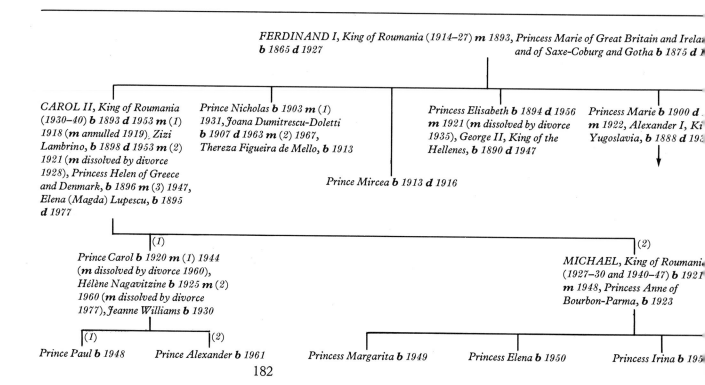

FERDINAND I, King of Roumania (1914–27) **m** 1893, Princess Marie of Great Britain and Irela
b 1865 **d** 1927   and of Saxe-Coburg and Gotha **b** 1875 **d**

CAROL II, King of Roumania (1930–40) **b** 1893 **d** 1953 **m** (1) 1918 (**m** annulled 1919), Zizi Lambrino, **b** 1898 **d** 1953 **m** (2) 1921 (**m** dissolved by divorce 1928), Princess Helen of Greece and Denmark, **b** 1896 **m** (3) 1947, Elena (Magda) Lupescu, **b** 1895 **d** 1977

Prince Nicholas **b** 1903 **m** (1) 1931, Joana Dumitrescu-Doletti **b** 1907 **d** 1963 **m** (2) 1967, Thereza Figueira de Mello, **b** 1913

Princess Elisabeth **b** 1894 **d** 1956 **m** 1921 (**m** dissolved by divorce 1935), George II, King of the Hellenes, **b** 1890 **d** 1947

Princess Marie **b** 1900 **m** 1922, Alexander I, Ki Yugoslavia, **b** 1888 **d** 19

Prince Mircea **b** 1913 **d** 1916

(1)

Prince Carol **b** 1920 **m** (1) 1944 (**m** dissolved by divorce 1960), Hélène Nagavitzine **b** 1925 **m** (2) 1960 (**m** dissolved by divorce 1977), Jeanne Williams **b** 1930

(2)

MICHAEL, King of Roumani (1927–30 and 1940–47) **b** 192 **m** 1948, Princess Anne of Bourbon-Parma, **b** 1923

(1)
Prince Paul **b** 1948

(2)
Prince Alexander **b** 1961

Princess Margarita **b** 1949

Princess Elena **b** 1950

Princess Irina **b** 195

King Michael has a vast, comfortable house above Versoix in Switzerland. Having never gone about as a has-been shrouded in regret, but diligently pursued his career, he has made a singular success of being an ex-King. His daughters now almost independent, he can give more time to the problems of exiled Roumanians. His wife Anne is delightfully unpretentious and versatile, capable of anything from cleaning a carburettor to baking a roll. During the Second World War she was an assistant at a New York City department store. "Customers are always wrong," she says, "particularly if they happen to be friends." Later she helped in the French Resistance, and was awarded the Croix de Guerre. The family call her Nane.

a hair-raising coup against Antonescu by having him and his son arrested, detained in a ventilated safe (used formerly for the royal stamp collection), and executed.

Soon after, Roumania was fully under communist control, a puppet state of Moscow. It was a measure of King Michael's popularity with the Roumanian people that the government kept him a King behind the Iron Curtain for another two years. But an opportunity to remove him was found in 1947 while he was attending his cousin Princess Elizabeth's wedding to Prince Philip in London. His forced abdication occurred as soon as he returned to Roumania.

Still much-loved by his people, King Michael was compelled to go into exile with little means of support, most of his personal property having been confiscated. He settled in Switzerland, and to support his new wife and family, went to work. With an inventive mind, especially in technology, he quickly adapted. For a time he worked as a test pilot, showing a special

Above, Princess Elena and Princess Irina, two of King Michael's five daughters. Few outside the family are aware of who they are. All attended school in Britain. Margarita does social work in Edinburgh; Elena teaches in London; Irina works with retarded and partially sighted children in Lausanne; Sophie is a student and Maria, still in her teens, is at a boarding school in North Wales.

Left, King Michael's mother, Queen Helen, lives in a villa at San Domenico, near Florence. Although she was ill-used by King Carol, she is as patiently sweet as if she had never had a care. She refused several good offers of a second marriage. A woman of deep religious conviction, she forgives those who abused her, though continuing to remember in a detached way, as if the unhappiness were someone else's.

Princess Ileana (Mother Alexandra) b 1909 m (1) 1931 (m dissolved by divorce 1954), Archduke Anton of Austria b 1901 m (2) 1954 (m dissolved by divorce 1965), Stefan Issarescu, b 1906

rincess Sophie b 1957   *Princess Maria b 1964*

183

talent for testing equipment, then using his knowledge of aviation to branch out into the business world as a consultant for several British and American companies.

In 1822, the two old Danubian principalities of Moldavia and Wallachia rose in revolt against Turkey their overlord, which consequently allowed the appointment of native rulers. In 1856, Turkey, France, Great Britain and Austria naively signed a treaty declaring the principalities should never be united. The people saw this as an infringement of their rights and in 1859 elected the same candidate, Alexander Cuza, as ruler of both principalities. United, Moldavia and Wallachia were proclaimed the Principality of Roumania in 1859. They were, however, still essentially under Turkish control.

Cuza's slipshod private life, combined with increasingly autocratic tendencies resulted in his unceremonious deposition in 1866. By agreement of the major European powers, Prince Karl of Hohenzollern, a twenty-seven-year old officer in the Prussian army, was nominated hereditary prince and confirmed in his position by a referendum.

Karl, or Carol as he was now known, turned out a good politician at home and abroad. In the Russo-Turkish War of 1877, Roumania fought as Russia's ally and as a result gained independence from Turkey. The proclamation of Carol as King followed. At the coronation, he himself placed the crown, made from captured Turkish cannon, on his head. He was the builder of modern Roumania. With an immense capacity for hard work, he developed Roumania's natural resources, the rich arable land, the coal, iron and later oil, so that what had in 1866 been a backward, impoverished Turkish province was transformed by the end of the nineteenth century into a wealthy European state.

In complete contrast to the austere and down-to-earth King Carol was his Queen, Elisabeth of Wied, a high romantic who was a poet and writer of fairy tales under the pen name of Carmen Sylva. Tall and buxom, with bright blue eyes and prematurely grey hair cut short, usually dressed in flowing white mourning after the death of her only child, she would sit discoursing in lofty tones on all manner of subjects to an admiring circle of writers, artists and musicians. She loved the wind and the sea and she would stand, on the terrace of her house overlooking the Constanza harbour calling out blessings to the departing ships through a megaphone.

King Carol adopted his nephew Ferdinand, a son of his elder brother, as heir. He became King in 1914: modest and unassuming, he suffered from indecision, but reigned through the First World War, managing, unlike so many other European monarchs, to keep his throne. Also, he won his people's affection, so that he is remembered as Ferdinand the Good or The King of the Peasants.

He was greatly helped by his Queen, the beautiful Marie, daughter of Queen Victoria's second son. She, like her mother-in-law, wrote fairy tales, but she was in addition highly practical. During the Balkan Wars, she ran a cholera camp, and in the First World War, nursed the wounded. This was not simply a matter of rolling bandages and making stately progresses through the wards: she actually performed the work of a hospital nurse, cleaning gangrenous wounds, assisting in operating theatres and administering enemas.

Ferdinand and Marie's eldest son was Prince Carol. He had every chance of being a popular, successful monarch. Tall, handsome and

Queen Elisabeth

intelligent, he was not lacking in sense of duty—at the age of nineteen he had helped his mother in the cholera camp. But there was an instability about him, and he was fatally weak as far as women were concerned. A socialist Swiss tutor had sown doubts in his mind about being a prince, so it was easy for him to decide to renounce the throne when in 1918 he made a runaway marriage to a colonel's daughter, Jeanne Marie Valentine Lambrino, known as Zizi. After this marriage had been annulled, he resumed his position as heir apparent, fell in love with the beautiful Princess Helen of Greece and married her, much to his family's rejoicing.

To their despair, he eloped again with the red-haired Elena Lupescu, whose romantic, apparently Roumanian surname was a translation of the German Wolf. This time, his family regarded renunciation as final, and when King Ferdinand died in 1927, his son Michael, in his sixth year, became King. Then in 1930 the Prime Minister decided the Regency situation was unsatisfactorary, and called back Carol.

Before and after his reign, Carol behaved haphazardly, but during it he did show a sense of purpose which surprised his friends and enemies, going some way to leading Roumania out of the reigning political and economic chaos; sponsoring the arts and rebuilding his capital and his palace. On the other hand, he was rude and dismissive to his mother and unkind to his wife, with the result that his goodname was irretrievably spoilt. In the last three years of his reign, he assumed the dictatorial powers of an absolute monarch. This greatly contributed to his downfall. For when in 1940 Hitler engineered his abdication, Carol had few friends to support him.

Elena Lupescu, or Magda, as she was usually called, never lost her allure for Carol. They were married in a civil ceremony in 1947 and a religious one in 1949. When Carol died in 1953, she continued to live in exile in Portugal, dying in 1977.

Carol as Crown Prince

185

RUSSIA

Autocracy, Tempered by Assassination

When Grand Duke Vladimir succeeded in 1938 as head of the Romanov family, and as would-be Emperor and Autocrat of All the Russias, he issued a manifesto stating that he was assuming all the rights and duties inherent in these titles, according to the Fundamental Law of Russia and the statutes of the imperial family. He accepted the oath of allegiance from monarchists, reasoning that "if one is born to a certain position, there is nothing one can do about it." He rejects the term Pretender—"one pretends nothing"—and says that if there is a likelihood of his being useful to his country, he must be as well prepared as possible.

The Grand Duke is a great-grandson of the Russian Emperor Alexander II, and the eldest son of Grand Duke Kirill, a cousin of the last Russian Emperor, Nicholas II. His mother, Victoria Melita, was a daughter of Alfred, Duke of Edinburgh and thus one of Queen Victoria's grand-daughters. He was born in Finland, where his parents and two elder sisters had fled during the Russian Revolution, and there he spent the first three years of his life. After several moves—Coburg, Zürich, the Cote d'Azur—the family settled at St. Briac in Brittany. It was here, in 1922, after it had been established to the satisfaction of all but a handful of romantics that the Emperor Nicholas and all his children had indeed been murdered, that the Grand Duke Kirill proclaimed himself head of the Imperial House.

Vladimir was educated in Paris and at London University, and in 1939 returned to England to work in a machine-shop in the Midlands, under the pseudonym of Mikhailov, a name which more than two centuries earlier had done service for Peter the Great during his stint at the shipyards in Deptford. During the Second World War, he spent some time in France

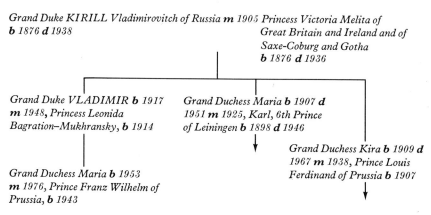

*Grand Duke KIRILL Vladimirovitch of Russia **m** 1905 Princess Victoria Melita of*
***b** 1876 **d** 1938*   *Great Britain and Ireland and of*
Saxe-Coburg and Gotha
***b** 1876 **d** 1936*

*Grand Duke VLADIMIR **b** 1917*   *Grand Duchess Maria **b** 1907 **d***
***m** 1948, Princess Leonida*   *1951 **m** 1925, Karl, 6th Prince*
*Bagration–Mukhransky, **b** 1914*   *of Leiningen **b** 1898 **d** 1946*

*Grand Duchess Kira **b** 1909 **d***
*1967 **m** 1938, Prince Louis*
*Ferdinand of Prussia **b** 1907*

*Grand Duchess Maria **b** 1953*
***m** 1976, Prince Franz Wilhelm of*
*Prussia, **b** 1943*

186

before being deported to Germany and then went to Austria. He categorically denied rumours to the effect that he had entered into negotiations with Hitler concerning the return of the Romanovs to a puppet-throne, stressing his opposition to the Axis powers. After the war, he moved to Spain, where he still lives with his wife, Princess Leonida, a descendant of the former royal family of Georgia.

It was in 1613 that the Romanovs came to power in Russia, after Muscovy, traditionally thought to have been founded by a ninth-century norseman called Rurik, had become an immense empire, stretching from the Arctic to the Caspian Sea, and from the Dniepr deep into Siberia.

The title of tsar—derived from Caesar—was first adopted by Ivan the Great, who ruled from 1462 to 1505. Among the Russian tsars, many of whom went in for murders and massacres, and none of whom, although they were pious to the point of mysticism, were particularly characterized by the quality of mercy, some were good and some were bad, but Ivan IV, grandson of the Great, has the reputation of having been truly terrible. Responsible for repeated waves of atrocities, bloodbaths and torments which killed his subjects in tens of thousands, he also carelessly killed his eldest son, also named Ivan.

This left Theodore, the proverbial "Holy Fool", as his heir, and since this gentle, smiling figure was too simple-minded to rule in anything but name, his brother-in-law, Boris Godunov, eventually became master. When Theodore died in 1598, Boris Godunov proclaimed himself Tsar and was regarded as a usurper by pretenders who sprung up on all sides. The fight for the throne gained momentum after Godunov's death. This period is known as the time of trouble and devastation in the country. When it became clear that the situation had to be regularized, delegates of the National Assembly met for an election. Their choice fell on the sixteen-year old Michael Romanov, a nobleman related by marriage to the imperial family. His reign, and that of his son Alexis, saw a slow recovery from the chaos. It also saw the complete enserfment of the peasants, and the beginnings of western influence.

Russia's window towards the west was decisively flung open by Michael's grandson, Peter I, the son of Alexis by his second wife. He had been preceded by a dim elder half-brother, on whose death he had been crowned as co-Tsar with a younger and even dimmer half-brother, Ivan. Soon after the boys' double coronation, both princes were sent to the country while the Tsarevna Sophie, their sister, ruled instead.

In 1696 Peter I made a successful bid for power. The Regent Sophie,

Vladimir, Grand Duke of Russia, divides his time between an imposing residence in Madrid and an even grander villa in Brittany. His claim to the Romanov throne cannot be faulted: Vladimir's father, the Grand Duke Kirill, was the son of Tsar Alexander III's brother. Other possible claimants long ago renounced their rights for themselves and their descendants. Steeped in the tsarist tradition from infancy, Vladimir is in constant touch with many sources inside Russia who have persuaded him that there is a well-founded longing for a return to Romanov rule.

Leonida, the wife of Grand Duke Vladimir, descends from the Bagrations, the former royal family of Georgia, whose own descent, it has been claimed, is from the Old Testament King David. Indeed, a Bagration princess was once heard questioning the presence of strangers at a Good Friday service in a Russian Orthodox church. "Don't they understand," she grumbled, "that this is a private family funeral mass?" In fact, the Bagrations are the oldest traceable Christian family of the East, probably descending from fourth-century B.C. Armenian rulers.

187

Grand Duchess Maria of Russia, the daughter of Grand Duke Vladimir, lives at St. Briac-sur-Mer in Brittany, and is married to a great-grandson of Kaiser Wilhelm II, Prince Franz Wilhelm of Prussia. She has the stately looks typical of the Bagration ladies, her maternal ancestors, and the resourcefulness of the Romanovs. When she was younger, she became, on her own initiative, a valued employee of the noted fashion house of Grès in Paris.

Prince Andrew of Russia is a great-grandson of Tsar Nicholas I. He lives with his second wife, Nadine, near Faversham in England's Kent countryside. She is familiarly known by the Russian colony in England as "the self-raising princess", because she is the daughter of Herbert McDougall, a member of the flour family. Prince Andrew has five children and a number of grandchildren living in countries as far-flung as France, California and Australia.

who had assumed the title of Autocrat, was banished to a convent. Her lovers and supporters were disposed of, while Ivan, the co-Tsar, continued to lead a cabbage-like existence in the country, leaving Peter to become the Great.

At the age of twenty-five, Peter left his wife Eudoxia and his son Alexei, for neither of whom he cared a great deal, and set out on his journey to explore western civilization for himself. It was a large party, two hundred and fifty strong, not counting the court dwarf, who accompanied Peter on his mission. The grand embassy attracted much attention by their exotic dress, their enormous capacity for alcohol, and their interest in every detail of western administration and technology. During his journey, Peter I studied twenty-seven trades including engineering, turnery, carpentry and shipbuilding.

The Tsar's grand tour ended suddenly. In Vienna, Peter learned of a mutiny in the Streltsy regiment—once the loyal guard of his half-sister, but forgiven by Peter when they had supported him in 1696. On his arrival in Moscow, the mutiny had been bloodily suppressed, but Peter meted out the most savage punishment: gibbets at every city gate; tortures and mountains of corpses left unburied to discourage future disobedience. For all his desire for a new Russia, Peter the Great was an old Russian at heart.

Peter I reorganized the army, built a navy and defeated Charles XII of Sweden, the greatest warrior of the age, at the Battle of Poltava in 1709. Now Russia really did have her window on to Europe. To go with it, she needed a new capital and Moscow, with its hundreds of onion domed churches, was too steeped in ancient superstitions to serve the modern state, so Peter ordered the erection of a city, St. Petersburg, more fitting for a westernizing Tsar.

While Peter did not concern himself much with his wife, preferring an ever-changing supply of mistresses, he had in fact formed an attachment during the Swedish war: a Lithuanian servant girl, who travelled with the army, and was the mistress of Alexander Menshikov, Peter's great favourite. It was this girl whom he married, after sending Eudoxia to a convent, and whom he crowned as Empress Catherine. His niece, and his daughter, of this marriage, Anna and Elizabeth, in turn ruled Russia after his death

Prince Dimitri of Russia, brother of Prince Andrew (opposite page), is one of the most likeable and highly respected members of the Russian colony in Britain. During the Second World War he served with distinction in the British navy. He has been honorary president of the Russian Benevolent Society, and although in frail health for some years, continues to be an effective head of the Russian Refugees Relief Association, which annually sponsors a colourful and remunerative Russian bazaar in London.

Prince Nicholas Romanoff, a great-grandson of Tsar Nicholas I, is a successful farmer—cattle, vineyards and grain—of a vast acreage near Rome which has been in his wife's family for more than six hundred years. He succeeded as head of his branch of the family on the death of his father, Prince Roman of Russia, in October 1978. Nicholas Romanoff is an expansive man, who entertains well: with him, an impromptu lunch becomes, without apparent effort, an exercise in gracious dining.

in 1725. Eudoxia's son, the disappointing Alexei, who had been discovered in a plot and was known to abhor all his father's western reforms, was imprisoned and strangled to death.

Peter III, the son of Anna and her husband the Duke of Holstein-Gottorp had been married by his aunt the Empress Elizabeth (whom he briefly succeeded) to Sophie of Anhalt-Zerbst—who unsurped his throne to become known as Catherine the Great.

There is no doubt that Catherine the Great belongs to the species of enlightened despot, and that she further dragged Russia out of her orientalism; though there is some doubt as to whether she was more despotic than enlightened, at least in practice. "It may be just, but is it useful" was her cry, for which the French philosophers with whom she corresponded had no answer. She may be forgiven for thinking her people happier than they actually were: like other Russian monarchs before or since, she was surrounded by clouds of sycophants. On her progress south into the Crimea (a new conquest which she called New Russia), and which she visited in enormous state, she found that all was prosperous: the resourceful Potemkin had built his famous two-dimensional villages along the route, and peopled them with commandeered peasantry put into new clothes for the occasion. However, what with the triple partition of Poland, which was Catherine's inspiration, she left Russia much aggrandised for her son and successor, Paul I.

This prince had been snatched out of his cradle by the Empress Elizabeth and brought up under her supervision. Whether Catherine minded this as much as she claims in her memoirs is open to doubt: certainly, she had meant to leave her throne to Paul's son Alexander, but death overtook her before she could finalise arrangements.

When Catherine died in 1796, and the officers bringing the news to Paul were seen galloping up to his house, Paul thought that his last hour had come: too many potential tsars had met mysterious deaths during Catherine's reign. Paul had never made a secret of his dislike of his mother and all her ideas. Where she had been enlightened, he was narrow. Where she had valued education and the free exchange of ideas, he banned foreign books. His reign was one of terror and the Emperor himself seemed to be the most frightened man in the realm. What is regarded as his paranoia made him distrust his ministers and his subjects. It accounts for the wholesale deportations to Siberia, the executions and the dreadful punishments which he inflicted even on the middle-classes who had in the past been exempt from knoutings, nose-splittings and the like. To extend tyranny to this degree, when the shockwaves of the French and American revolu-

Paul I

tions still hung in the air, naturally led to the formation of secret societies concerned with civil rights and constitutional government. Thoughtful people—his sons among them—began to regard him as a madman. He died by assassination in a highly secure house that he had built precisely to save him from such a fate. His death was greeted by general celebration. "Paul is dead", people said, kissing each other, "Alexander is risen".

The cause of Paul's death was given as apoplexy. That of his father's had been given as colic—and neither was believed. Whether the new Emperor, Alexander I, was guilty of his father's death will never be clear. It is certain however, that he suffered from a sense of sin. This enveloped him in a grey mist throughout his life and many loves, even when, after he had pursued the remnants of Napoleon's *Grande Armée* on its retreat from Moscow in 1812, he rode into Paris fêted as the hero of the day.

His mysticism, mixed with political and diplomatic adroitness, gained him, in the West, the title of Sphinx of the North. To his own people, he was the Blessed One, the Little Father who had delivered Europe from a monster, but who did not, in the event, deliver his own children from bondage. Alexander I, like Russian monarchs before and since, was afraid of a conflict with the land-owning classes, so the Fundamental Rights of Russia, with which he was much concerned, remained unimplemented. Having succumbed to typhoid during a Crimean journey with his ailing Empress, he was for years thought to have mysteriously disappeared, and to have lived on as a holy hermit.

There were no surviving children of Alexander I's marriage, and the succession fell to one of his brothers—but just which one needed clarification. There were two senior grand dukes, and amazingly, each seemed more anxious to pass up the crown than the other. Constantine, the elder, who was Viceroy of Poland, had in fact secretly renounced his rights. Nicholas, the younger grand duke, lost no time in swearing allegiance to Constantine and was surprised to receive Constantine's allegiance to himself by return post. It took all of three weeks to clear up the misunderstanding. Nicholas was in fact as anxious to rule as Constantine was to remain in Poland: however, knowing that his severity as a commander had made him not beloved by the guards regiments on whose loyalty any Emperor depended, he hesitated to present himself to the Senate in that capacity. Only when he learned of a rebellion in the making, headed by a group of officers who had tasted liberty when they had accompanied Alexander I to Paris, did he go to the Senate to accept its allegiance.

On the next day, 14th December 1825, the great square in front of the Winter Palace slowly filled with people. Some called for Constantine; others for a constitution. None knew that it was too late, and that Nicholas I had just become ruler of All the Russias. They learned this news when he appeared among them on his charger and his cannons fired, leaving two hundred dead and wounded. "Mes amis du quatorze", as Nicholas was to refer to the ring-leaders, were arrested as were two hundred and fifty of those who survived the massacre. There were five executions, and the rest were marched off to Siberia with their families. The victims were remembered as the Decembrists, martyrs of the abortive revolt that is sometimes called the First Russian Revolution. The Duke of Wellington, who remarked at the time "where kings know how to ride and to punish, there will be no revolution", was sadly mistaken. Nicholas I's dark reign was characterised by systematic oppression. In order to be well informed, he founded the notorious Third Section—his secret police, whom he

Nicholas I

aided by personal acts of surveillance, and surprise public appearances.

That all was not well with Russia became clear after Turkey had declared war on her in 1853. England, together with her allies, came to Turkey's aid in order to prevent Russian domination of the Balkans. The struggle became known as the Crimean War. Nicholas died before peace was made, but not before the "Omnipotent Russian Colossus" had revealed its feet of clay. For all that this Emperor had been known as the Gendarme of Europe, his system had failed, and despotism and its attendant corruption were doomed. When Nicholas I handed over what he called "his command" to his eldest son Alexander, he regretted that it was not in so fortunate a state as he might have wished.

Alexander II was a benevolent man of thirty-six when he succeeded. The signs of kindness that had been read in his features when he had been Tsarevitch (he is the man after whom the Cesarevitch race at Newmarket had been named in honour of a Russian state visit to England), were soon transformed into actions: amnesties, a relaxation of taxes and the act for which he came to be called Alexander the Liberator—the freeing of the serfs. This, however, took so long to achieve, and in the event granted such restricted liberties, that neither the freed peasants nor the liberal elements were pleased, while the erstwhile serf-owners were of course disgusted.

Alexander was aghast at "so much ingratitude". Again there was a tightening of police regulations, and again there were executions and transportations to Siberia, which unfriendly province he was the first emperor to visit in person.

A new breed of revolutionary came into being—that of the Nihilist. Their aim—to the amazement of an English visitor—was simply to do away with the old order. As for reforms, these would have to be suggested by people in power. What was needed now was a clean sweep and an annihilation of all that had gone before. This, naturally, included the person of the Autocrat himself. Alexander II survived all assassination attempts—a bomb in the Winter Palace that wrecked his white marble dining room, mysterious fires, even a pistol shot at close range while he was in a carriage with the Napoléons during a visit to the Paris Exhibition of 1867.

Alexander II's eldest son died quite suddenly in 1863. The royal family of England pitied his parents, but most of all they pitied his fiancée Dagmar, a sister of Alexandra, the Princess of Wales. However, after a decent interval, she married the second Grand Duke instead, and it is he who succeeded as Alexander III in 1881, after bombs thrown into his sleigh had finally done for the Liberator—who was even then considering sweeping reforms.

Alexander III's manifesto mentioned "the great reforms of the past", but went on to say that "God's voice demands that we take the helm trusting in divine providence and believing in the strength and truth of . . . autocratic power". He reintroduced some of his grandfather's sterner measures and reinforced the personal security of the imperial family. He was hostile to all ideas of change and evolution, and his thirteen-year reign—reactionary but for Russia's industrial development—proved to be the Indian summer of autocracy, orthodoxy and nationalism. Fond of Dagmar, called Minnie by the English royals, and of his son and heir, Nicholas, Alexander III was said to favour the simple life. Although he liked to think of himself as a peasant, the splendour and frantic extravagance at the

Alexander III

Imperial Palace continued unabated—making a strange, glittering oasis in a country over which hung "a dull, heavy, silent melancholy". Alexander III, having survived the train derailment of 1888 that might have been caused by terrorists or might have been accidental, died five years later from a kidney injury sustained at the occasion. He was succeeded in 1894 by the last of the reigning emperors, Nicholas II.

"How sad that Nicky is so young for this responsible position" wrote Queen Victoria's daughter. She thought Nicholas II had a great mission, and prayed "that he may be rightly inspired to fulfil it . . . The unfortunate nation is groaning and thirsting for simple liberties as every other country now enjoys. Will Nicky be allowed to understand all this? No-one is more dependant than an absolute monarch for if the truth does not reach his ears, wrong decisions are taken even with the best intentions." The English royal ladies hoped that dear Nicky's life, unlike his father's, would not be constantly in danger. The young man, they felt, could escape it all, kill Nihilism with one blow, and rest in safety if only he took up the plans for radical reforms that his grandfather Alexander II had prepared but never quite introduced. However, Nicky's manifesto pledged him also to the principle of absolute autocracy. This caused disappointment to his well-wishers in the west who grieved that "he had crushed all hopes, and perhaps lost the valuable confidence and affection of his many suffering subjects".

Worse, the grand dukes, Nicholas's wicked uncles, treated the hapless Nicky to some extremely bad advice. After a catastrophic stampede for the presents that newly-crowned emperors traditionally distributed among the populace had left over a thousand people trampled to death, it was the uncles who urged Nicholas and Alexandra at attend a dance in their honour at the French Embassy: this established him from the start as a man who cared nothing for his people. As for his ministers, there was little rapport between them and the monarch. Fearful and indecisive, Nicholas II said that he did not understand affairs of state, and "I don't

even know how to address ministers"—as he had amply proved before his father's death, when he had attended some of their meetings.

In 1904, again following the uncles' advice, Nicholas senselessly went to war against Japan (it failed for the same reason as had the Crimean war: out-dated weapons and lack of organisation). Moreover, one of the admirals found the Emperor strangely absent-minded, more so than usual, when he reported the disposition of his ships, and was surprised when the Emperor turned to him with a happy smile, saying "he weighs fourteen pounds". Nicholas II's thoughts were in the nursery, where his four daughters had at last been joined by the longed-for son and heir to All the Russias.

Sadly, the baby was seen to suffer from haemophilia—as did several of Queen Victoria's descendants. This was a great sorrow to his parents, and even before the notorious Rasputin appeared, faith healers and spiritual-ists—particularly a French medium—began to haunt the superstitious court.

Rasputin, the drunken monk with hypnotic powers, was to play his part in the family's downfall, but first, in January 1905, there came the Bloody Sunday which effectively sealed their fate. It was on the 9th that a large crowd of peaceful people, carrying ikons and portraits of the Emperor, were on their way to the Winter Palace to watch the presentation of a petition to Nicholas II, who had in fact absented himself to avoid receiving it. The authorities had been informed, and on the orders of the Emperor's uncles, soldiers fired upon the crowd. Cossacks charged, there were over a hundred dead, and the unrest that had been simmering burst out all over the country.

One of the uncles, the handsome Sergey, was assassinated a month later. Strikes were called. Leon Trotsky emerged as the leader of a Soviet, or council, that threatened to paralyse the entire country by strikes. Troops, which Nicholas I was only too ready to send to the trouble-spots, brought the threat of civil war only closer. In the end, when begged to so by the

More than a furlong in length, the
façade of the main palace at Pushkin,
formerly Tsarskoye Selo, presents
a perfectly balanced pattern of
porticoes, balconies, pilasters, pediments,
windows, urns, pillars and statues.
Except for the pilasters, pillars and four
statues, every ornament is gilded, and
before the Revolution, people in their
innocence used to say that the roof was
solid gold. During the Second World
War, the Germans burned and mutilated
Tsarskoye Selo, but now it is restored to

its former grandeur. The abundance of
gold is still there, however, in the same
doubtful taste as before, and the whole
structure (which is perhaps too heavy
and too long), continues to astonish
visitors. The present palace was
designed for Empress Elizabeth by
Rastrelli in 1748-62, and considerably
embellished for Catherine the Great by
the Scottish architect, Charles Cameron.
He was responsible for the collonade,
which is now an open-air museum, and a
great many of the charming interiors.

Like Tsarskoye Selo (opposite page), The Great Palace at Petrodvorets (formerly the Peterhof), is on the outskirts of Leningrad. Under construction throughout most of the eighteenth century, its style belongs to the Russian Baroque period. The exterior has too much gold paint for some people's taste. In the famous gardens is a superabundance of fountains, some of which torture water into unlikely shapes.

more liberal of his ministers, Nicholas agreed to grant a constitution, and to form a parliament called the Duma.

The Emperor, "looking smaller, yellower, more helpless", was now, in the words of a Prussian attaché, furious against everybody and everything. "I've made so many concessions and now they want that I positively sanction anarchy. It's no good giving in; I've done too much already", he said. Searching for the proverb that would illustrate his dilemma, he rejected the one about the little finger and the whole hand and said "no, its the one about inviting pigs to dine—and being certain that they'll put all their trotters into the dishes."

In 1914, when she had not yet recovered from the Japanese debacle, Russia went in to World War I in the cause of Panslavism. An anti-German wave swept over Russia; the Empress Alexandra became a target for abuse; the sinister presence of Rasputin, never understood, added to the unpopularity of the imperial family. In February 1917, Petrograd—renamed because the German version was no longer acceptable—was short of bread. Riots broke out which developed into the February Revolution, which lasted for nine days and ended with the Emperor's abdication in favour of his brother Michael.

Nicholas II and his family: left to right, Grand Duchess Olga; Grand Duchess Marie; the Tsar; the Tsarina; Grand Duchess Anastasia; the Tsarevitch Alexis and Grand Duchess Tatiana.

The Imperial family were taken to Tsarskoye Selo. In October 1918 came the Bolshevik Revolution. Civil war broke out between reds and whites, and in the night between the 16th and 17th of July came the hideous murder of the Imperial family.

Europe was shocked, and although the ghastly incident has been the subject of much investigation, some of it official, it is to this day shrouded in some mystery. Need all have died? Were all six of them massacred together? Or were the ex-Empress and her daughters, as some authorities say, spared and carried away after the ex-Emperor and his son had died, only mysteriously to disappear later? Did Anastasia escape, or not? What had happened to the secret rescue plans? Of King George of England's promise of friendship to his cousin, who so strikingly resembled him? And why did the Kaiser's rescue attempt fail? All these questions, like so many in Russia's history—which has been called the history of autocracy tempered by assassination—remain unanswered.

THE TWO SICILIES
House Divided

The Royal House of The Two Sicilies is a house divided: there are two claimants for the dynastic leadership, both Bourbon princes, first cousins once removed. One is Prince Don Carlos, who would be the undisputed head of the family had not his grandfather, Don Carlo, renounced the succession on his and his descendants' behalf in 1900—albeit conditionally. The condition was that the Bourbon throne of Spain would unite with that of The Two Sicilies. To this end Carlo adopted Spanish nationality and was granted the title of Infante of Spain. He married a Spanish princess, Mercedes, Princess of the Asturias, sister of King Alfonso XIII. His son Alfonso was born in Madrid, where his son Don Carlos, the present claimant, still lives.

The second claimant is Prince Don Ferdinand. He belongs to the generation previous to that of Don Carlos, for he is the son of Carlo's younger brother Don Ranieri.

The quarrel started when the last undisputed head of the family, Don

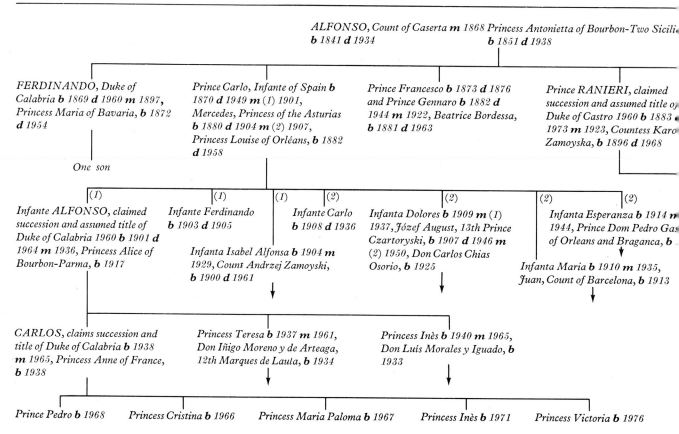

ALFONSO, Count of Caserta **m** 1868 Princess Antonietta of Bourbon-Two Sicili
b 1841 **d** 1934 **b** 1851 **d** 1938

FERDINANDO, Duke of Calabria **b** 1869 **d** 1960 **m** 1897, Princess Maria of Bavaria, **b** 1872 **d** 1954

One son

Prince Carlo, Infante of Spain **b** 1870 **d** 1949 **m** (1) 1901, Mercedes, Princess of the Asturias **b** 1880 **d** 1904 **m** (2) 1907, Princess Louise of Orléans, **b** 1882 **d** 1958

Prince Francesco **b** 1873 **d** 1876 and Prince Gennaro **b** 1882 **d** 1944 **m** 1922, Beatrice Bordessa, **b** 1881 **d** 1963

Prince RANIERI, claimed succession and assumed title o, Duke of Castro 1960 **b** 1883 1973 **m** 1923, Countess Karo Zamoyska, **b** 1896 **d** 1968

(1) Infante ALFONSO, claimed succession and assumed title of Duke of Calabria 1960 **b** 1901 **d** 1964 **m** 1936, Princess Alice of Bourbon-Parma, **b** 1917

(1) Infante Ferdinando **b** 1903 **d** 1905

Infanta Isabel Alfonsa **b** 1904 **m** 1929, Count Andrzej Zamoyski, **b** 1900 **d** 1961

(1) Infante Carlo **b** 1908 **d** 1936

(2) Infanta Dolores **b** 1909 **m** (1) 1937, Józef August, 13th Prince Czartoryski, **b** 1907 **d** 1946 **m** (2) 1950, Don Carlos Chias Osorio, **b** 1925

(2) Infanta Esperanza **b** 1914 *n* 1944, Prince Dom Pedro Gas of Orleans and Braganca, **b**

Infanta Maria **b** 1910 **m** 1935, Juan, Count of Barcelona, **b** 1913

CARLOS, claims succession and title of Duke of Calabria **b** 1938 **m** 1965, Princess Anne of France, **b** 1938

Princess Teresa **b** 1937 **m** 1961, Don Iñigo Moreno y de Arteaga, 12th Marques de Laula, **b** 1934

Princess Inès **b** 1940 **m** 1965, Don Luís Morales y Iguado, **b** 1933

Prince Pedro **b** 1968   Princess Cristina **b** 1966   Princess Maria Paloma **b** 1967   Princess Inès **b** 1971   Princess Victoria **b** 1976

Ferdinando, elder brother of Don Carlo and Don Ranieri, died in 1960. The fathers of the present contenders each immediately claimed the vacant post. One side argued that the renunciation of 1900 was merely a formal statement, operative only if and when the crowns of Sicily and Spain were united; the other side argued that the renunciation had been valid from the moment it had been signed. As there is no authority in the world empowered to settle the matter, and as there seems little chance of agreement between the factions, the dispute looks like going on forever.

The Kingdom of The Two Sicilies ceased to exist just a hundred years before the start of the quarrel, having in 1860 been incorporated into the Kingdom of Sardinia which, ten years later, became the Kingdom of Italy.

The Bourbons themselves were comparative newcomers to The Two Sicilies which, until 1816, were known as the Kingdom of Naples and Sicily. These two territories, comprising Naples and the south of Italy up to the border of the Vatican lands, plus the island of Sicily, had been gathered into a single kingdom in the eleventh century by Roger I, son of Tancred de Hauteville, the Norman knight celebrated as the deliverer of Jerusalem. Roger had made his kingdom the centre of the civilized world, and ruled with all the skill necessary to keep in check the hostile groups that were his subjects. Roger's successors were less successful than he in keeping the balance. So were the Hohenstaufen kings that followed him—with the exception of Frederick II, King and Emperor.

After the Hohenstaufens, the French House of Anjou came to Sicily, but on Easter Day 1282, in a rising known as the Sicilian Vespers, the French were defeated and the crown passed to the Spanish House of Aragon. Early in the sixteenth century, Spain finally united under King Ferdinand the Catholic and his wife Isabella of Castile. The crown then

Prince Don Ferdinando, Duke of Castro, is married with three children, and lives in Provence. His financial circumstances are not so fortunate as those of his rival claimant, the Duke of Calabria, which lends poignancy to the fact that he continues to press his claim. His cause, like that of the Duke of Calabria, has its supporters, and relations between the two factions are uneasy.

Three other sons   *Four daughters*

DINANDO, claims
ssion and title of Duke of
~o b 1926 m 1949, Chantal
hevron-Villette, b 1925

Princess Carmen,
b 1924

e Carlo b 1963

Princess Beatrice b 1950

Princess Anna b 1957 m 1977,
Jaques Cochin

Prince Don Carlos, Duke of Calabria, one of the two claimants to the throne of The Two Sicilies, photographed on the occasion of the birth of his son and heir, Pedro, in 1968. His two elder daughters Cristina, left, and Maria, were then aged three and two. Don Carlos and his wife Anne, a daughter of the Count of Paris, are well known in Madrid society. He devotes much of his time to his farm about two hours from Madrid and is president of a number of charities, including a college with five hundred non-paying students; the Spanish Wildlife Preservation Society and a home for old people. He has one particularly interesting business interest: a scheme to create a fishing industry for Mexico, whose shores are exploited mainly by the United States and Japan. The dispute between himself and Don Ferdinando over who is the true claimant to the throne of The Two Sicilies hangs on whether Don Carlos's grandfather's renunciation of of the crown was provisional or absolute. There is no way to settle the question, and the dispute looks as if it will continue indefinitely.

passed by marriage to the Habsburgs, and Naples and Sicily were to be ruled by viceroys in the reigns of the subsequent Habsburg kings of Spain. In the eighteenth century, after the War of the Spanish Succession, Naples and Sicily went to the Austrian Habsburg Emperor, but later he was obliged to cede the Kingdom to the Spanish Bourbons. King Philip V of Spain in turn gave it in 1735 to his younger son Infante Carlos, or Charles of Bourbon.

When Charles of Bourbon took up his residence in the Kingdom, his subjects were more than pleased to have a king holding court in their midst—and Charles' was nothing if not splendid. The royal Palace at Naples was the repository of the Farnese treasures which Charles had prudently removed from the northern duchies before his departure. Charles was also the king who vigorously recommenced the excavations at Herculaneum and who started the digging at Pompeii. And with its superb buildings—Capodimonte, Caserta and the Opera House of San Carlo—Naples came to be considered, after Paris, the most elegant place in Europe.

In 1759, Charles III and his wife exchanged the crown of Naples and Sicily for that of Spain, whose throne had fallen unexpectedly vacant through the death of the King's half-brother.

Charles' son Ferdinand accordingly became King Ferdinand I of The Two Sicilies. Ferdinand, of the bulbous nose, was fondly called Nasone by his subjects. His wife Maria Caroline, the sister of Marie Antoinette, called him "an amiable fool" and after the wedding night, his only comment about her had been "she sleeps like the dead and sweats like a pig".

This was according to Sir William Hamilton, the English diplomat, who presented his credentials as minister in 1764. He also relates that it was His Majesty's friendly custom to invite selected courtiers to attend him on his close-stool.

In 1786, Sir William was joined in Naples by the notorious Emma Hart, whom he married in 1791. In time, Emma became the Queen of Naples' intimate friend and when Nelson, the hero of the Nile, put in at Naples in 1799, he became not only Emma's but the Queen's hero, too.

Before Naples fell to France, the King and Queen, innumerable children and Emma were on their way to Palermo in Nelson's flagship. It was the worst voyage in Nelson's experience, during which the six year-old Alberto died of seasickness and exhaustion in Emma's arms. Napoleon at first allowed Ferdinand to return to and stay in Naples, but in 1806 Napoleon announced his intention "that the Bourbons shall cease to reign" and sent first his brother Joseph, and after him Joachim Murat to

Naples. Ferdinand, under British protection, stayed on in Sicily. Although the King claimed to enjoy the woodcock shooting. Nelson said he was worn to a shadow of his former ebullient self, and his heart bled for him. With Napoleon's power at an end, the King returned to the mainland in 1814, to be succeeded in 1825 by his shambling, stooping son Francis (who was chiefly famous for being irritable because he suffered from what his doctors diagnosed as "the flying gout"). He was in turn succeeded by his son, Ferdinand II—King Bomba, whose rule Gladstone called "a negation of God". His first Queen on the other hand—Maria Christina, daughter of Victor Emanuel I of Savoy—was thought to be an angel. She spent her life with lowered eyes; having been brought up in a convent, she truly wished she had become a nun. On discovering that she was pregnant, she gave all her possessions to her maids and got ready "to be delivered and to quit this life". Having given birth to a son, she promptly died. Such was the memory of her holiness that the Pope declared her Venerable and initiated the Cause for her Beatification.

Although the King has the reputation of having been a monster of debauchery, he had been a faithful husband to Maria Christina, just as he was to his second wife, the Archduchess Maria Theresa. In spite of this Austrian connection, King Bomba, because he wished to keep Naples independent, had no wish to be bolstered by Austrian military might. Nor did he respond favourably to the suggestion, made by Italian liberal radicals, that he might become King of all Italy. Instead, following the example of the Papal States, he sent troops off to the King of Sardinia, Charles Albert of Savoy, to combat Austria. The liberal radicals, however, reluctantly turned against King Bomba and swelled the revolutionary element which in the 1840s swept Europe from the North Sea to the Mediterranean. Revolution broke out in Sicily in 1848, followed by a rising on the mainland.

A constitution was demanded, and at length granted. Perhaps the King really wanted to make it work, but anarchy followed. Barricades went up in Naples proper, but the rising was quelled by the King's troops, for all that he had a horror of bloodshed. For the remaining ten years of his life, Ferdinand reigned more or less peacefully, still as an absolute monarch, and by the time that the partisans of a United Italy made their next move—the first, unsuccessful one had been in 1857—Ferdinand was dead.

His son Francis II was called Little Job by the Pope, and the Neapolitan Hamlet by Sir Harold Acton, biographer of the Bourbons of Naples. But when Garibaldi and the Thousand landed in Sicily a year after the King had come to the throne, Francis chiefly relied on prayer. As the crisis worsened, he telegraphed five times in twenty-four hours for papal blessings—the last three were telegraphed back by a cardinal. He led no army to defend his kingdom, and he, also too late, granted a constitution. Garibaldi conquered first the island and then the mainland, and when many of the people surrounding the King defected, he and his wife sailed away to Gaeta. There, with a few stalwart loyal troops, the couple endured a three-month siege. The young Queen herself manned the guns against the rebels, but in 1861 the standard of The Two Sicilies was lowered for the last time.

The royal couple kept a sombre court in Rome at the Farnese palace, which had remained the family's property. The Two Sicilies became one of the territories of Victor Emmanuel of Savoy, the subsequent King of Italy. King Francis died in 1894. His Queen, who had added to his gloom by leaving him, lived on until 1925.

Ferdinand II

Francis II

199

YUGOSLAVIA
Black George's Dynasty

Crown Prince Alexander of Yugoslavia declined the title of King when his father, King Peter, died in 1970. The reasons he gave were that he was serving in the British army and was thus in no position to make political declarations. Also, he had become a naturalised British subject and wished to avoid being the cause of political friction in Britain or among Yugoslavs in their native country or abroad.

His lack of interest in the cause of Yugoslav royalism disappointed its supporters, whose brightest hopes turned to the dead King's brother, Prince Tomislav. He lives in England and is considered a serious upholder of the Karadjordjević family cause.

Yugoslavia is the largest country in the Balkan peninsula, a sprawling hybrid created by the peace treaties of 1919 out of states administered by Austria, Hungary or both that were, notoriously, some of Europe's oldest trouble spots.

Chief among the new nation's ill-matched constituents was the old Kingdom of Serbia. For decades, Serbia had been beset by the rival claims of two dynasties, both of peasant origin, the Karadjordjevićs (Kara Djordje or "Black George" was the nickname of its founder) and the Obrenovićs. In 1903, the existing Obrenović King, Alexander, had made himself unpopular with the army and powerful Radical Party by marrying his mistress, the fascinating Draga Masin. They met a particularly gruesome end. Troops broke into the Palace in Belgrade, murdered Alexander and Draga and threw the bodies out into the garden where they lay exposed

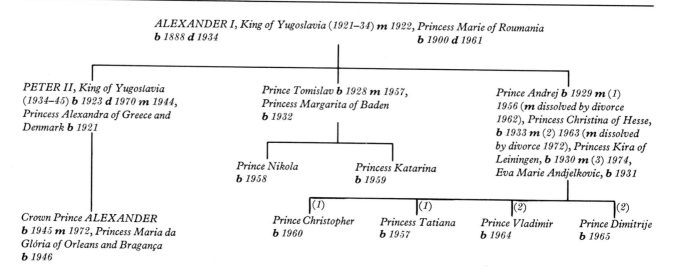

The head of the family, a carefree, likeable man, is known as Crown Prince Alexander: he deliberately declined the title of King when his father, King Peter, died in 1970. The Prince was not interested in the job, preferring to leave the cause to his uncle, Prince Tomislav. Alexander works as an investment broker, and for many years made his home in the beautiful old Imperial summer capital of Brazil, Petropol is. Recently he has moved, with his wife Maria da Gloria, to the United States.

while officers sat at tables drinking to the new King, Peter Karadjordjević.

It was Peter Kardjordjević who in 1919 was promoted to the throne of the new Serbo-Croat-Slovene Kingdom—the name of Yugoslavia not coming into use until 1929. In addition to Serbia, the new kingdom consisted of the old Kingdom of Montenegro together with Bosnia-Herzegovina, Croatia-Slavonia, Slovenia and Dalmatia. King Peter, aged 74 and in uncertain health, was only titular King, with his son Alexander acting as Prince-Regent. This was an unfortunate start, for the old man at least believed in constitutional rule but the son, although possessed of good intentions, had dictatorial tendencies.

Small, serious, looking older than his years with professorial pince-nez glasses and loose-fitting starched collars, Alexander succeeded his father

Prince Tomislav, standing, who farms in England's Kent countryside, is the Yugoslav royal family's ambassador in lieu of his nephew Alexander. He is the brother of the late King Peter II and with his children is in line of succession to the British throne. On his wife Margarita seems to have fallen the mantle of her relations, Princess Andrew and the Grand Duchess Serge, both of whom were in religious orders: the very religious Margarita was a nurse at St. George's Hospital, London, and known as Sister George.

Princess Elisabeth of Yugoslavia, daughter of Prince Paul, late Regent of Yugoslavia, lives in London. She has been married twice and had a widely reported friendship with Richard Burton. Her first husband was Howard Oxenberg, New York and Miami socialite; her second was English banker Neil Balfour.

King Alexander

as King in 1921. He immediately ran into trouble, with the Croats seeking independence. Determined that the various nationalisms which threatened to destroy the country should give way to a wider loyalty, he decided in 1929 to take over himself. He suspended the constitution, changed the country's name to Yugoslavia and dismissed the parliament, declaring that the time had come when no one should stand between people and King. Further, he divided Yugoslavia into nine countries, which were no more than arbitrary divisions. His police were brutal, the Peasant and Communist Parties were victimised and it was only a matter of time before Croatian frustration turned to violence. In 1934, minutes after his arrival in Marseille for a state visit to France, Alexander was shot dead by a Bulgarian assassin hired by a Croatian terrorist group. The French foreign minister was also killed in the attack.

The new King of Yugoslavia was Alexander's eleven-year old son, Peter, and his cousin Prince Paul, an accomplished man more interested in the arts than government, was obliged to act as Regent until the boy should reach his eighteenth birthday. Paul had been close to King Alexander, but did not admire his methods. He did not have the chance to reconcile Yugoslavia's internal troublemakers, as well he might had he succeeded as King.

As the Second World War loomed in the Balkans, with the young King Peter still two years away from his majority, Prince Paul found himself in a frightening position. He had strongly pro-British sympathies, having been at Oxford, lived in London as a young man and married a sister of the Duchess of Kent. But six of the seven states bordering Yugoslavia had, to a greater or lesser degree, thrown in their lot with Nazi Germany. The country was unprepared to defend itself and the Croats ready to defect.

Entering the Royal Palace in Belgrade it is easy to feel that one is slipping in by a seldom-used side door, for the house is one of those architectural peculiarities which seem to lack an entrance in keeping with the elaborateness of the fabric. Inside, although the rooms are comparatively small and dark and suffocatingly over-stuffed with furniture and bric-a-brac, the foyer and grand staircase hold great promise. The establishment, which is actually a pair of palaces with a connecting facade on the garden side, owes much to Garnier, and is greatly reminiscent of the Casino at Monte Carlo and somewhat so of L'Opera in Paris. It is sad that the genuinely elegant touches about the Palace are somehow tarnished and tawdry: the velours are dusty, the real marble looks fake, the paintings are forgettable, and everywhere there is the cold, brassy smell of the butler's pantry. The Palace is like a once-proud Edwardian luxury hotel under new and slipshod management. Beograd, the Serbian name for Belgrade, means white castle: what a pity its Palace could not have lived up to the name.

It seemed that the only alternatives were German or Russian domination. While having no illusions about Hitler, Germany seemed the lesser of the two evils, so with a heavy heart, Paul signed a pact with Germany and Italy in March 1941. Two days later there was a military revolt, encouraged by the British government, in which the Yugoslav government was overthrown, the Regency abolished at a stroke, and young King Peter II invested with the powers which six months later he would have assumed on his eighteenth birthday.

Hitler did not wait to see whether the new regime would be friendly or otherwise, but ordered an immediate attack on Yugoslavia and Greece. Belgrade had nine days of unreal peace, when the King was crowned amid scenes of rejoicing. Then, on April 6th, the Luftwaffe struck. The country was not even able to hold out a fortnight, which was the King's gloomy forecast, but surrendered on April 17th, shortly after King Peter had followed Prince Paul into exile.

King Peter headed a Yugoslav government-in-exile in London and won his wings in the British Royal Air Force. When he asked to be parachuted into Yugoslavia to join the resistance movement led by Tito, he was refused. For in 1943, the British government gave its support to Tito's partisans, and had King Peter fought with his strongly monarchist people against the Nazi occupier, it would not have been so easy for Tito to win over the Yugoslavs by mounting a propaganda campaign against the King.

At the close of the war, King Peter was not allowed to return to his country. By the end of 1945, the Communist Party was dominant and Yugoslavia a Federal People's Republic. King Peter went into exile in the U.S.A. living with unrelieved unhappiness until his death virtually alone, in Denver, Colorado, in 1970.

King Peter in 1960, aged 37

INDEX

INDEX

Every effort has been made to trace copyright holders of photographs appearing in Europe's Royal Families. *The publishers wish to apologise to any photographer or agency whose work has been used, but not listed below.*

Picture acknowledgements

8-15 Roger Gorringe **19** Baudouin and Fabiola, Camera Press; Prince Albert etc, Camera Press **20** Baudouin etc, Camera Press; Leopold, Press Association **21** Marie-Christine etc, Press Association; Liliane, Press Association; Count of Flanders, Popper **22** palace, Spectrum; Leopold, Maurice Quick **23** Carlotta, Maurice Quick **24** palace, Keystone **25** all pictures, Maurice Quick **27**; Ingrid, Rigmor Mydtskov **28** Prince Georg etc, Dmitri Kasterine; Henrik, Butt Lindemann **29** Benedikte, Rigmor Mydtskov **30** palace, H. Kanus; Christian IX, Maurice Quick **32** palace, Spectrum Colour Library; Alexandra, Maurice Quick **33** Frederik IX, Maurice Quick **35** Queen, Tim Graham; Duke, Tim Graham **36** Prince of Wales, Anwar Hussein; Princess Anne etc, Snowdon; Prince Andrew, Anwar Hussein; Prince Edward, Anwar Hussein **37** Queen Mother, Country Life Books; Princess Margaret etc, Norman Parkinson **38** Gloucesters, Norman Parkinson; Alice, Duchess of Gloucester, Tom Blair; Prince Michael etc, Keystone Press **39** Princess Alexandra etc, Norman Parkinson; Countess of Athlone, Keystone; Kents, Norman Parkinson **40** Windsor, Spectrum; George, Popper **41** George, Popper **43** Balmoral, Lichfield **43** palace, Angelo Hornak; Victoria, Maurice Quick **44** palace, Angelo Hornak; George V, Maurice Quick **45** palace, Brighton Pavilion; Edward, Maurice Quick **47-9** Lichfield **49** Karl Eusebius, courtesy of Prince Franz Joseph **50** palace, Bavaria Verlag; Anton Florian, courtesy Prince Franz Joseph **51** Johann, courtesy Prince Franz Joseph **53** Grand Duke etc, Camera Press; Henri, Camera Press; Grand Duchess Charlotte, Camera Press **54** Marie Astrid, Rex Features **55** group, Rex Features **56** palace, Spectrum; Adolph, Maurice Quick **57** palace, Camera Press; Marie Adelaide, Maurice Quick **59** Rainier, Anthony Howarth; Grace, Snowdon; Albert, Rex Features **60** Caroline etc, Keystone Press **61** Stephanie, Rex Features; **62** Albert, Maurice Quick **63** palace, Angelo Hornak; Alice, Popper **64** palace, Angelo Hornak; Polignac, Popper **67** Queen, Rex Features; Prince Bernhard, Karsh of Ottawa **68** William the Silent, Popperfoto; Beatrix etc, Press Association **69** Margriet etc, Camera Press **70** William II, Popperfoto; three princes, Max Koot **71** Irene etc, Camera Press; Christina etc, Keystone **72** palace, Keystone **74** palace, Bart Hojmeester; Wilhelmina, Maurice Quick **75** Emma, Maurice Quick **77-9** Lichfield **79** Ragnhild, courtesy Princess Ragnhild **80** palace, Camera Press; Haakon, Maurice Quick **81** Maud, Maurice Quick **83** group, Rex Features; King, Sipa Press/Rex Features **84** Countess, Europa Press/P.A.; Elena and Cristina, Europa Press/P.A.; Felipe, Europa Press/P.A. **85** Maria del Pilar, Agencia Efe; Margarita, Europa Press/P.A.; Duke of Cadiz etc, Europa Press/P.A. **86** Philip V, Mansell Collection; Marie Louise, Popper; Godoy, Mansell Collection **87** palace, Spectrum **88** Isabella, Popper; palace, Spectrum **89** Alfonso, Maurice Quick **91** King, Camera Bild/ Camera Press; Princess, King Carl Gustav/Pressens Bild; Queen, Jan Collsioo/ Pressens Bild **92** Christina etc, Lewenhaupt/Pressens Bild; Bernadotte etc, Archiv Henry Guttman **93** Bertil etc, Jan Collsioo/Pressens Bild; Margaretha, Mirrorpic **94** palace, H. Kanus/Elisabeth Photo Library **96** palace, Camera Press; Solliden, Camera Press **97** both pictures, Maurice Quick **101** Leka etc, Camera Press; Geraldine, Popper **102** both pictures, Maurice Quick **103** palace and princess, Popper **105** Dr. Habsburg etc, Tor Eigeland/Daily Telegraph Picture Library **106** Empress, courtesy Dr. Habsburg; Karl Thomas etc, Daily Telegraph Library **107** Carl Ludwig, courtesy Archduke Carl Ludwig; Geza, courtesy Archduke Geza **108** palace, Peter Baker **110** Hofburg, J. Allan Cash; **111** palace, Peter Baker; Emperor etc, Maurice Quick **113** Simeon etc, courtesy King Simeon; Kardam, courtesy King Simeon; group, Camera Press/Gyenes; Giovanna, courtesy King Simeon **114** palace, Popper **115** Ferdinand, Popper; Boris, Maurice Quick **117** Count etc, Frank Spooner Pictures **118** Count, Presse Seeger; Thibaut etc, Frank Spooner Pictures **119** Duchess, Liverani/Camera Press **120** Louvre, La Documentation Francaise; Versailles, J. P. Durel/La Documentation Française; Louis, Mary Evans **121** Mme de Maintenon, Popper **122** Louis, Popper **123** palace, Spectrum; King, Popper **125** Napoleons, Keystone; Napoleon, Maurice Quick **126** Duke, Maurice Quick **127** Napoleon, Maurice Quick **129** Louis Ferdinand, Tor Eigeland/Daily Telegraph Colour Library **130** Georg Friedrich etc, courtesy Prince Louis Ferdinand **131** Viktoria Louise, courtesy Prince Louis Ferdinand; Princess Antonia etc, Keystone **132** palace, Bavaria Verlag; Friedrich, Popper **133** Friedrich Wilhelm, Popper **134** Kaiser, Maurice Quick **135** palace, Spectrum; Kaiser, Maurice Quick **137** Duke etc, Keystone; Franz, Bavaria Verlag; Max Emanuel, Press Association **147** all pictures, Bavaria Verlag **148** palace, Bavaria Verlag **149** Sophie, Popper **150** Ernst August, Maurice Quick **151** Duke, Maurice Quick **153** Margrave, etc. Presse Seeger/Camera Press **154** palace, Hulton; August, Mansell Collection **155** Luise etc, Maurice Quick **157** Duke etc, Presse Seeger; Duchess, Bavaria Verlag; Marquis etc, by courtesy the Marquess of Cambridge **158** Duke, Bavaria Verlag; Duke, Mansell Collection **159** palace, Bavaria Verlag; King, Maurice Quick **161** Constantine etc, Colin Davey/Camera Press; group, courtesy King Constantine; Frederika, Central Press; Prince Peter, courtesy Prince Peter; Lady Katherine Brandram, Central Press Photos **162** palace, Camera Press **163** King, Maurice Quick **164** palace, Peter Baker; Sophie, Maurice Quick **165** King, Maurice Quick **167** King, Rex Features; Prince, Rex Features; Duke etc, Keystone **169** palace, Spectrum **170** palace, Italian State Tourist Office **171** Umberto, Maurice Quick **173** King, courtesy King Umberto of Italy **174** palace, Camera Press **175** King, Maurice Quick **177** group, courtesy Duke of Braganza **179** palace, Peter Baker **180** palace, Peter Baker **181** Dom Carlos, Maurice Quick; Dom Duarte, courtesy, Duke of Braganza **183** King etc and Princesses, Lichfield; Queen, Popper **184** Queen, Maurice Quick **185** palace, Elisabeth Photo Library; Carol, Maurice Quick **187** Grand Duke, Tor Eigeland/ Daily Telegraph Colour Library; Grand Duchess, Rex Features **189** Grand Duchess etc, Rex Features; Prince, Lee Garmes, courtesy Prince Andrew **189** Prince Dimitri, courtesy Prince Dimitri; Prince Nicholas Romanoff, P. G. Valdoni **190** both pictures, Popper **191** Tsar, Maurice Quick **192** palace, Spectrum **194** palace, Spectrum **195** palace, B. Leidmann/Bavaria Verlag; group, Maurice Quick **197** Don Ferdinando, courtesy Prince Don Ferdinand; Don Carlos, Europa Press/Press Association **198** palace, Spectrum **199** Ferdinand, Radio Times Hulton Picture Library; Francis, Mary Evans **201** Alexander etc, Richard Slade/Camera Press; group, Camera Press; Princess, Rex Features **202** palace, Radio Times Hulton Picture Library **203** King, Popper.

James I, King of England (d. 1625)

Elizabeth m Friedrich V, Elector Palatine, King of Bohemia

Karl Ludwig, Elector Palatine

Elisabeth Charlotte m Philippe, Duke of Orleans

Elisabeth Charlotte m Leopold, Duke of Lorraine

Philippe II, Duke of Orleans

Franz I, Holy Roman Emperor

Louis, Duke of Orleans

Leopold II, Holy Roman Emperor

Louis-Philippe, Duke of Orleans

Ferdinand III, Grand Duke of Tuscany

Franz I, Emperor of Austria

Louis Philippe, Duke of Orleans

Leopold II, Grand Duke of Tuscany

Franz Karl

Louis Philippe I, King of the French

Augusta m Franz Luitpold of Bavaria

Karl Ludwig

Ferdinand, Clementine m Prince August of Saxe-Coburg and Gotha

Duke of Orleans

Edward VII, King of Great Britain

Maria Immaculata m King of Italy

Elisabeth Amalie m Prince Aloys of Liechtenstein

Otto

Ferdinand I, King of the Bulgarians

Robert, Duke of Chartres

Ludwig III, King of Bavaria

Umberto I, King of Italy

Karl I, Emperor of Austria

Boris III, King of the Bulgarians

Jean, Duke of Guise

Rupprecht, Crown Prince of Bavaria

Elisabeth II, Queen of Great Britain

Olav V, King of Norway

Prince Louis Napoleon

Umberto II, King of Italy

Albrecht, Duke of Bavaria

Franz Joseph II, Prince of Liechtenstein

Otto, Archduke of Austria

Simeon II, King of the Bulgarians

Henri, Count of Paris

James I, King of England (*d* 1625)

Elizabeth *m* Friedrich V, Elector Palatine, King of Bohemia

Karl Ludwig, Elector Palatine

Elisabeth Charlotte *m* Philippe, Duke of Orléans

Philippe II,
Duke of Orléans

Elisabeth Charlotte
m Leopold, Duke of Lorraine

Louis
Duke of Orléans

Franz I,
Holy Roman Emperor

Louis Philippe,
Duke of Orléans

Leopold II,
Holy Roman Emperor

Louis Philippe,
Duke of Orléans

Franz I,
Emperor of Austria

Ferdinando III,
Grand Duke of Tuscany

Louis Philippe I,
King of the French

Franz Karl

Leopoldo II,
Grand Duke
of Tuscany

Theresa
m Carlo Alberto,
King of Sardinia

Edward VII, King
of Great Britain, etc,

Ferdinand,
Duke of
Orléans

Clementine
m Prince
August of
Saxe-Coburg
and Gotha

Karl Ludwig

Augusta
m Prince
Luitpold
of Bavaria

Vittorio Emanuele II,
King of Italy

Robert,
Duke of
Chartres

Ferdinand I,
King of the
Bulgarians

Otto

Elisabeth Amalia
m Prince Aloys of
Liechtenstein

Ludwig III,
King of
Bavaria

Umberto I,
King of Italy

Clotilda
m Prince
Napoléon

George V,
King of
Great Britain

Maud
m Haakon VII,
King of Norway

Jean,
Duke of
Guise

Boris III,
King of the
Bulgarians

Karl I,
Emperor
of Austria

Rupprecht,
Crown
Prince of
Bavaria

Vittorio
Emanuele III,
King of Italy

Prince
Victor
Napoléon

George VI,
King of
Great Britain

Henri,
Count of
Paris

Simeon II,
King of the
Bulgarians

Otto,
Archduke
of Austria

Franz Joseph II,
Prince of
Liechtenstein

Albrecht,
Duke of
Bavaria

Umberto II,
King of Italy

Prince Louis
Napoléon

Elizabeth II,
Queen of
Great Britain

Olav V, King
of Norway